SOCIAL EXCLUSION AND THE WAY OUT

SOCIAL EXCLUSION AND THE WAY OUT
An individual and community response to human social dysfunction

Adrian Bonner

Kent Institute of Medicine and Health Sciences, University of Kent, UK

John Wiley & Sons, Ltd

Copyright © 2006   John Wiley & Sons Ltd, The Atrium, Southern Gate, Chichester, West Sussex PO19 8SQ, England

Telephone   (+44) 1243 779777

Email (for orders and customer service enquiries): cs-books@wiley.co.uk
Visit our Home Page on www.wiley.com

Other Wiley Editorial Offices

John Wiley & Sons Inc., 111 River Street, Hoboken, NJ 07030, USA

Jossey-Bass, 989 Market Street, San Francisco, CA 94103-1741, USA

Wiley-VCH Verlag GmbH, Boschstr. 12, D-69469 Weinheim, Germany

John Wiley & Sons Australia Ltd, 42 McDougall Street, Milton, Queensland 4064, Australia

John Wiley & Sons (Asia) Pte Ltd, 2 Clementi Loop #02-01, Jin Xing Distripark, Singapore 129809

John Wiley & Sons Canada Ltd, 22 Worcester Road, Etobicoke, Ontario, Canada M9W 1L1

Wiley also publishes its books in a variety of electronic formats. Some content that appears in print may not be available in electronic books.

Library of Congress Cataloging-in-Publication Data

British Library Cataloguing in Publication Data

A catalogue record for this book is available from the British Library

ISBN-13 978-0-470-01935-1
ISBN-10 0-470-01935-2

Typeset in 10/12pt Palatino by Integra Software Services Pvt. Ltd, Pondicherry, India
Printed and bound in Great Britain by TJ International Ltd, Padstow, Cornwall
This book is printed on acid-free paper responsibly manufactured from sustainable forestry in which at least two trees are planted for each one used for paper production.

CONTENTS

PART II: HEALTH AND ILLNESS IN SOCIAL GROUPS

ABOUT THE AUTHOR

Dr Adrian Bonner is Reader in the Institute of Medicine and Health Sciences, University of Kent. As founder and director of the Addictive Behaviour Group he has facilitated the development of undergraduate and postgraduate teaching and research activities aimed at practitioners and managers working in social and healthcare services. He has been a member of various UK government working groups, including Skills for Health, a workforce development group set up to support the UK Anti-Drugs Strategy and is a director of the Institute for Alcohol Studies. Adrian's principal research has focused on mechanisms of brain damage and the role of nutritional factors in cognitive function. This biomedical research has become more integrated with psychological and social approaches during the development of innovative screening, assessment and outcome monitoring systems for use in the delivery of services for vulnerable people.

Adrian provides health-related support for The Salvation Army Social Services in the UK; he also represents The International Salvation Army on various bodies, including the United Nations (UN).

PREFACE

Social Exclusion and the Way Out is an attempt to provide a critical appraisal of the complex nature of social exclusion, which has not changed, in many ways, since the nineteenth-century philosophers began to diagnose problems of the 'deserving and undeserving' poor. In 2006 poverty still exists but, in the analysis of the social dimensions of poverty and social exclusion, it is essential to focus on the nature of human dysfunction. Irrespective of an individual's income and wealth or poverty, the person's perception of their *social identity* and *quality of life* will be significant determinants of their response to their social situation. One of the long-lasting objectives of The Salvation Army's Social Services is to *work with people where they are* and to help them develop a sense of *meaning and belonging*. Hopefully, a greater understanding of individual functioning and the underlying issues of mental health, illness and the pervasive problems of alcohol dependency will provide some insight into new ways of identifying individual needs and help to inspire new interventions to support the vulnerable members of the community.

ACKNOWLEDGEMENTS

The author would like to thank the following people for their help in preparing this text. First to my family: to Gill for her great patience and proof-reading skills; to Adam and Kirsten for their insights into youth culture and medicine; to Gemma for her help with the illustrations; and to Jake, for his insight into the biosocial and political perspectives of contemporary life. Special thanks go to colleagues working within The Salvation Army, in particular Major Dean Logan and Claire Luscombe for their regular discussions on the strategic developments of the social programme in the UK, and also to Lieutenant Colonel Paul Bollwahn (National Headquarters, US) and Commissioner Christine MacMillan (National Headquarters, Canada) for their continued support and encouragement. I am also grateful to the UK Social Services management team: Lieutenant Colonel Keith Burridge, Majors Ian Harris and Ray Irving. Other people who have added to discussions relating to the book include Major David Emery, OBE, Colonel Paul DuPlessis, Majors Paul Kingscott, Richard Mingay and Norman Piper, and Reverend David Day.

I have been supported by colleagues at the University of Kent in undertaking this work within the *Kent Institute of Medicine and Health Sciences* (KIMHS). Particular thanks go to Professor Cornelius Katona (Dean of KIMHS), Professor Tony Hales, head of the Division of Psychiatry and consultant psychiatrist for Kent NHS, and to Alexi Brook for research assistance. I am particularly grateful to Professor Victor Preedy (King's College), Dr Colin Martin (University of Sheffield) and Reverend/Professor Chris Cook (University of Durham) for their friendship and collaboration in ongoing research initiatives over many years. Very special thanks go to Professor David Melville, vice chancellor, who has expressed a great interest in this research linking the University of Kent to the work of The Salvation Army.

INTRODUCTION

In the second half of the nineteenth century poverty was a political and moral issue. A social consequence of the industrial revolution was the growth of slums in the shadows of the factories and warehouses, in the expanding English towns. In the country the paupers were thought to have the opportunity to help themselves out of poverty, but in the industrial towns destitution was considered to be inevitable. The malnourished and disease-ridden urban populations were becoming a growing problem. From a health perspective only a third of the men who took the 'Queen's shilling' passed a very basic medical examination (Himmelfarb 1984). Marx, Ruskin and other philosophers at the time warned that poverty would be the catalyst of a revolution. Prior to the publication of *Das Kapital* by Marx, Engels (1844) had written *The Conditions of the Working Class in England* and Henry Mayhew had published *London's Labouring Poor* in 1850.

Charles Booth's 30-year survey of the causes of poverty, published in *The Life and Labour of the People of London*, added to this concern that something must be done about the growing problems within urban society. Booth used a rational scientific approach to diagnose the problem, but made a limited attempt to provide a solution to the complex range of problems that he observed. He classified the population of London according to their poverty or affluence, and concluded that 8.4% of people in London lived in very poor conditions, 'at all times more or less in want'. In East London he found 35% in poverty. Charles Booth's finding was that 'those deemed very poor [class B, in his survey]... were of a wretched and casual character... and... at all times more or less in want', and he suggested that they should be removed from the society of the deserving poor, 'to prevent them from infecting industrious workers with their feckless ways'. Booth suggested that, 'they should be placed in state-created communes where their children, temporarily separated from their parents, would be educated to become useful members of society'. Despite this capitalist-based view of the contemporary social problems, Booth did comment on the observation that only 30% of the households in London included grandparents, whereas in Barking, Essex, families showed 'a very wonderful and beautiful loyalty to parents in households... which was clearly lacking in London'.

The work of the Rowntree Foundation began at this time, with Seebohm Rowntree attempting to define poverty more precisely than Charles Booth had done. Rowntree described 10% of the working-class households in York as living below the poverty line in *primary poverty* and 17.93% were living in *secondary poverty*, defined as living above the poverty line but 'obviously living in a state of poverty . . . in obvious want and squalor'. (For more information on these early studies on the urban and rural poor, see Thane, 1982 and Chapter 1.)

In his book about the lives of William and Catherine Booth, Roy Hattersley (1999) has provided a useful review of the socio-political events of this period and has observed that William Booth (1829–1912) did not have the analytical skills of his unrelated peer Charles Booth, but that he was concerned with the linkages between moral and physical degeneration, poverty and depravity. William was energetically engaged in evangelical and social enterprises and founded The Salvation Army (originally called the Christian Mission) in 1865. The Christian Mission set up soup kitchens in the 1860s and the 'social ministry' expanded to provide 'shelters' for men and 'refuges' for women. William's helpers' expression of social action was to provide cheap food and material help for the poor. Despite considerable opposition from the establishment for these evangelical and social welfare activities, The Salvation Army's social services expanded. William was very disturbed at finding the existing social policies of the day to be 'lamentably inadequate' – a new radical approach was needed.

Using the model of Henry Morton Stanley's accounts of his travels across Africa in *Through a Dark Continent*, William Booth documented his radical strategy to 'present help for the actual need' in a far-reaching and, what appeared at the time, aspirational strategy of nearly 300 pages, published in 1890. The book was entitled *In Darkest England and the Way Out*. This wide-ranging set of observations, certainly informed by Charles Booth and other commentators at the time, provided innovation and far-sighted approaches in addressing prostitution and other social ills, and was based on an impressive 'Great Scheme', which included three parts.

The first component of the scheme was the 'city colony', a refuge in the 'very ocean of misery'. The city colony consisted of shelters, where the destitute were to be taken, provided with food and shelter and exposed to 'moral and religious influences'. Access into a shelter required a small payment, obtained by work either in a Salvation Army enterprise or as a temporary day labourer sent out by a Salvation Army employment service to employers friendly to the scheme. The plan was that most men who passed through these agencies would be 'floated off to permanent employment'. Those who remained with the Salvation Army would be checked for 'health and character' and sent to the second part of the Great Scheme, the 'farm colony'. Personal improvement from the benefits of a healthy rural environment, supplemented by 'industrial (agricultural) . . . moral and religious methods' would equip the men to return to their earlier honest employment or to settle in the country as agricultural labourers. It was expected that the majority of 'reclaimed' men would be transferred by the Salvation Army authorities to the third part of the scheme, the 'overseas colony', where they would be assisted to emigrate to Salvation Army agricultural communities to be established in underpopulated British colonies, such as Canada, Western Australia and South Africa, 'the final home for these destitute multitudes'. A print of the fascinating coloured picture showing the ocean of misery, a lighthouse, and the city, farm and overseas colonies overlaid with a large amount of demographics describing the main socially excluded groups (of criminal, homeless, prostitutes, etc.) was included in *In Darkest England and the Way Out*.

This book was more than an aspiration strategy as many of these ideas did materialise. By 1890, not only had a considerable number of shelters/hostels been established, but The Salvation Army also opened its first labour exchange in the East End of London and within the year 20 similar exchanges had been established throughout Britain. Expansion into the United States and many other countries was even faster (Bollwahn 2000). In 2007 The Salvation Army is one of the two largest social support agencies working collaboratively with the US government in many hundreds of community projects. A similar situation exists in Australia, Sweden, Norway and many other countries.

One of the common features that seemed to be exacerbating the problems of the vulnerable people was alcohol abuse. In *In Darkest England and the Way Out* Booth comments: 'drunkenness . . . nine tenths of our poverty, squalor, vice and crime spring from this poisonous tap-root. Many of our social evils, which over shadow the land like so many Upas trees (poisonous) would dwindle away and die if they were not constantly watered with strong drink'. The many Salvation Army programmes addressed the problem of alcohol dependence in various ways, but an abstinent approach was used throughout this work. At this time the Temperance Movement attracted more members, became a mass movement and helped to create an ethos now described as *social capital*. Although often regarded as an outdated approach to managing the problems of alcohol in society, Virginia Berridge (2005) argues that the various expressions of *temperance* provide important models for developing current strategies in 2007.

William Booth's legacy in 2007 is an organisation operating in 111 countries with some very impressive statistics, which include: 31 769 beds in residential hostels; 10 333 beds in emergency lodges; 206 children's homes (capacity 9377); 175 homes for the elderly (capacity 12 036). Over the years specialist alcohol dependence services have been established. Currently there are 71 non-residential programmes (with a capacity of 2383), 209 residential programmes (with a capacity of 12 513), 40 Harbour Light centres (with a capacity of 3951), and 44 other services (with a capacity of 3716). More detailed international statistics are given in Appendix A.

William Booth was one of several social reformers, including Shaftesbury, Rowntree and Barnardo, whose ideas began to shape the community response to poverty alleviation, and address the links between moral and physical degeneration in England and other countries. Booth's influence can be measured in terms of the many millions of people who have directly benefited from this unique form of social action.

This volume is dedicated to the work of William Booth and to the current 25 000 officers, 110 000 staff and approximately 1.5 million members and volunteers of The Salvation Army, which still provides help for the 'submerged tenth of the population'. In the developing world the 'submerged tenth' refers to those in absolute poverty; in the developed world the 'submerged tenth' includes those in relative poverty but who are socially excluded.

REFERENCES

Berridge, V. (2005). *Temperance: Its History and Impact on Current and Future Alcohol Policy*. York: Joseph Rowntree Foundation.

Bollwahn, P. (2000). *William Booth: The Development of his Social Concern*. Washington: National Headquarters, The Salvation Army.

Hattersley, R. (1999). *Blood and Fire: William and Catherine Booth and their Salvation Army*. London: Abacus.

Himmelfarb, G. (1984). *England in the Early Industrial Age*. London: Faber and Faber.

Thane, P. (1982). *The Foundations of the Welfare State*. Harlow: Longman.

ABOUT THIS BOOK

Social exclusion is a highly complex phenomenon that involves a wide range of complex needs. From a holistic viewpoint individual needs will be highly specific and require a detailed assessment of the individual's particular health and social circumstances. To tackle the problems of *social exclusion*, therefore, a multidisciplinary evidence-based approach is required. The main disciplines contributing to this approach have arisen from the biological sciences (including medicine, psychiatry, psychopharmacology, health, ethology), psychology (including social psychology, perception, cognition, learning, developmental psychology) and social science (including socialisation, deviance, social policy, economics). All of these subdisciplines could potentially contribute to the *biopsychosocial* model of social exclusion. Each of these areas of enquiry has its own language and methodology, leading to problems in interdisciplinary communication. This book is an attempt to provide a link between these approaches by considering the nature of *meaning and belonging*, from a multidisciplinary perspective. As a number of the concepts contributing to this *biopsychosocial* model are complex, many of the sections are cross-referenced to other sections of the book where fuller explanations are provided.

Parts I and II of this book provide an overview of the mechanisms and functions of social groups and some speculations as to the reasons why some individuals do not function well within a social context. The term 'complex needs' is frequently used to describe the range of interacting problems that mitigate against inclusion. In some people, addressing one problem, for instance deficits in basic skills, might unlock a combination of complex needs. Stigmatisation, despair and hopelessness, exacerbated by poverty and poor living conditions, can lead to social exclusion. However, inclusion problems can occur in those who are materially well off and have access to adequate resources. In both of these situations motivational issues, compounded by physical and mental health problems, need to be understood and appropriate interventions offered. The main theme being developed in Part II is the link between biopsychosocial aspects of stress, which, if it becomes chronic, can lead to mental illness and problematic alcohol and drug misuse. These negative health behaviours become reflected in lifestyle choices, which can be destructive, for instance inadequate feeding and other aspects of personal organisation. There is increasing evidence of problematic alcohol and drug use affecting neuropsychological functioning. This linked set of actions and consequences underpins the cycle of social exclusion; this is particularly significant from a transgenerational perspective in view of the developmental sequelae, which is commonly found in socially deprived communities.

Part III consists of a brief review of statutory and non-statutory responses to the complex needs of the socially excluded, which have developed during the last two centuries. Well before the establishment of the welfare state the community responded to vulnerable people in a variety of ways, many of which were aimed at protecting the community. Nevertheless, care of the needy was gradually recognised as a function of a civil society. The welfare state developed as a consequence of the actions of benefactors and social reformers and also as a response to the consequences of industrialisation.

Part III begins with an introduction to screening and assessment. The need to clearly identify the primary and secondary causes of social exclusion is a prerequisite for the development of appropriate services and the creation of a programme of support for the client. In developing either statutory or non-statutory support services the guiding philosophy of the project/service needs to be carefully considered in order to provide the most effective support to enable the service user to change his or her behaviour, and become motivated to step out of the exclusion trap and be included in mainstream society.

The process of change and limitations due to neurocognitive deficits is the main topic of Chapter 11. Here the link between psychosocial interventions, brain function and nutritional deficits in the socially excluded is highlighted. Chapters 12 and 13 present the highly complex and ever-changing health and social care infrastructures in the UK. The reader will notice the evolving socio-political attitudes to the 'deserving and undeserving poor' during the last two centuries. Currently the speed of health and social care reform appears to be increasing, by the month. Although the initiatives from the Department of Health, Department of Work and Pensions, the Office of the Deputy Prime Minister and other departments are well documented on government websites, this section of the book is intended to highlight the main changes and place these within an historical context. An emerging theme in these chapters is the creation of very large governmental budgets and the apparent state intervention in providing support that was previously generated by the community. Statutory interventions are expensive and not always the most appropriate ways to engage with hard-to-reach vulnerable people. A way forward appears to be the development of partnerships between public-financed and voluntary sector organisations.

Some readers of this book might wish to use a 'pick and mix approach', for instance those who are less familiar with life science perspectives might find it useful to read Part I, followed by Part III, and then explore the more detailed aspects of Part II.

The author hopes that this wide-ranging approach to social exclusion will provide an important insight into *meaning and belonging* in the UK in the twenty-first century.

Part I

Individual Functioning and Social Exclusion

CHAPTER 1

EXCLUSION FROM SOCIETY

WHAT IS SOCIAL EXCLUSION?

Early definitions of social exclusion were quite broad and described the consequences of the associated problems of unemployment, poor skills, low incomes, poor housing, high crime, bad health and family breakdown. The UK government's Department of Culture, Media and Sport used operational definitions such as:

> Social exclusion takes many forms. It can be direct or indirect, and can embrace both groups and individuals. Exclusion also has a geographical dimension embracing rural, urban and suburban areas alike (DCMS 1999).

The government's definition of social exclusion was extended in 2001 to include:

> Social exclusion is something that *can* happen to anyone. But some people are significantly more at risk than others. Research has found that people with certain backgrounds and experiences are disproportionately likely to suffer social exclusion. The key risk factors include: low income; family conflict; being in care; school problems; being an ex-prisoner; being from an ethnic minority; living in a deprived neighbourhood in urban and rural areas; mental health problems, age and disability (DfES 2005).

Although UK government definitions have been broadened during recent years, social exclusion is still couched in anti-poverty work. Percy-Smith (2000) has argued against the narrowing of definitions to poverty and spatial issues, she defines seven 'dimensions' of social exclusion:

- Economic (e.g. long-term unemployment; workless households; income poverty).
- Social (e.g. homelessness; crime; disaffected youth).
- Political (e.g. disempowerment; lack of political rights; alienation from/lack of confidence in political processes).
- Neighbourhood (e.g. decaying housing stock; environmental degradation).

- Individual (e.g. mental and physical ill health; educational underachievement).

- Spatial (e.g. concentration/marginalisation of vulnerable groups).

- Group (concentration of above characteristics in particular groups, e.g. disabled, elderly, ethnic minorities).

Social exclusion policies should address the needs of groups and individuals, as listed above, and those who do not have access to the relevant support services, and are disempowered from civil society. Social *inclusion* occurs when those in need engage with and begin to benefit from statutory and nonstatutory support structures and services. However, inclusion involves more than 'support', participation in the community is a key aspect of *meaning* and *belonging.*

Social cohesion or *community cohesion* are mechanisms for creating a society that is not fractured by poverty, racism and violence. However, it is important to keep the individual as the central focus. This is engendered in the concept of *capacity building*, which promotes the idea that it is the ability of people to equip themselves and bring about local change. This latter approach comes from within communities (cf. externally led initiatives). In discussing the community response to HIV/AIDS, Campbell and Campbell (2005) suggest that sustained change comes from the learning experience of the community and the capacity of the individuals to believe in their ability to overcome the challenge. One of the principal factors in the exclusion of HIV/AIDS and other disease-related problems such as leprosy is *stigma.*

SOCIAL POLICY PERSPECTIVES ON SOCIAL EXCLUSION

In the first part of the nineteenth century socialists, such as Robert Owen, and conservatives, such as Thomas Carlyle, were beginning to analyse the unequal distribution of wealth and income being generated from industrial capitalism. They identified strength originating from competitive rather than cooperative effort and self-help emerging at the expense of mutual obligation and responsibility for the poor.

These ideas were influential in organisational management and the political establishment supporting the Poor Law Amendment Act of 1834, described by Engels as 'the most open declaration of war by the bourgeoisie upon the proletariat' (Engels 1944). The implications of this act were that anyone who was physically capable of work had no alternative but to support him/herself. Public help was only given to the aged and disabled. The view at that time was that there were sufficient employment opportunities for everyone, but if not, other developing economies in America and Australia provided opportunities in this *laissez-faire* view of the international economic community.

Between the 1830s and 1860s even those employers who believed that poverty was self-inflicted tended not to stick to the letter of the Poor Law, sometimes supplementing wages and providing relief to those not employed. While some employers overtly exploited their employees, others provided better working conditions, shorter hours, improved housing and medical care. This combination of philanthropy and optimising of the work force (an early application of human resource management strategy) led to the growth of private charities and institutions, providing some alleviation of poverty. The role of evangelical Anglicans and Nonconformists to *save souls* was a significant aspect of this philanthropic movement. The reference to *souls* reflected the poor moral state and depravity observed in many of those in abject poverty.

This increasing socio-political awareness of poverty and its links with social degeneration, as described by Marx, Engels, Mayhew, Charles Booth, William Booth and others in the late nineteenth century, caused governments from then until the present day to respond in various ways to the issues of social inequality. These responses include fiscal, employment, educational initiatives and addressing the needs of vulnerable groups, in particular children, the elderly, ethnic minorities and those who might be disadvantaged and suffer discrimination.

Overcoming the problems of social exclusion is a core aim of the current government policy, as documented in the *UK National Action Plan on Social Inclusion*, and *Tackling Social Exclusion* (SEU 2004). In 2006, when an increasing number of government strategies are being devised, some important questions are:

- To what extent are government and non-governmental agencies responsible for addressing the problems of social exclusion?

- What is the responsibility of the community in understanding and responding to the needs of individuals?

- What are the key features of inclusion in the community?

- How can the complex needs of individuals be assessed?

- What innovations can be supported within a human capacity building context?

The earlier association between poverty, *per se*, and social exclusion is clearly a simplistic view of a highly complex multidimensional set of causes and consequences. Socio-economic factors are highly significant, however, and a social policy perspective needs to be informed by the needs of the individuals and should recognise the importance of the appropriate assessment of these in relation to the interactions of biological, psychological and social factors operating during the development, growth and ageing of the individual.

WHO IS RESPONSIBLE?

Contrary to the expectations of many political commentators of the late nineteenth century, there were only a limited number of riots resulting from the severe unemployment and shortages of job opportunities, as exemplified by the Lancashire 'cotton famine'. Some riots did occur such as the 'Sheffield Outrages' of 1866. At this time self-help groups began to emerge. These included 'Friendly', mutual aid societies and savings banks. *Deserving* workers were given the vote and the Trade Union Act, for the first time, gave legal protection to Trade Union funds, and the Criminal Law Act of 1875 legalised peaceful picketing. These social advances were seen as benefits of the increasingly affluent British society in the mid-twentieth century. They were paralleled by the problems of excessive alcohol consumption, resulting from increased personal wealth for some, and the increasing levels of personal stress related to the competitive nature of employment in the industrial world and the increasing possibility, towards the end of the century, of mass unemployment in the face of growing competition from other economies of the United States and Western Europe. In response to the problems of heavy drinking, temperance organisations began to develop and expanded rapidly.

After the Second World War the Welfare State was developed as a response to a recognition of the inadequacies in health care and living conditions of the vast majority of people in Britain. Beveridge's Report of 1942 on *Social Insurance and Allied Services* laid down the basic concepts of the free *National Health Service*, which was introduced after the war (Thane 1982; Fraser 1984). The vulnerable and needy had previously only received support from charitable organisations, benefactors and volunteers. This was now supplemented by state-based services. Paradoxically, in 2006, the statutory services still provide the main support for people in need, but increasingly the government is relying on the private and voluntary sectors to deliver services. This presents a number of problems, not the least is the ability of charitable organisations to maintain a sustained service in a contract culture where short-term funding cycles frequently mitigate against long-term strategic planning.

Systems of care provision are changing at a time when social and economic environments are co-evolving in relation to greater individuality, for example more single people and single parents are presenting increased accommodation needs. Other demographic changes include the greater number of people living longer at a time when the traditional extended family (support) structure is becoming uncommon. A survey, *The Responsibility Gap*, by the Henley Centre (2004) revealed that a large number of people have no obligation to care for members of their extended family, their local community or vulnerable members of society. The report highlights the changing attitudes towards more individual responsibility for the individual's own health and social care, but less responsibility for that of others, due to a range of drivers including 'time squeeze', the changing roles of women, and 'hypermobility'.

In the UK the economy has grown steadily during the last 12 years and incomes have increased, unemployment has fallen. There has been a change in the distribution of income from 1979, when 10% of the population accounted for 20% and 4.4% of top and bottom incomes, respectively, compared to 17 years later when 24% had the highest, 3.5% had the lowest incomes. This change has been extrapolated by the Office for National Statistics to predict that by 2010, these high and low income sectors will be 30% and 3% of the population. The Henley report highlights the *Responsibility Gap* and the need to reflect on the respective roles of government, corporate organisation, charities and volunteering.

Putnam (2000) has documented changes in American society during the last 25 years. He has plotted the reductions in civic, religious, volunteering and philanthropic activities and growth in individualism and its various consequences. These include increasing disconnection of the individual American from his/her family, friends and social groups. This contraction in social capital is the product of reductions in social bonding, which is reflected in reduced satisfaction in life, growing social problems and negative health indicators (see Chapters 4 and 5 of this book) and increasing neighbourhood anxiety related to criminal behaviour. This period of apparent decline in *social capital* in the US should be compared with socio-political changes in the UK.

The Macmillan years during which 'we had never had it so good', followed by global economic crises, associated with energy supplies, and then 'individualism' encouraged by the Thatcherite policies of the 1980s have been superseded by a New Labour approach which has catalysed a large number of state interventions, developed within a performance management culture.

The well-intentioned target setting of this government has focused existing and new resources on key areas of need, but often targets have been set in the absence of evidence of their effectiveness, as seen for instance in the UK Anti-Drugs Strategy. Here we see inappropriate targets being set, such as the *Drug Treatment and Testing Orders* (DTTOs), which have been implemented without evidence from pilot schemes; and presently a major change in the licensing laws, which is vehemently opposed by the medical profession, the police establishment and large sectors of the community. The Licensing Act, which came into force in November 2005 is based on a number of false premises. These include the local control of licensing applications, which was heralded as the community having some measure of control over the granting of licences, and the encouragement of a Mediterranean café culture to replace the traditional British booze-culture drinking style. In the first instance, media reports in the media since the Act came into force have demonstrated a complete lack of success of community opposition to licence applications with evidence of the power of the drinks industry influencing local decision making. The movement towards a French-style café culture has already been undermined by the recent reports of high levels of alcohol-related damage in the French population (1 in 10 with a serious alcohol problem, and a much higher incidence of alcohol liver disease than found in the UK population).

The French paradox (relating to the health benefits of wine drinking) does not exist, as reported by senior French alcohol scientists at the European conference on alcoholism, held at the University of Kent in 2005. The emerging British paradox is that while this government is pursuing a criminal justice agenda in tackling the problems of alcohol and other drugs it is ignoring the health and social consequences of increasing the availability of alcohol, which will impact on individuals and society and mitigate against the government's efforts to address social exclusion.

The contemporary debates relating to alcohol and other drugs in society pivot around the balance of personal versus community responsibility. The need to protect communities is shifting policy towards a community/criminal justice agenda.

The Social Exclusion Unit, established with the office of the Deputy Prime Minister, in 1997 and a wide range of *joined-up* new initiatives including anti-poverty schemes, employment schemes and the targeting of resources to vulnerable children, have been developed. In 2005 a government department for *Respect* was established. These initiatives are reflections of the loss of social capital described by Putnam.

POVERTY AND SOCIAL EXCLUSION

Poverty is a significant, but not necessarily the most important, dimension of social exclusion. Poverty is relative and highly variable across the world and is linked to the state of the world's socio-economic development. In addressing the issue of 'Globalisation and Marginalisation', Bundell (1999) presents the following argument:

> It is now widely recognised that poor (and not so poor) communities – both North and South – are sharing an increasingly common experience as a result of recent global economic forces. Nowadays corporations, investors and financial dealers – those with wealth and resources – communicate and do business on a global basis. They manufacture where costs are lowest and they invest or deal where profits are highest. Financial dealers in particular move their money in and out of countries and local markets at a moment's notice as computers communicate across the globe . . .

This forms the rationale for the Christian Aid and Church Action on Poverty advocacy campaigns, which have today culminated in the heavily publicised and widely supported *Make Poverty History* initiative, among others. In September 2000, at the United Nations Millennium Summit (UN 2002), world leaders agreed to a set of time-bound and measurable goals and targets for combating poverty, hunger, disease, illiteracy, environmental degradation and discrimination against women. The Millennium Development Goals (MDGS) have provided a focus for international development. These aims are clearly defined, measurable and have time-bound outcomes:

• halve extreme poverty and hunger;

• achieve universal primary education;

• empower women and promote equality between men and women;

• reduce under-fives mortality by two-thirds;

• reduce maternal mortality by three-quarters;

• reverse the spread of diseases, especially HIV/AIDS and malaria;

• ensure environmental sustainability;

• create a global partnership for development, with targets for aid, trade and debt relief.

The focus on the problems of the third world should not detract from the high levels of poverty which exist in the western world. In monitoring changes in levels of poverty and social exclusion in the UK the Joseph Rowntree Foundation have reviewed 50 indicators of poverty and social exclusion (in reports covering the last five years; 2000–4). A summary of these indicators demonstrates that although 18 of the 50 indicators have improved or remained stable in recent years, increases have been reported in: the number of low birth-weight babies (25% higher among mothers in social class IIIM); the number of young offenders (3000 in England and Wales); the number of 16–18 year olds not in training (150,000); mental health problems (3.5 million, 1.5 times more prevalent in the poorest two-fifths of the population); excess winter deaths (20,000–50,000 each year); non-participation in civic organisations (10 million); and households in temporary accommodation (80,000). The main conclusions from the current Joseph Rowntree Foundation reports (JRF 2003) are that poverty is decreasing in families and in the elderly but the number of childless adults below the poverty threshold (based on 60% of median income of £200 per week for a couple with no children, £122 per week for a single person, £291 for a couple with two children, £241 for a lone parent) has increased. Furthermore 22% (12.4 million people) are living below the 'poverty line'.

The improvement, noted in the 1990s, in reducing the number of young people with few qualifications has flattened out and there is no change in 16 year olds who failed to gain five or more GCSE passes. However, the introduction of the National Literacy and Numeracy Strategies has led to significant improvements according to the DfES (DfES 2005), which states that in 2005, pupils aged 11, achieving the expected level in English was increased by 14 points, compared to 1998 and in mathematics there was a 16-point increase.

From a health perspective premature deaths in adults under 65 fell by a sixth, but premature death rates in Scotland are significantly higher than in England and Wales. There has been no change in long-term illness and inequalities in children's health and there is growing concern about increasing levels of obesity (see Chapter 9), an increase of two-fifths during the last 10 years, with women receiving below-average incomes being twice as likely to be obese as those on higher incomes.

SOCIAL GROUPS: BEHAVIOURAL PERSPECTIVES

The previous summary of the social policy context of social exclusion provides an insight into the development of support services, which are already available or should be developed in the community. However, other disciplines contribute to a wider appreciation of this multidimensional problem. The disciplines of psychology and ethology provide useful insights into human social behaviour, perspectives that increase our understanding of the nature of groups, how they function and how individuals might be included or excluded from them.

Human social behaviour has been studied by psychologists and ethologists, using two different approaches to the scientific study of behaviour. Psychological studies were developed from philosophy and initially were concerned with *vitalism*, which considered human behaviour to be the result of 'entelechial soul-like factors and inexplicable instincts' (Bierens De Haan 1940). This *vitalistic* concept was significant in the American school of psychology, which emphasised that behaviour is purposefully directed at a specific goal. Here the animal or human is motivated by expectancies that require no further explanation (Tolman 1932).

Gestalt psychologists were concerned with *wholeness* (Krueger 1948) in contrast to the American behaviourists who focused on specific stimuli and reactions and their interactions. The latter view developed from the mechanistic schools and the work of Descartes, which viewed all behaviour as being derived from physical laws. Here subjective phenomena are ignored and *wholeness* is considered to be misused by the *vitalists*.

This psychology *without mind* led to the search for elements out of which complex behaviours would arise, an approach that was closed to subjective inner experiences. The overwhelming influence of the environment, and the role of learning, was studied by Watson (1919), the father of *behaviourism* and other Americans including Thorndike (1911), Lashley (1938) and Skinner

(1953). *Behaviourists* tended to overlook the innate basis of behaviour and the possible influence of genetic background. This biological dimension of behaviour was developed by the ethologists.

Ethology emerged in Europe in the 1930s and was concerned with understanding the nature of behaviour. Although this approach was largely based on animal studies, insights into human behaviour have complemented the more extensive work undertaken by the various schools of psychology. Ethology had its origins in the work of Darwin (1872), who described the expressive movements of man and animals, but Lorenz (1931) was the first of a number of workers in this field to recognise the spontaneity underpinning *instinctive actions*. Ethology provides a biological perspective on behaviour, however, analytical methods for studying the *causality* of behaviour in other animals have been applied to human behaviour (Eibl-Eibesfeldt 1970) for instance in the study of human development and nonverbal communication. This approach has been used for the development of predictive indices of child abuse (Browne and Madely 1985).

Living in groups

The most common groups found in animals and humans are families. Such groups, originating from *kin selection*, have common sets of genes and display *altruistic* (self-sacrificing) behaviour. Other types of group exist (e.g., aggregations, anonymous groups) but *altruism* is only likely to occur in closed groups (Hamilton 1964).

The concepts of *selfish genes* (Dawkins 1976) and the fundamental drivers of altruistic and selfish behaviours have been used to explain some aspects of human behaviour. For instance a wide range of ethological studies have given an insight into aggression, which occurs within and between groups, and the role of social hierarchies. Explanations of aggressive behaviour include *learning theory* (aggressive behaviour is learned) and *frustration-aggression* (a reaction to impediments or external influences that prevent a goal being attained).

These studies demonstrate not only the influence of inherited factors but also of the various developmental factors, such as isolation and maternal deprivation, on the development of behaviour exhibited in a group setting. Individual aggression is generally suppressed in groups and women and children are more protected than men, although there are reports in the anthropological literature and contemporary media about the killing of children in wartime. Comparative studies have shown an innate inhibition to killing and suggest that binding norms of ethical behaviour seem to be programmed into humankind. Furthermore, the origin of culturally defined greeting ceremonies and other appeasement gestures provide safeguards against the possible release of aggression in group members.

A little-studied form of aggression is the *expulsion reaction*, which is directed towards a member of the group. Examples of this behaviour have been found in penguins (Kearton 1935) and chimpanzee (Lawick-Goodall 1971). In these examples group members will attack one member of the group and even kill it, if it deviates from the norm in bearing some unusual physical characteristic or deformity.

The biological basis of social structures is clearly significant in human societies. Even such fundamental aspects of group identity in animals as odours, which reduce aggression in group members, occur in humans who, despite masking their pheromones by the use of deodorants, exploit this subconscious sensory system by the use of musk, in perfumes, to attract members of the opposite sex.

Advantages of living in groups

A comparative view of group living suggests that the main advantages of groups are: to facilitate mating and the controlled interchange of genetic material; caring for the young; increased probability of individual survival by altruistic behaviours and the protection against predators; division of labour; social facilitation of individual behaviour (individuals tend to eat more when in groups) and the regulation of population size. These features can be generalised across animal and human groups, and although group structures, parenting styles and individual responses are quite diverse, an insight into the fundamental aspects of group living can be gleaned by such comparisons. Complex social groups require organisation and work. This is most exquisitely demonstrated in honeybee colonies where resource collection, building and maintenance are highly organised activities carried out by individuals specially equipped for particular functions. Although this social organisation is controlled to a large degree by genetic factors the idea of being *fit for work* and *mutual benefit* by participating in community functions are reflected in human groups.

Group cohesion

Group attraction might result from a favourable resting place offering shelter and protection, however, social attraction will form the basis of a true association that might involve one signal to attract a partner, such as a pheromone or visual signal. In the absence of aggression, bonding is likely. The nature of bonding in animals and humans has common origins, which are related to the processes concerned with reducing aggression, as discussed above.

Comparative studies of the social behaviour of man and other animals indicate that aggression is modulated by rank order, disruption of this order can release intense outbursts of aggression within a previously stable group. *Social disorganisation* occurs in human societies as revolutions, in which aggression occurs between members of the group (Scott 1960). Conversely aggressiveness against strangers is increased by group consciousness in a well-organised group. With increased group size recognition of members is achieved by a variety of mechanisms, such as *symbol identification* in humans. This is important in *appeasement gestures*, which in themselves do not keep the group together, but enable the individuals to live together. Appeasement gestures form the basis of *display behaviour* as seen in a wide range of animal and human groups.

In established groups with a ranked structure, the highest-ranking individuals often provide a unifying function, and the young, inadvertently, often increase group cohesiveness in that attraction of the young keeps the adults together. Increased *social bonding* results from the friendly reactions released by the signals produced by other young. Here physical contact is important as all gregarious animals (including humans) demonstrate a need for contact.

Appetitive behaviour (see under section Human Motivation and Reward on p. 32, Figure 2.4) for contact is evident in all primates, which deteriorate if left in isolation. When contact is established, social grooming usually occurs. Bonding can develop and be strengthened through aggression, fear, sexual activity and care of the young. With regard to sexual activity Freud traced all human social relationships to sexual origins, however, Eibl-Eibesfeldt (1970) suggests that the affectionate behaviour of a mother to her child (hugging, kissing, stroking) is not sexual in nature, as implied by Freud, since ethological studies indicate that this behaviour is a *mother–child interaction* and distinct from the sexual bonding in human social life.

Comparative ethological studies have identified *incest taboos* in a wide range of animals, including humans. The strong inhibition against mating with parents, offspring or siblings has probably evolved in family groups, which stay together for long periods, as a safeguard against inbreeding, which could have catastrophic consequences for the health of the group in subsequent generations. However, the biological basis of incest taboo in humans is controversial (David *et al.* 1963; Kortmulder 1968; Livingstone 1969). There is evidence that *not* engaging in sexual relationships with peers is learned. Children reared in Kibbutzim from early childhood, in small peer groups, engage in sexual play in the early years but by 10 years of age inhibitions occur and relationships between the sexes become tense. In adolescence the tenseness disappears and a brother–sister type bond develops. No marriages occurred in the 2769 cases studied (Shepherd 1971). The high levels of domestic violence and child sexual abuse, in our present society (see Chapter 14) suggest that these destructive behaviours, which are expressions of primary biological drives, have their origins in a biological basis of group behaviour.

SOCIAL IDENTIFICATION

'The individual's knowledge that he/she belongs to certain social groups together with some emotional and value significance to him of the group membership' is a definition of *social identity* according to Taifel (1972). Here differentiation is made between individual and group behaviour in that the latter is represented in the mind, implying a sense of *belonging*. This social psychological perspective suggests that *belonging* is more than a knowledge of the characteristics of the group. By focusing on *the group within the individual*, this social identity approach is a development of traditional social psychology, which was concerned with *the individual in the group*.

Social identity assumes that the nature of people and the interrelationships are influenced by social categories, which stand in power and status in relation to one another. *Categories* include subgroups of people of different races (Inuit, Celt), nationalities (Swedish/British), religion (Muslim/Christian) and 'power and status' suggests that some categories have more power, status and prestige. A particular social structure, therefore, will be determined by the relationship of the categories to one another. Social structures are continually changing in response to economic and political forces and individuals are born into a particular set of circumstances determined by the relationship of various social categories.

Groups are identified by deep differences in beliefs, ideology and values. These characteristics increase the competition between groups, dominant groups being able to generate and enforce a *status quo*, masking and subduing conflict (Parkin 1971). This *conflict* view, as understood via the *social identity* approach, is in contrast to the *social consensus* concept, in which 'the rules of the game' provide order and stability. Here, those who do not share common societal values or do not fit society's roles are considered to be deviant individuals who are abnormal as a result of inappropriate socialisation (Sherif 1936; Farr and Moscovici 1984).

Symbolic interactionism (Mead 1934; Meltzer *et al.* 1975) implies that the 'self' is a self-conception resulting from the influence of society on the individual. In order to facilitate effective communication, symbols have a common meaning, understood by members of the group. In this way individuals construct themselves as social objects by displaying specific symbols such as tattoos, skin piercing, crucifixes and so on. Labelling theory, concerned with the social processes that give rise to 'deviant identities', has been used to explore the mentally disturbed (Lemert 1951; Szasz 1961), drug addiction (Becker 1963) and institutionalised identities (Goffman 1968).

Social identity and group cohesion

There are two types of theories which attempt to explain the way in which people come together and stay together in groups; these relate to *interindividual interdependency* and *interindividuality*. Interindividual interdependency, as discussed by Lewin (1943), Sherif (1936) and Deutsch and Gerrard (1955), suggests that interdependency of individuals, as opposed to similarities or dissimilarities, provides the dynamic which develops and maintains group cohesion, as a result of the satisfaction of individual needs.

This mutual satisfying of need has a positive, psychological value and makes the group attractive, encouraging members to maintain their contribution to the group. Interdependence and attraction are crucial in social exchange and social reinforcement. The rewards experienced by members of the group maintain its cohesiveness. *Interindividuality* theories (Festinger 1954; Suls and Miller 1977) focus on the role of pre-existing similarities in attitudes and values between people in the formation of groups. The validation of personal values and attitudes gives reassurance to group members and satisfies a basic need to evaluate the group members, an important feature in *self-esteem*.

In addition to *interdependency of group members* and *interindividuality, social impact theory* (Latane and Wolf 1981) postulates that specific interindividual factors have an impact on the group members. These include group size (greater impact on the individual by large group size), immediacy (greater impact on the individual by shorter distances in time and space), strength of source (characteristics of the group which make it attractive to group members). Hogg and Abrams (1992) have critically reviewed the various theories regarding the social psychology of groups (see Figure 1.1), and have

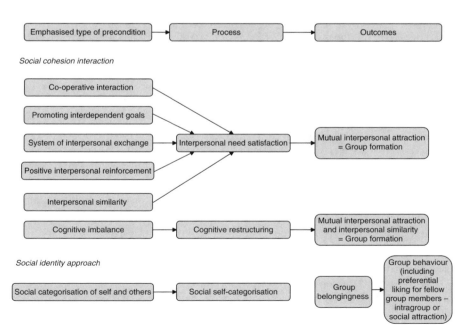

Figure 1.1   Social psychological perspectives on how groups form.
Source: Reprinted with permission from Hogg and Abrams (1988). *Social Identifications*. London: Routledge.

provided a helpful commentary on *conformity and social influence* and the role of language, speech and communication in social identification.

The discussions above indicate that being a member of a social group requires a complex set of skills, which are dependent on a range of biological and cognitive processes, effective communication, and abstract factors which make the group attractive to the individual and vice versa. Social inclusion has both physical (e.g. shelter, food, etc.) and psychological (e.g. reward and reinforcing) benefits and is a valuable mechanism for ensuring personal survival. In summary, the biological basis of individuality provides the infrastructure (the hardwiring) which, through the process of learning and socialisation, results in the uniqueness of individuals. An increased understanding of individual and group dynamics will, hopefully, give a greater insight into the complex processes of inclusion and exclusion.

REFERENCES

Becker, H. S. (1963). *Outsiders*. New York: Free Press.

Bierens De Haan, J. A. (1940). *Die tierischen Instinkte und ihr Umbau durch Erfahrung*. Leiden.

Browne, K. D. and R. Madely (1985). Ethogram: an event recorder software package. *Journal of Child Psychology and Psychiatry*, **26**, Software Section 3.

Bundell, K. (1999). *Local Lives and Livelihoods in a Global Economy*. London: Church Action on Poverty Educational Trust.

Campbell, I. and A. R. Campbell (2005). Responding to HIV/Aids, alcohol and drug misuse – developing local community capacity for care, prevention and transfer. *Alcohol and Alcoholism*, **40**(S 1), i 3.

Darwin, C. (1872). *The Expression of Emotions in Man and Animals*. London.

David, F. A., U. Bronfenbrenner, E. H. Hess, D. R. Miller, D. M. Schneider and J. N. Sphuler (1963). The incest taboo and the mating patterns of animals. *American Anthropologist*, **65**, 253–65.

Dawkins, R. (1976). *The Selfish Gene*. Oxford: Oxford University Press.

DCMS (1999). Libraries for all: social inclusion in public libraries. Policy Guidance for Local Authorities in England.

Deutsch, M. and H. B. Gerrard (1955). A study of normative and informational influences upon individual judgement. *Journal of Abnormal and Social Psychology*, **51**, 629–36.

DfES (2005). *Press Notice: Literacy and Numeracy Standards*. Department for Education and Schools.

Eibl-Eibesfeldt, I. (1970). *Ethology: The Biology of Behavior*. New York: Holt, Rinehart and Winston.

Engels, F. O. (1944). *The Conditions of the Working Class in England*. Oxford: Blackwell.

Farr, R. M. and S. Moscovici (1984). *Social Representations*. Cambridge: Cambridge University Press.

Festinger, L. (1954). A theory of social comparison processes. *Human Relations*, **7**, 117–40.

Fraser, D. (1984). *The Evolution of the British Welfare State* (2nd edn). Basingstoke: Macmillan.

Goffman, E. (1968). *Asylums*. London: Pelican.

Hamilton, W. D. (1964). The genetic evolution of social behaviour. *Journal of Theoretical Biology*, **7**, 1–52.

Henley Centre (2004). *The Responsibility Gap*. London: The Henley Centre/The Salvation Army.

Hogg, M. and D. Abrams (1992). *Social Identification*. London: Routledge.

JRF (2003). *Monitoring Poverty and Social Exclusion 2003*. York: Joseph Rowntree Foundation.

Kearton, C. (1935). *Die Insel der funf Millionen Pinguine*. Stuttgart.

Kortmulder, K. (1968). An ethological theory of the incest taboo and exogamy. *Current Anthropology*, **9**, 437–49.

Krueger, F. (1948). *Lehre von dem Ganzen*. Bern: Huber.

Lashley, K. S. (1938). Experimental analysis of instinctive behaviour. *Psychological Review*, **45**, 445–71.

Latane, B. and S. Wolf (1981). The social impact of majorities and minorities. *Psychological Review*, **88**, 438–53.

Lawick-Goodall, J. (1971). *In the Shadow of Man*. London: Collins.

Lemert, E. M. (1951). *Social Pathology*. New York: McGraw-Hill.

Lewin, K. (1943). Psychology and the process of group living. *Journal of Social Psychology*, **17**, 119–29.

Livingstone, F. B. (1969). Genetics, ecology and the origins of incest and exogamy. *Current Anthropology*, **10**, 45–61.

Lorenz, K. (1931). Beitrage zur Ethologie Sozialer Corviden. *Journal of Ornithology*, **76**, 137–413.

Mead, G. H. (1934). *Mind, Self and Society*. Chicago: University of Chicago Press.

Meltzer, M., J. W. Petras and L. T. Reynolds (1975). *Symbolic Interactionism: Genesis, Varieties and Criticisms*. London: Routledge & Kegan Paul.

Parkin, F. (1971). *Class Inequality and Political Order, Social Stratification in Capitalist and Communist Societies*. London: MacGibbon and Kee.

Percy-Smith, J. ed. (2000). *Policy Responses to Social Exclusion: Towards Inclusion?* Milton Keynes: Open University Press.

Putnam, R. (2000). *Bowling Alone: The Collapse and Revival of American Community*. New York: Simon Schuster.

Scott, J. P. (1960). *Aggression*. Chicago: Chicago University Press.

SEU (2004). *Tackling Social Exclusion: Taking Stock and Looking to the Future. Emerging Findings*. London: Social Exclusion Unit, Office of the Deputy Prime Minister.

Shepherd, J. (1971). Mate selection among second generation kibbutz adolescents and adults: incest avoidance and negative imprinting. *Archives of Sexual Behavior*, **I**, 293–307.

Sherif, M. (1936). *The Psychology of Social Norms*. New York: Harper & Bros.

Skinner, B. F. (1953). *Science and Human Behaviour*. New York: Macmillan.

Suls, J. M. and R. L. Miller (eds) (1977). *Social Comparison Processes: Theoretical and Empirical Perspectives*. Washington: Hemisphere.

Szasz, T. (1961). *The Myth of Mental Illness*. New York: Hoeber.

Taifel, H. (1972). Social categorisation. In S. Moscovici (ed.), *Introduction à la Psychologie Sociale*, Vol. 1. Paris: Larousse.

Thane, P. (1982). *The Foundations of the Welfare State*. Harlow: Longman.

Thorndike, E. L. (1911). *Animal Intelligence*. New York: Macmillan.

Tolman, E. C. (1932). *Purposive Behaviour in Animals and Man*. New York: Appleton.

UN (2002). *Implementing the Millennium Declaration*. United Nations Department of Public Information http://www.un.org/millenniumgoals/MDGs-FACTSHEET1.pdf.

Watson, J. B. (1919). *Psychology from the Standpoint of a Behaviourist*. Philadelphia: Lippincott.

CHAPTER 2

INDIVIDUAL FUNCTIONING

THE CONCEPT OF SELF

In the previous chapter it is clear that groups are complex organisations which are dynamic, changing with time, and an individual in a group becomes transformed by membership of that group. He/she assumes a *social identity*. The concept of *social identity* focuses on *the group within the individual.* This mind-centred approach to social behaviour provides an insight into the person's inner experience of being a group member or, alternatively, the subjective experience of being excluded from a group. This chapter attempts to provide a review of the subjective experiences of *self*, and provides an insight into *meaning and belonging*, from a neuropsychological viewpoint. This will include a brief review of brain mechanisms, which provide the substrate for consciousness, through which individual identity is established and maintained. This will be followed by a review of behavioural and neural mechanisms of reward-mediated behaviour.

The emerging discipline of neuropsychology attempts to investigate the basis of clinical diseases of the brain, it involves the study and treatment of cognitive, emotional and behavioural problems caused by neurological disorders. Traditionally, psychological and neurological studies rarely take account of decision making or *judgement* as seen in patients with frontal-lobe syndromes such as those with Korsakov's syndrome. These patients have an inability to make judgements. While man and other animals can survive without abstract reasoning and thought, *judgement* is perhaps the most important, life-preserving faculty.

The loss of specific neurological functions, through disease or injury, results in disability or impairment of speech, vision, dexterity, memory and other behaviours, which are needed for the person to function independently, and as part of a group. Of these various losses memory is particularly devastating due to its central role in maintaining *personality*, and *social identity*. This is exemplified by the loss of visual memory suffered after, for example, road accidents; the resulting *Traumatic Brain Injury* (TBI) may lead to the inability of a patient to recognise his/her family and subsequent consequences for *social identity* and functioning within the family group.

Sacks (1985) describes a number of cases in which patients lose awareness of themselves. In the case of the 'disembodied lady', Christina, a confident and competent 27-year-old with two young children developed an infection leading to polyneuritis and lost an awareness of her own body. This 'disembodying' involved a total loss of all bodily sensations. All awareness of self (*proprioception*) had been lost leaving no sense of state and position of muscles, tendons or joints, an extreme situation in which the inflammation had affected her *proprioception*, one of the three sensory inputs which provide a sense of the position of our body in time and space. The other two sensory inputs are vision and balance. This loss of the somatic basis of identity, described by Freud as 'body ego', results in depersonalisation or de-realisation. Sacks notes similar body image disturbances, resulting from severe neuropathies, which occur in people who have overdosed on vitamin B6 (pyridoxine).

In addition to TBI, brain damage can result from other clinical conditions that have a nutritional basis. For instance diabetes can result in neuropathy which very occasionally develops beyond a severe 'glove and stocking' neuropathy to a complete numbness and feeling of nothingness or de-realisation. In these cases, and in the loss of *proprioception*, the loss of subjective awareness is due to reduced or loss of electrical activity in the nervous system.

Korsakov's syndrome is one of the more acute examples of loss of identity. In most cases, chronic use of alcohol causes neurotoxicity (death of neurons in the brain), which is exacerbated by nutritional deficiencies. This frequent problem in socially excluded people will be considered in more detail in Chapter 8, however, a brief comment on this condition will be given here as it provides a fascinating insight into the concept of personal and social identity.

People suffering from Korsakov's psychosis suffer severe memory loss but replace what has been lost by *confabulating*. Sometimes quite remarkable powers of invention are used to create a world literally moment by moment in order to provide a life story which has been lost and compensate for a world which is continually disappearing, losing meaning and value. This example of confabulation, to replace what has been lost, indicates the importance of our own personal narrative, the story of our lives which is continually being added to, unconsciously, informed by our perceptions, thoughts and actions and significantly via dialogue with other people in the social group and beyond. We have a basic need to possess a story, sometimes the external view of our historical identity is an edited version of our innermost story. This is a central aspect of our concept of *self*. In the case of someone who has lost significant parts of their narrative, the loss of reality leads to the question as to whether the person has lost their *soul*. Is it possible that severe amnesia such as found in a range of conditions resulting from accidental, degenerative or nutritional/toxic induced brain

damage can lead to a person being *de-souled*? In such amnesic conditions
it is not only a matter of loss of a personal narrative but also a central
capacity for feeling that has disappeared, which may be described as being
de-souled. Luria (1976) described this as the final pathology, the ultimate
destroyer of the world. In *Neuropsychology of Memory* he presents a range
of frontal-lobe syndromes and their catastrophic consequences in shattering
lives. Those who have lost their reality, who appear not to be suffering, are
possibly the most Godforsaken. From a theological perspective an immortal
soul could be *lost*, which might be redeemed or found. Kierkegaard used
the term *despair*, a concept which suggests that a person who is in *despair*
has the possibility of regaining a sense of reality and meaning through the
process of salvation. This metaphysical approach is widely used in treatment programmes for addressing dependency on alcohol and other drugs.
A more detailed review of this application of the spiritual dimension of
treatment is given in Chapter 11. However, before we leave these key aspects
of *being human* we will review the ideas on the *soul* through the history of
neuroscience.

THE MIND, BODY AND SOUL

During the last 20 years there have been major advances in our understanding of the brain and its functions (Carlsson 1990). These advances
have resulted from technological developments in neuroscience, in particular through new approaches to brain imaging and molecular studies
of neurotransmitter systems and the underlying genetic mechanisms.
The human genome has been mapped and we now have a very
detailed understanding of information processing in the brain. With so
much new information long-standing philosophical questions are being
readdressed:

• Can the neurosciences explain the mind?

• Is the soul a redundant concept?

Around 600–400 BC Greek philosophers were concerned with early
concepts of the mind and soul. There was an ongoing debate on the location
of the process of *thinking*. Did this occur in the brain or the most centralised
organ in the body, the heart? Plato and Galen added to this debate by
considering the relationship between the body and the soul. The rational
soul was considered to have its seat in the brain. From these discussions
Galen developed the idea of the *psychic pneuma*: which he suggested was
produced and stored in the vesicles of the brain. This liquid became known
as the 'animal spirits' and later 'nervous fluid' in the eighteenth century.
Galen asked whether the 'psychic pneuma' could be the substance of the
soul or the soul itself? During the sixteenth century the early anatomists

contributed to this ongoing debate by providing an understanding of the structures and functioning of the body. Vesalius (1543) carried out anatomical observations and described the gross anatomy of the nervous system. Descartes (1649) was impressed by the flow of *animal spirits* from the heart to the ventricles and made comparisons with machines and developed a hydraulic model of function. From the anatomical observations he noted the central position of the pineal gland in the head and suggested that this might be the seat of the soul (Figure 2.1). This was an intriguing comment, which had significance in the 1960s when the pineal gland was shown to produce a complex mixture of hormone-like compounds (e.g. melatonin and related behaviourally active metabolites) that play a role in the biochemical basis of mental illness (see Chapter 7).

From these early ideas on the functioning of the brain major strides have been made in the advancement of neuroscience.

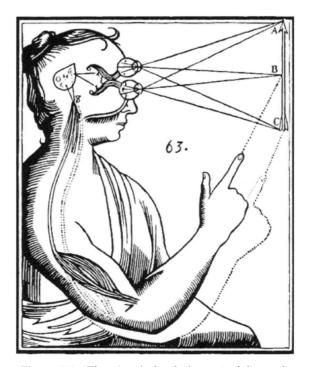

Figure 2.1 The pineal gland: the seat of the soul.
Source: Descartes, R. (1664). *L'Homme*. Paris. (In French). Digitised photographic reproduction available online. Reprinted in Adam and Tannery vol. XI. Partial English translation in CSM vol. I. Complete English translation in Hall 1972.

CONTEMPORARY VIEWS ON BRAIN FUNCTION

The ideas presented above demonstrate that an understanding of body, mind and soul has preoccupied the thoughts of philosophers and scientists since the dawn of academic enquiry. Some of the greatest thinkers have attempted to understand the material basis of the universe and the nature of creation, through scientific and metaphysical enquiry. Einstein, for instance, developed a 'theory of everything', which included the revolutionary concepts of *relativity*, but could not reconcile his ideas with the probabilistic concepts contained in the theory of quantum mechanics on the basis that *creation* could not be explained by such a theory. The brain is considered to be the most complex material in the universe, consisting of a layering of structures ranging from molecules to neurons, conductors of information in the brain, to entire regions from which behaviour is generated. A detailed explanation of structure and function is required in order to answer questions such as:

• How is the brain affected by the environment during development?

• How are normal and abnormal behaviours determined?

• What effect does (social) isolation have on brain function?

• Why are some individuals more vulnerable to alcohol and other drugs than others and become dependent on them?

   It has been estimated that about 30 billion neurons, or nerve cells, form the wrinkled and convoluted cerebral cortex (Figure 2.2). If unfolded the cortex would be approximately the same size as an A3 piece of paper. The neurons (Figure 2.3) are functionally linked together via one million *synapses*, small gaps between individual neurons (see Chapter 7 for more detail), forming a dense network described as *grey matter*. Communication is possible over longer distances by means of the extended parts of the neurones called *axons*, forming the *white matter*.

The management of information from the external world

Sensory information from the external world is relayed inwards and, after processing, behaviour is produced via *motor systems*. This *sensorimotor* information is managed by subdivisions in the cortex that mediate hearing, touch, taste and sight. These sensory modalities are linked to motor regions, the activity of which is reflected in muscular movements resulting in locomotion, speech and other behaviour outputs. The synaptic organisation of the brain provides a system whereby the vast flow of information is modulated and channelled into appropriate behaviour responses. These multiple sites of information control are the target areas through which medications and

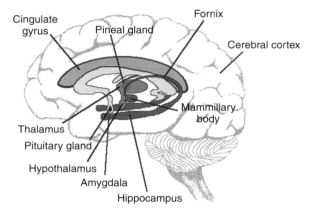

The Limbic system

Figure 2.2 Diagrammatic display of external convolutions and some main components of the limbic system, the 'emotion' centre of the brain (see also Figure 7.4, for cellular basis of learning in the hippocampus).
Source: http://normandy.sandhills.cc.nc.us/psy150/brlimbic.html. Reprinted with permission from Judson Scott Lewis.

drugs of abuse have their effect (see Chapter 7, 'Neurotransmission and Information Management', p. 104).

In considering the nature of consciousness (see section 'Consciousness: A Unique Function of the Human Brain', p. 27), a wide range of brain regions is involved, one of the most important structures of which is the thalamus. This small structure (about 1.5 square centimetres) is located in the centre of the brain, and is served by nerves from the various sensory receptors (e.g. retina, inner ear, skin and so on) forming clusters called nuclei. Neurons from each of these clusters project extensions, called *axons*, to specific areas of the cortex. An example of this is the link between the primary visual cortex area (named Visual Area I, VI) and the optic nerves from the retina, which are linked to the lateral geniculate nucleus in the thalamus. Thalamocortical tracts consist of neurons from the cortex, which feed back to the thalamus. One such fibre bundle is the corpus callosum, which connects the two hemispheres, and consists of 200 million reciprocal axons. Two different consciousnesses can be produced by cutting the corpus callosum, leading to a split-brain syndrome. The reticular nucleus surrounds the thalamus and, by connecting to each specific nucleus, can inhibit their activity. It is thought that the *reticular nucleus* provides a gate or switching mechanism thereby regulating the expressions of sensory functions such as sight, hearing and touch. Another thalamic nucleus is the *intralaminar nucleus* which is implicated in consciousness in that it establishes appropriate thresholds or levels of cortical response; if set too high, consciousness is lost.

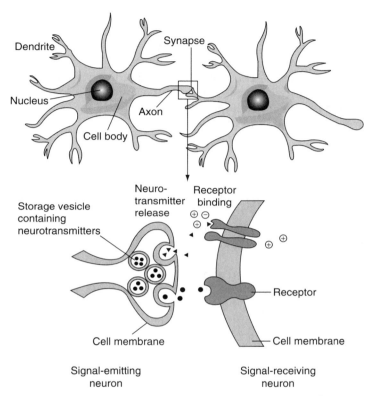

Figure 2.3   View of neurons and detail of the synaptic junctions showing the release of neurotransmitters from the pre-synaptic neuron and activation of the receptors on the post-synaptic neuron.
Source: NIH/NIAAA.

The neural basis of emotional behaviour

A complex set of structures known as the *limbic system* (Figure 2.2) is found deep within the centre of the brain. This is considered to be the emotional core of the brain, consisting of the subcortical regions which include the hippocampus, the basal ganglia and the amygdala. The *basal ganglia* are the primary structures concerned with motor control and its sequencing. Loss of the synaptic neurotransmitter, dopamine, from these structures results in Parkinson's disease. In this condition patients have difficulties in initiating motor activity, show muscular rigidity and express certain mental symptoms. The basal ganglia are therefore critically important in initiation and control of motor patterns and also *procedural memory*. This form of memory is important in learning to drive a car and other non-conscious learned activities. Furthermore, the basal ganglia are involved in forming categories of perceptions during experience (Greenfield 2000).

In addition to sensory and cognitive functioning, the brain's motor functions are critically important in forming images and concepts as well as the regulation of movement. The *motor cortex* is involved in these outputs by, for example, the production of signals via the spinal cord to the muscles. By this means the cerebellum, a large bulge at the rear of the brain, coordinates and controls movement and the various sensory loops.

Learning and memory

The hippocampus, appearing like a pair of seahorses, contains the synaptic mechanisms responsible for cellular location of memory, a property of the system which depends on specific neuronal connections (see Chapter 7). The initial ideas for this most important brain function were developed by Hebb (1955, 1976), who suggested that memory was established when pre- and post-synaptic neurons fired in close temporal order (i.e. within a few milliseconds), which increased synaptic efficiency. Later studies pointed to the role of the NMDA receptors (Muller *et al.* 2002) via a mechanism called *long-term potentiation* (LTP). Many studies of the properties of LTP have shown that this form of plasticity is central to the cellular basis of learning and memory. Contemporary work indicates that modifications of NMDA receptors (see Figure 7.5, p. 106), found in the hippocampus, account for the *potentiation* of synaptic transmission. Furthermore, recent studies suggest that LTP, in addition to changes in synaptic function, is also associated with the growth of synapses (synaptogenesis) (Muller *et al.* 2002).

The hippocampus provides for the memory of specific episodes or experiences of life. An important set of structures that are critical to learning and maintaining consciousness are the ascending systems. Edelman (2004) has labelled these *value systems* because their activity is related to rewards and responses essential for survival. These systems include the *locus coeruleus*, a small number of neurones which release noradrenaline; the *raphe nucleus*, which releases serotonin; various cholinergic nuclei, which release acetylcholine; the dopaminergic nuclei, which release dopamine; and the histaminergic system, found in the hypothalamus, a subcortical region which has many functions including the main linkage between the central nervous system and the endocrine (hormonal) system (noradrenaline, serotonin, acetylcholine, dopamine and glutamate are *neurotransmitters*; important in information management in the brain, see Chapter 7). These *value systems* influence large populations of neurons simultaneously by releasing neurotransmitters in an aerosol manner, thus affecting the probability that neurons regionally located to the value system will fire, after receiving glutamatergic input. In this way responses for survival are produced by learning and memory systems which are tuned to the existing physiological and behaviour states of the individual.

In the brain other loci release neuropeptides, such as enkelp, an endogenous opioid, which regulates an individual's response to pain. This mechanism is important in dependent drug users, an understanding of which is pertinent to perceptions of pain and pleasure, key aspects of the bio-psycho-social theory of opioid dependence (see section, 'Reward Mediated Behaviour and Substance Misuse', p. 33). This topic will be developed further in considering the role of opioid systems in mother–infant interactions during development. Another aspect of the development of dependency is the role of emotion, in particular fear. The amygdala, within the limbic system, mediates this response. These aspects of brain function will be discussed later in this chapter.

In summary, the three main neuroanatomical systems in the brain consist of the *thalamocortical* set of local and regional reciprocal loops, the polysynaptic inhibitory loop of the *basal ganglia* and the diffuse ascending projection of the various *value systems*, located in the limbic system.

CONSCIOUSNESS: A UNIQUE FUNCTION OF THE HUMAN BRAIN

Consciousness is thought to be a specific feature of the human animal and its loss considered to be equivalent to death. To understand it requires a knowledge of brain structure and function (see the section 'Contemporary Views on Brain Function', p. 23 above). James (1981), in *Principles of Psychology*, explored the properties of consciousness. He argued that an understanding of consciousness requires a metaphysical approach. While this may be important, advances in the science of the brain suggest the benefits in understanding and alleviating suffering may be progressed by advances in neurobiological and neuropsychological methods and new technologies. For instance studying how the firing of the neurons gives rise to subjective sensations, thoughts and emotions, provides an explanation and a treatment rationale for a range of emotional (affective) disorders. This suggests that both metaphysical and scientific approaches should be reconciled to provide a holistic view of the human conditions such as stigma, feelings of exclusion and other complex conditions, which lie across the boundaries of several disciplines.

As discussed earlier the Ancient Greeks believed that consciousness resided in the heart, an idea that is still implied in many contemporary metaphors. However, there is strong support for the idea that the organisation and operation of the brain underpin consciousness, as evidenced by loss of consciousness when brain function ceases during anaesthesia, following stroke and traumatic events. Studies of sleep (Empson 1993) also provide some insight into the nature of consciousness. Consciousness is a process not a thing. Although an area of the brain may be essential or necessary for consciousness this does not mean that consciousness is solely dependent on it; the process of consciousness is more likely to be reliant on the distributed activities of populations of neurons in various regions of the brain.

Value systems in the central nervous system

The *Theory of Neuronal Group Selection* (TNGS) provides a global brain theory to explain some key aspects of brain function and contributes to our understanding of consciousness. TNGS suggests that memory is the capacity to repeat or suppress a specific mental or physical response, resulting from changes in synaptic efficacy (synaptic strength) in groups of neurons. Edelman (2004) has proposed that in the evolutionary transition between reptiles and birds and reptiles and mammals a new reciprocal set of neuronal connections appeared in the form of the *thalamocortical system*. The increased connective capacity between the cortical areas, involved in perceptual categorisation, and the more frontal areas, responsible for value category memory have resulted in the emergence of extensive *re-entry corticocortical connections* linking wide areas of the cortex. This and other developments in brain structure and function have resulted in the origin of *value-category memory* facilitating the ability to construct a complex scene and to make discriminations between components of that scene. This provides the functional basis of *primary consciousness*.

The concept of primary consciousness is consistent with the view that it is an active process which gives rise to *higher order consciousness* and the ability to imagine the future, explicitly recall the past and the awareness of being conscious. A remarkable feature of consciousness is that it is unitary, i.e., it is in one piece. Conscious moments simultaneously include sensory input, consequential motor activity, emotions, fleeting memories, imagery, bodily sensations (proprioception) and a peripheral fringe. With such complex sets of information it is not surprising that individuals have an inability to undertake three or more conscious acts at the same time. The evolutionary importance of this limitation is possibly linked to the need of the individual to complete motor actions and strategies without interruption, a strategy which has survival value.

The term *quale* has been used to describe the phenomenal experience or specific conscious state such as craving, pain, warmth, pleasure. Philosophers regard an understanding of *qualia* as central to the concept of consciousness. Neuroscientists have contributed to this debate by suggesting the neurobiological basis of *qualia* that produce difference subjective experiences. TNGS suggests that *qualia* are higher order discriminations in a complex domain.

The unitary nature of *qualia* is thought to emerge from the dynamic *thalamocortical* system, which can change its functional connectivity within milliseconds. The possibility of rapidly relating *value-category memory* to perceptual categorisation allows for the connection of conceptual and memory maps. Consciousness involves sensory inputs from the external world as well as internal signals, via proprioceptors, aspects of kinaes-thetic somato-sensory awareness. These subconscious functions provide salience for the various internal and external events related to a partic-ular *quale*. That is, higher order consciousness is based on a set of refer-ences, which are related to the neuronal status of the body. These neuronal explanations provide an insight into how the individual is aware of his or her changing circumstances and underline the need to consider primary consciousness as a fundamental state, which underpins higher order consciousness.

CONSCIOUSNESS AND NONCONSCIOUSNESS

The organisation of behaviour, which involves the relationship between movement and time, results from the activities of the subcortical struc-tures; the basal ganglia, the cerebellum and the hippocampus. The perfor-mance of habitual and automated behaviours, for instance playing a musical instrument, is possible due to transactions between the basal ganglia and the cortex. This provides a link between conscious and nonconscious functions. Motor circuits in the basal ganglia modulate movement by enhancing some cortical responses and suppressing others. This offers an explanation as to why Parkinson's patients show cognitive defects in addi-tion to the problems of initiating and controlling movement (see Arcin-iegas and Bereford 2001). Basal ganglia are associated with defects and repetitive actions connected with obsessive-compulsive disorders. Further-more absent-mindedness and the severe cognitive defects in dementia are thought to result from the disease process impacting on the basal ganglia projections to the prefrontal cortex. In considering the links between the basal ganglia and the cortex an explanation for the emergence of complex behaviours emerges. This can be exemplified by learning to play a piano concerto, for instance. Here detailed attention is required to learn a particular section of the music, which, after many repetitions becomes automated. Later, two or more sections, which have become learnt, may be joined by conscious effort and further practice, again leading to automated execution. In the performance of the concerto the pianist will perform without conscious attention but will be planning consciously ahead for the next sections of the concerto. This example indi-cates that the operation of the dynamic nonconscious part of the brain can operate in isolation from the cortex, working at a higher level of organisation.

Human values

The above examples provide an insight into *primary consciousness*, a property which is shared between man and other members of the animal kingdom. A sense of the past and a concept of the future, and awareness of nameable *self* is, as far as can be determined, not possessed by animals with only *primary consciousness*. It appears that the added features which have evolved in humans, setting them apart from other animals, are the abilities to use symbols as tokens and link meaning (i.e. value) to acts and events and to contemplate future events. This semantic capability has allowed the development of *high-order consciousness*. Humans are conscious of being conscious. *High-order consciousness* depends in part on the episodic memory, established in the hippocampus, providing semantic activity but *primary consciousness* is also required. The evolution of semantic and then linguistic abilities is clearly critical for the development of *high-order consciousness*.

Bruner (see Edelman 2004, p. 100) has highlighted the great expansion in consciousness made possible by the *re-entrant* interactions between maps of concepts and linguistic tokens and the nonconscious parts of the brain. With the acquisition of a true language and an expanding lexicon, *high-order consciousness* can lead to more precise categorisation of interpersonal (between individuals) and intrapersonal (within the individual) experience. This high level analysis of *social identity* and increasing powers of narrative allows a socially constructed *self* which can be referenced to past recollections and future insights. In this way *high-order consciousness* makes possible representation *in the mind.*

Philosophers and neuroscientists have a common interest in understanding the relationship between *qualia* and *the mind*, however, an important question addressed within this text is how such abstract concepts contribute to our understanding of *self* in terms of *meaning and belonging* from an individual's perspective. One immediate response to this is to recognise the enormous variation in human experience made possible by the possession of *high-order consciousness*. The answer to this question must surely take account of emotional responses interacting with *value systems* and the processes giving rise to *primary consciousness* and *high-order consciousness*. Individual emotional responses are modulated by the diffuse *ascending-value systems*, such as the locus coeruleus, the raphe nuclei, various cholinergic and dopaminergic systems and some hypothalamic systems.

The earliest conscious experiences arise from the combination of inputs from value, proprioceptor and sensory systems; with ongoing experience adaptive systems result in the generation of new *qualia*. This aspect of individual development, providing a unique point of view of *self* within the world, will clearly be influenced by biological psychological and social factors during development, adolescence and later life maturation. Whatever positive and negative experiences have impacted on the development of the individual, the conscious brain, in health and disease will integrate what can be integrated and resist a shattered view of reality.

HUMAN MOTIVATION AND REWARD

Miller (1962) defined motivation as 'all those pushes and prods – biological, social and psychological – that defeat our laziness and move us, either eagerly or reluctantly, to action'. This aspect of human functioning deserves comment because, without this *goal-directed*, purposeful behaviour both humans and other animals would not survive. Maslow's hierarchy of needs (Maslow 1954) is a helpful framework to consider the basic biological, homeostatic, drives required for survival, within the context of a hierarchy of other drives leading to *self-actualisation*. The spectrum of motivational dynamics includes internal and external; innate and learned; mechanistic and cognitive; and conscious and unconscious elements. These may be grouped as survival or physiological motives and competence or cognitive motives (Gross 2006).

Maslow's *humanistic* psychological approach to motivation is concerned with high-level human functioning (including being conscious), but the pyramid-shaped model emphasises the importance of the fundamental events in the central nervous system, the autonomic system and the endocrine system, and interactions within and between these biological subsystems, on which higher functions depend.

Other approaches to the study of motivation include *psychodynamic* and *behavioural* perspectives. Freud's attempts to discover the internal unconscious drives and motives are encapsulated in *psychoanalytical* theory (see Gross, 2006). Observations of *schedules of reinforcement* in rats and pigeons laid down the foundations of our current understanding of the nature of motivation and conditioned learning as described by Skinner (1953).

An understanding of both homeostatic, survival-based drives and higher level factors related to self-actualisation is important in working with socially excluded people because frequently harm-reducing, life-saving strategies and interventions are required in the initial contact phase, see p. 159. Motivational dimensions of *self-esteem* and *self-actualisation* are important in the development of *social identity* (see the section 'Social Identification' in Chapter 1, p. 13) and the process of social exclusion.

Maintaining homeostasis

Cannon (1929) used the term homeostasis (*homos* meaning the same; *stasis* meaning stoppage) to describe the process whereby an organism maintains a near constant internal (bodily) environment. The regulation of body

temperature, salt concentration, blood sugar levels and many other physiological parameters is essential for survival. Imbalances in the physiological
status are normally compensated by a reaction such as sweating to reduce
body heat, or consuming food to adjust for decreases in sugar concentrations. These automatic, unconscious, responses are regarded as homeostatic
drives, which lead to appropriate *gaol-directed* behaviours. In the maintenance of the internal environment breathing results in oxygen intake and the
exhalation of carbon dioxide, these are *involuntary* and *continuous*, whereas
eating, drinking and sexual behaviour are *voluntary* and *discontinuous*. An
example of a *discontinuous* behaviour is shown in Figure 2.4.

Goal-directed behaviour is cyclical and consists of searching (appetitive),
goal-seeking, goal-finding, consummatory and quiescent (recovery) phases
before the next cycle of behaviour begins. The time between successive
phases of goal-directed behaviour will be determined by the internal needs
of the human or other animal. These needs are monitored in the case of
sugar, carbon dioxide in the blood and other physiological parameters by
the hypothalamus, a small structure at the base of the limbic system. The
hypothalamus (see Figure 5.2, p. 74) is linked with the pituitary gland,
which responds to activities in the central nervous system (primarily the
hypothalamus) by producing one or more of a range of releasing factors
which control the activity of the endocrine system. Feedback systems (see
the section 'Stress in Children and Families', Chapter 5, p. 73) are central to
addressing the motivation of hunger and eating, as suggested by the glucostatic (Mayer 1955) and the lipostatic theories (Green 1994). These theories
assume that the central nervous system responds to physiological *set points*.

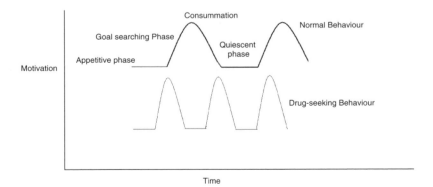

Figure 2.4   Diagrammatic representation of the change in motivational state in goal-
directed behaviour. A comparison between normal behaviour and drug-seeking
behaviour is displayed. The increased amplitude and high frequency of consummatory acts are typically found in those with addictive behaviours.

Contemporary views suggest that, rather than the original mechanical thermostat model, various physiological factors drift around a set point until they achieve balance or equilibrium. Pinel's analogy is that set points are achieved as in the case of a leaky barrel, the amount of fat in the body is regulated around a naturally regulated set point, rather than a predetermined set point, as suggested by the earlier thermostat model.

The limbic system is involved in decision making in relation to external and internal stimuli. The activity of this system is suppressed in PAP syndrome (athymhormic syndrome), which results in 'loss of mental self-activation'. In these patients, the various nervous stimuli have no emotional content, so the patient remains non-motivated. They act immediately when spoken to, as neural information passes directly from the language centre (Wernicke's area) to the frontal lobe, bypassing the limbic system. Lack of motivation in depressed patients results from a nonfunctioning caudate nucleus (in the limbic system), which dampens responses in the frontal lobe. Conversely, in some schizophrenics, abnormalities in receptors that respond to the neurotransmitter dopamine decrease the effectiveness of the limbic system (Laplane and Dubois 1998).

Reward-mediated behaviour and substance misuse

Figure 2.4 shows the cyclic changes in motivation characteristic of *voluntary* and *discontinuous* behaviours. This model of *goal-seeking* behaviour can also be used to explain drug-seeking behaviour, which is either directed at reducing pain or increasing pleasure. Drug seeking and drug consumption are thought to subvert the natural processes which maintain the equilibrium of pain and pleasure. This occurs by a reduction in *appetitive* and *goal-seeking* periods and obtaining a 'hit' or a 'high' (the consummatory act) by short-circuiting the natural processes of reward-mediated behaviour (Figure 2.4). When this occurs the activity of the *dopamine-mesolimbic reward system*, in the brain, responds to drugs which activate these dopamine-containing neurones giving very significant elevated sensations of intense pleasure. This is particularly evident in the response to ingestion of crack cocaine resulting in 'orgasmic-like highs', which reduce within minutes and require further drug intake to maintain the feelings of intense pleasure. The individual responses to drug and other direct stimulations of the brain involve the complex limbic system, the emotional centre of the brain (see Chapter 7, section 'Neurobiological Basis of Substance Use and Dependence', p. 114).

An explanation for dependence on opioids, such as heroin and related compounds is that these compounds have natural receptors in the central nervous system, predominantly occurring in the reward and pain pathways of the brain. The body's natural opioid system has important functions in inhibiting breathing, mobility and other behaviours of the foetus in the later stages of conception and the initiation and maintenance of the infant–mother bond, postnatally. In this case homeostasis is maintained by an increase in endogenous opiates (morphine) when anxiety is reduced after resumption of the infant–mother bond (see Chapter 5, section 'Anxiety, Socialisation and Mental Health', p. 78, and also Figure 11.1, p. 185). This pharmacological explanation of *affiliative* behaviours, as described by Bowlby (1977), can now be extended to suggest increased vulnerabilities of those who experienced poor mother–infant bonding, perhaps leading to later life psychopathologies including vulnerability to opiate dependence. Aspects of maternal and paternal deprivation together with a wide range of negative childhood experiences are commonly reported in clients using homeless and addiction services in the community.

This behavioural pharmacological perspective on social exclusion, then, should be considered from a development viewpoint (see Chapter 3) in that early experiences not only shape the developing central nervous system, by establishing homeostatic balances of neurotransmitters and their respective receptors, but also provide a growing reservoir of memories against which current challenges are compared via the activity of the limbic system. An interesting question arises from these discussions as to whether this disrupted developmental progression should be considered to be *brain damage* per se or a *maladaptive behaviour*. No matter which description is used, the reality of irreversibility of this process strongly suggests the overwhelming influence of child abuse on later life behaviours and antecedents of psychiatric morbidity (Teichner *et al.* 2000).

This chapter has briefly reviewed a number of processes relating to normal neuropsychological functioning and the underlying physiological mechanisms which provide homeostasis, the development of consciousness and self-actualisation. These physiological and mental states are determined by a complex set of interdependent biological, psychological and social factors, which become perturbed as a result of the many threats and challenges from the external world. Understanding this huge array of sensory (external) information requires complex information processing in the brain, and a value system which allows appropriate responses to be made. The processes of decision making (judgements) require the various components of the brain to work effectively, and provide the substrate of our understanding of the concepts of *meaning and belonging*. The attribution of value to information being processed in the brain requires *value-category memory*. An historical record of past neural and related behavioural experiences is, therefore, important in making an appropriate response today. Negative memories generated in childhood, subversion of the natural processes of reward and punishment and cognitive changes, and damage, resulting from the use and abuse of alcohol and other drugs will all contribute to a person's ability to function independently and in social groups.

REFERENCES

Arciniegas, D. B. and T. P. Bereford (2001). *Neuropsychiatry: An Introductory Approach.* Cambridge: Cambridge University Press.

Bowlby, J. (1977). The making and breaking of affectional bonds. I. Aetiology and psychopathology in the light of attachment theory. An expanded version of the Fiftieth Maudsley Lecture, delivered before the Royal College of Psychiatrists, 19 November 1976. *British Journal of Psychiatry*, **130**, 201–10.

Cannon, W. B. (1929). *Bodily Changes in Pain, Hunger, Fear and Rage.* New York: Appleton.

Carlsson, A. (1990). Early psychopharmacology and the rise of modern brain research. *Journal of Psychopharmacology*, **4**(3), 120–6.

Descartes, R. (1649). *Les passions de l'ame.* Vol. XI. Amsterdam: Reprinted in Adam Tannery.

Edelman, G. M. (2004). *Wider than the Sky: The Phenomenal Gift of Consciousness.* London: Penguin.

Empson, J. (1993). *Sleep and Dreaming* (2nd edn). Hemel Hempstead: Wheatsheaf.

Green, S. (1994). *Principles of Biopsychology.* Sussex: Lawrence Erlbaum Associates.

Greenfield, S. (2000). *The Private Life of the Brain.* London: Penguin.

Gross, R. (2006). *Psychology, The Science of Mind and Behaviour.* Chichester, UK: John Wiley & Sons, Ltd.

Hebb, D. O. (1955). Drives and the CNS (conceptual nervous system). *Psychological Review*, **62**(4), 243–54.

Hebb, D. O. (1976). Physiological learning theory. *Journal of Abnormal Child Psychology*, **4**(4), 309–14.

James, W. (1981). *The Principles of Psychology.* Cambridge: Harvard University Press.

Laplane, D. and B. Dubois (1998). Affective disorders due to loss of mental self-activation. *Review of Neurology*, **54**(1), 35–9.

Luria, A. R. (1976). *The Neuropsychology of Memory.* New York: Basic Books.

Maslow, A. (1954). *Motivation and Personality.* New York: Harper & Row.

Mayer, J. (1955). Regulation of energy intake and the body weight: the glucostatic theory and lipostatic hypothesis. *Annals of the New York Academy of Sciences*, **63**, 15–43.

Miller, G. A. (1962). *Psychology: The Science of Mental Life.* Harmondsworth: Penguin.

Muller, D., I. Nikonenko, P. Jourdain and S. Alberi (2002). LTP, memory and structural plasticity. *Current Molecular Medicine*, **2**(7), 605–11.

Sacks, O. (1985). *The Man Who Mistook His Wife for a Hat.* London: Picador.

Skinner, B. F. (1953). *Science and Human Behaviour.* New York: Macmillan.

Teichner, G., B. Donnhue, T. Crum, N. Azrin and C. Golden (2000). The relationship of neuropsychological functioning to measures of substance use in an adolescent drug abusing sample. *International Journal of Neuroscience*, **104**(1–4), 113–24.

Vesalius, A. (1543). *De Humani Corporis Fabrica.* In D. Garrison & M. Hast (Eds) *On the Fabric of the Human Body* http://vesalius.northwestern.edu

CHAPTER 3

LIFE-CYCLE PERSPECTIVES ON SOCIAL EXCLUSION

In consideration of an individual at any one point in time, previous experiences, life events and the complex interactions between environmental factors and biological factors will influence the person's response to a new challenge. In the case of a major life event, such as being made redundant, this might be a less traumatic experience if that person has a good family and social structure and is in good health, compared to a lone parent who depends upon a weekly wage to support him/her and a child and has poor social support. Although losing a job has a significant impact on *self-actualisation and self-esteem* (see Chapter 2, section 'Human Motivation and Reward', p. 31), in both of these situations impact on physical and mental health will be much greater in the second case. Individual responses to major and minor life events will depend not only on the present circumstances, but will also be influenced by previous experiences, coping skills and vulnerability to mental health problems. Each of these factors will be affected by early events, even before birth, and subject to the interplay of biological, psychological and social influences. Figure 3.1 shows the approximate relative changes in these domains throughout the life span. Physical and mental health dimensions of this interactional model will be discussed in Chapters 4 and 5.

This chapter focuses on the important inherited and environmental factors, which through the complex process of development, provide the uniqueness of humans and an insight into vulnerabilities which mitigate against a person being *included* in society.

For those who need help in integration into the community, addressing their basic skills for employment, their criminal behaviour or problematic alcohol or drug misuse will be important. A range of learning strategies and psychosocial interventions may be helpful as described in Chapter 12. Such interventions should take account of the developmental issues in the person's life cycle, which will influence their response to the intervention. This chapter will provide a developmental perspective on *inclusion in* or *exclusion from* social groups.

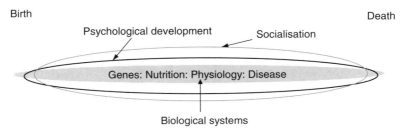

Figure 3.1   Interaction of biological, psychological and social factors from conception to death.

INHERITED AND ENVIRONMENTAL INFLUENCES ON HUMAN DEVELOPMENT

A multiplicity of mechanisms is involved in regulating the process of human development, maturation and ageing. These processes occur at molecular, cellular and systemic levels, with highly complex interactions within and between these three levels. There is a considerable heterogeneity in an individual's responses to these time-dependent processes, resulting from the contribution of both genetic and environmental factors in shaping the life span. Thus, the diversity of several trajectories of the life span, from incidence of disease and disability to absence of pathology and persistence of function, suggest that increasing our understanding of these many factors and their interactions will provide an insight into the human life cycle and the processes of social inclusion and exclusion.

In recent years, theoretical ideas of ageing, as an extremely complex multifactorial process, have replaced the earlier view that a specific cause such as a single gene or the decline of a key body system resulted in ageing. The biological aspects of molecular, cellular and systemic changes during the life span underpin and react to psychological and social processes. This bio-psycho-social model of ageing provides a useful insight into the major influences on the person's ability to thrive. For instance contemporary explanations of the transactional response to acute or chronic *stress* suggest that a person's perception of their ability to cope with a particular threat is dependent upon their perception of the challenge, previous experience, physical resources and aspects of their personality. This will be described in Chapter 5.

Perceptual and cognitive processes involve a complex set of information processes and memory systems as described in Chapter 2. These brain systems are vulnerable to damage by life-style choices such as consumption of mind-altering drugs and alcohol. Previous learning and memory will be important in the cognitive appraisal of the threat, which involves a highly complex set of brain processes and the functioning of neurons and neuroreceptors in specific regions of the brain including the hippocampus, cingulate gyrus, the amygdala and other components of the limbic system. The limbic system is considered to be the emotional centre of the brain and links the present threat to previous experiences, in an emotional context (see Figure 2.2 and Chapter 3, p. 48). Personality attributes such as novelty or sensation seeking appear to be correlated with the presence of gene polymorphisms for the dopamine neuroreceptors (DRD4), serotonin transporter and MAO-A (Serretti *et al.* 2005), and account for the individual differences in personality which respond differently to, for example alcohol (Lahti *et al.* 2005). In the example of the response to stress, clear links can be seen between molecular, cellular and systemic changes in that the cognitive aspects of this response depend upon functional cellular (neuronal systems) with functional neurotransmission involving mechanisms, fashioned during development by genetic and environmental influences. In the case of chronic stress, elevated levels of the stress hormone cortisol will cause damage to these cellular processes of learning and memory and increase vulnerability of the person to later life psychopathologies (see section 'Anxiety, Fear and Early Development' later in this chapter, p. 47). Childhood deprivation will impose these constraints on learning, exacerbated by poor living conditions and diet. In this scenario the molecular aspects of inadequate vitamins, cofactors and the accumulation of free radicals mitigate against *successful development and ageing.* Individuals, therefore, will vary considerably in their response to stress and successful strategies for dealing with stressors will include good family and social support and intact cognitive functioning. Less successful strategies involve an overdependence on alcohol and other drugs and limited social support, sometimes to the point of a person becoming socially excluded. The long-term consequences of this life style can be seen in the premature ageing observed in chronic alcohol dependent people.

NEUROPSYCHOLOGICAL DEVELOPMENT

Problems of cognitive dysfunction and mental ill health begin in the early developmental stages as a result of cumulative developmental issues such as poor nutrition and the presence of harmful substances in the prenatal blood supply. The impact of external stress in the mother, resulting in higher levels of the stress hormone cortisol has an important influence on cognitive functioning. This series of insults increases the vulnerability of the child, adding to a vicious circle of events exacerbated by alcohol misuse in the later years possibly leading to alcohol dependence or dependence on other drugs, which increase the probability of brain damage. The maximum rate of brain growth occurs during the first two years of life. Genetic information, inherited from the parents, directs growth and development of the nervous system, as is the case with other systems in the body. This information, encoded in DNA molecules is *translated* and *transcribed* into a diverse range of proteins, which form the material basis of body structures, such as skin, muscle and nervous tissue. Protein enzymes provide metabolic control, some of which are produced on a regular basis and others are induced briefly for specific purposes (see Chapter 7 for more details of this process).

Although the basic infrastructure of the brain is genetically pre-programmed, an overproduction of neurons occurs in some regions such as the olfactory and hippocampal regions, where the fine neuronal structure is tuned by the *pruning* of neuronal axons, dendrites and synapses which are not utilised. This process is influenced by sensory stimulation and increasing efficiency of specific neuronal pathways, an aspect of the process of learning. Neuronal pathways not used will degenerate according to the concept of Neural Darwinism (Edelman 1987), which provides an explanation, based on the principles of natural selection, of the way by which neurones are influenced by brain stimulation via sensory inputs from the environment. This physiological process of learning is perceived as a behavioural output originating from neurobiological mechanisms at cellular and molecular levels. The concept of *Long-Term Potential* (LTP) provides a useful conceptual framework for understanding the cellular basis of learning (Okada 2003; see also Figure 7.4). Emotional behaviour, a specific form of learning, results from sensory inputs, which are assimilated and processed in association within existing memories within the limbic system. Prenatally and postnatally, the development and maintenance of this neuronal infrastructure is significantly influenced by the internal biochemical status of the brain.

From a nutritional perspective the synthesis of proteins is a central element in the process of development. Proteins provide structural support, for example in combination with lipids (fats) in the membranes of all cells. Control of the many thousands of metabolic reactions in the body, from digestion of food to the control of brain neurochemistry is precisely catalysed and regulated by protein enzymes. Proteins are formed from the basic building blocks of 20 amino acids, most of which are obtained from the diet, and synthesised according to the genetic information (DNA) in each cell (see Figure 7.1). Krebs (1980) has pointed to the biochemical adaptation of the enzymes which degrade the amino acids tryptophan and tyrosine (precursors of the neurotransmitters serotonin and dopamine, respectively). These essential amino acids must be conserved when the diet is low in protein and must be removed when in excess, in order to prevent the formation of the physiologically destabilising compounds such as tyramine and tryptamine. In the presence of ethanol the capacity of the tissues to adapt and maintain a homeostatic state is inhibited. Within this internal environment the presence of growth factors, e.g. interleukin 1 (Bartfai and Schultzberg 1993), hormones (e.g. cortisol), neurotoxic compounds (e.g. nicotine and ethanol), and nutrients (e.g. amino acids and vitamins) will have major influences in this early development period. These internal factors can be affected by external stimulation, as evidenced by the early death of pre-programmed neurones in one-day-old rats, deprived of their mothers. This maternal deprivation and subsequent death is attributed to decreased levels of neurotrophic factors in the hippocampus of the infant rats (Zhang *et al.* 1997). An important conclusion from the concept of Neuronal Darwinism, as noted above, is that metabolic changes in brain cells throughout life, recognised or not, may predispose the individual to brain damage, or reduced brain development. A critical issue here relates to which changes are positive adaptations and which are detrimental in the developmental phase of the individual's life cycle.

Postnatally, the family environment can have significant negative influences on the developing child by inadequate parenting, poor nutritional provision, stress and abuse mediated by neuroendocrine responses. Thiamine deficiency, due to medically derived malnutrition, has been found in children and can lead to Wernicke encephalopathy, in the absence of alcohol consumption, if untreated (Seear *et al.* 1992). The biochemical outcome of chronic stress and abuse includes elevated stress hormone (cortisol) production which can chronically result in suppressed cognitive development due to damage to the hippocampus, a region of the brain concerned with learning and memory (Kalin 1993). Stress in this early period is thought to lead to late life psychiatric problems (Teicher 2002). Optimal development, therefore, depends upon a subtle interaction between behavioural events, in particular mother–infant interactions, and molecular phenomena, which require appropriate concentrations of precursors for synthesising structural and enzymatic proteins, required for brain structures, supplemented by a wide array of neurotrophic compounds and cofactors. When alcohol and other drugs are present in the pre- and postnatal environment this complex set of interactions becomes destabilised due to effects on cellular membranes and receptor signalling processes.

SOCIAL DEPRIVATION AND HUMAN DEVELOPMENT

There are methodological problems in studying early childhood influences and their outcomes. However, some useful insights have been obtained from a number of studies of children reared in deprived conditions. In a controlled study by Rubin *et al.* (1996), 102 children, aged 6 to 11 years, and their mothers living in shelters, were compared with 178 housed children and their mothers selected from the homeless child's classroom. He found no differences in cognitive functioning between homeless and housed children, but homeless children performed significantly more poorly than housed children in tests of academic performance. These marked differences in academic performance did not appear to be related to number of days missed from school or the length of homelessness, according to the mother's report, but were associated with the number of school changes. Davies-Netzley *et al.* (1996) found the burden of despair, in particular childhood abuse, to be a significant precursor of homelessness in women and was associated with severe mental illness. In this study of 120 homeless women with severe mental illness, the experience of childhood abuse was related to increased rates of suicidal tendencies and symptoms of post-traumatic stress disorder for some women. The likelihood of becoming homeless during childhood was greatly increased in women who had suffered abuse, suggesting that this is an important precursor to homelessness for many homeless women with chronic and severe mental illness. Vulnerability to the problems of homelessness differs considerably between younger and older individuals. The latter have more severe substance misuse problems and post-traumatic stress disorder (DeMallie 1997).

Social deprivation may be viewed from the perspectives of economic deprivation, stress-related factors, gender differences in vulnerability and psychological and sociological outcomes. While it is difficult to disentangle these various components of social deprivation, an attempt to understand the interplay between these and other influences on an individual's development will hopefully inform the availability of appropriate interventions, as discussed in Chapter 12. From early on in the prenatal stage the individual is subject to a continuous range of environmental physical and physiological threats, which include nutritional limitations, toxic substances and infectious agents in the embryonic environment.

Prenatal effects

Studies on Foetal Alcohol Syndrome (FAS) indicate that mechanisms of cellular damage resulting from heavy drinking in pregnant females may provide an insight into the more subtle effects on the nervous system, perhaps unrecognised, of lower levels of consumption of alcohol and other drugs which may predispose the individual to later life psychopathologies (Sokol 1981). Nutritional factors are important from the earliest time in the development of the foetus, particularly during the formation of the embryonic nervous system. Earlier studies suggested that the neurological problems of FAS were caused by reductions in blood flow leading to hypoxia, acidosis. These events were related to problems in cell replication, cell growth and cell death, the latter being specifically due to overstimulation of NMDA receptors (see Figure 7.4) found in the hippocampus and involved in the cellular basis of learning (see Chapter 2, section 'Learning and Memory', p. 26), with consequential excitotoxicity and cell death (Michaelis 1990).

A large literature has shown the confounding effect of ethanol on morphological development giving rise to Foetal Alcohol Syndrome (Halliday *et al.* 1995; Michaelis 1990; Randall *et al.* 1990) and brain damage in premature infants (West *et al.* 1994; Holzman *et al.* 1995). Experimentally, alcohol has been shown to interfere with many phases of brain development, via molecular, neurochemical and cellular events involved in the correct maturing of the central nervous system. The timing and concentration of alcohol exposure perturbs cell proliferation, migration, growth and differentiation and may cause cell death. Alcohol exposure during early embryogenesis can cause a reduction in the number of cells generated, including the neural stem cells (e.g. radial glia), and induces abnormal cell migration. In humans, drinking during this period is associated with a greater incidence of craniofacial defects and mental disabilities. Later exposure to alcohol, when cells are differentiating and synapses are establishing, may cause a reduction in the number of synapses formed and cause the death of brain cells. Neuroimaging studies indicate that some brain regions are more affected than others. Even within a given region some cell populations are more vulnerable than others. The neocortex, hippocampus, cerebellum and corpus callosum are especially susceptible to alcohol and have been associated with a range of behavioural deficits (Guerri 2005).

Although the link between prenatal exposure to alcohol and FAS is well established, it seems likely that the other drugs and nutritional effects will influence behaviour development. An emerging concern relates to high doses of vitamin A, prenatally, which can significantly affect the dopamine receptors in the developing foetal brain, a phenomenon which is thought to increase vulnerability to schizophrenia in later life (Maden 2001).

Postnatal effects

During postnatal development, nurturing and nutrition of the newborn continue to be important. Nurturing involves parental influences, which can be aversive as those present in substance-misusing parents (Kettinger *et al.* 2000), and the impact of peers. During the *critical periods* of learning in childhood, solitary play, likeability and peer rejection are associated with low positive emotion, high asocial behaviour and high peer exclusion (Spinrad *et al.* 2004). Hunger impacts on a child's physical and mental health and academic functioning, as observed by Weinreb *et al.* (2002), who found that in a study of 10-year-old children from homeless and low-income families in Massachusetts, 50 % experienced moderate hunger and 16 % severe hunger. Compared with those children who did not experience hunger, children with severe hunger had low birth weights (23 % vs. 6 %), were more likely to be homeless (56 % vs. 29 %) and had more stressful life events (9 % vs. 6 %). Those children assessed to have severe hunger scores had parent-reported anxiety scores that were more than double the scores for children with no hunger and significantly higher chronic illness counts (3.4 % cf. 1.8 %) and internalising behaviour problems when compared with children with no hunger.

Nutritional restrictions have an adverse effect on the growth of children (Fierman *et al.* 1991). This is particularly marked, as indicated by lower heights, in homeless children from larger families and in children with single mothers. Fierman *et al.* (1991) found that the period of homelessness appears not to be associated with decreased height or weight–height among homeless children, but homeless children in this study exhibited a pattern of stunting without wasting, characteristic of poor children experiencing moderate, chronic nutritional stress. These children exhibited a greater degree of nutritional stress than children living in stable accommodation, at a similar income level and than that reported in other groups of poor children in the United States. The issue of nutrition in early development will be reviewed in Chapter 9.

From a neurobiological perspective, recent research (Blakemore and Frith 2005) indicates that considerable changes occur in the brains of teenagers. These changes involve a dip in performance at puberty, which is reflected in a drop in educational performance at this time. Adolescence is a turbulent time due to physical, emotional and hormonal changes. These major changes in the prefrontal cortex might also explain the angst, aggression and mood swings, which are frequently reported in teenagers. Gender differences are significant at this time, again reflected in educational attainment, with boys maturing two years later and performing worse in educational tests than girls. This vulnerable time can also be when teenage antisocial behaviour becomes problematic. Such problematic behaviour is thought to have its origins in childhood, in that childhood nervousness and isolation have been shown to be negatively correlated with teenage antisocial behaviour and positively related with adult social dysfunction (Farrington 1993). Marianne van den Bree (2005) has published a major review of the risk factors for substance use in young people.

Ageing

During the various phases of the human life cycle, the process of ageing is influenced by events in the early stages of an individual's development. At this vulnerable stage in the life cycle an important question arises as to whether normal ageing can be separated from pathological processes causing disease and behavioural dysfunction in later life. A response to this suggestion is based on the assumption that ageing is the accumulation of damage to somatic cells, leading to cellular dysfunction, and culminates in organ dysfunction and an increased vulnerability to death. From a life-cycle viewpoint childhood events and the critical events in brain development are reflected in the ageing processes of the brain and impact on the rate of neurodegeneration (de Magalhaes and Sandberg 2005). This hypothesis involves brain plasticity in which the same mechanisms that shape the adult phenotype continue at later ages, contributing to cognitive dysfunction and possibly dementia. Common genetic influences that decrease brain plasticity at early ages, enabling our minds to focus on the immediate environment may be important in adulthood resulting in the ageing of brain processes by reducing plasticity. This perspective provides a helpful context for the understanding of successful *social inclusion*.

Ageing is associated with anatomical, chemical and functional changes in the brain. One of the most prominent changes occurs in the neuronal pathways which use the neurotransmitter acetylcholine to transmit information within the synapses (see Chapter 7, section 'Neurotransmission and Information Management', p. 104). The numbers of cholinergic neurons, receptors and afferent projections, in the parts of the brain involved in memory and related activities, decrease with age, and are thought to result in age-associated deficits observed in working memory and other cognitive tasks. Pharmacological potentiation of cholinergic neurotransmission has been shown to improve performance on working memory tasks in the elderly. Cognitive dysfunction can be treated by chronic treatment with cholinergic-enhancing drugs, but despite the well-documented clinical effects of cholinergic enhancement in the elderly, the underlying neural mechanisms remain to be elucidated (Pietrini *et al.* 2005).

The development of non-invasive methodologies, such as positron emission tomography (PET) and functional magnetic resonance imaging (fMRI), are now providing the opportunity to investigate the working brain in conscious patients (Hedden and Gabrieli 2005). These contemporary approaches to the investigation of the neural mechanisms of mental function in humans at different ages are providing an insight into physiological and psychopathological conditions. Such studies have been conducted in individuals whose brain function may have been affected by for example chronic exposure to alcohol, or impaired hormonal and nutritional states. Other studies have investigated brain function in relation to genetic risk factors such as alleles (genetic types) associated with increased susceptibility for developing dementia and high frequency of such alleles in Down's syndrome. The results of these studies have provided new insight on the interplay that genetic and environmental factors may exert on the brain during life as well as on the effects of therapeutic intervention strategies.

Ageing involves a number of degenerative processes and disruption of homeostasis in physiological systems. These include the desynchronisation of body rhythms including the sleep–wake cycle, which is a significant indicator of developing mental health problems. This can be partially addressed in therapeutic and care settings by means of *reality-orientation* practices which emphasise time and place cues, techniques which reduce disorientation in the elderly. Physical decline is reflected in social functioning in that lack of mobility decreases the opportunity for social interaction and increases social isolation. Additionally, reduced function of the sensory systems mitigates against social communication. Older people frequently have poor eyesight reducing their ability to identify facial expressions. Phillips *et al.* (2002) have observed an inability to assess displays of anger, sadness, and poorer ability to 'identify theory of mind from pictures of eyes'. The neuropsychological evidence from this study of 30 young adults (aged 20–40 years) and 30 older adults (aged 60–80 years) suggests potential impairments in processing emotions in older adults. Although there were no age effects on the ability to decode emotions from verbal material, age-related deficits in identifying some aspects of emotion from faces were found, but no age effects on the understanding of emotions in verbal descriptions were detected.

Social functioning involves complex activities of the brain. These include the creation of meaning from the world, as conceived via *theories of mind*. The use of sensory information to make sense of the (social) world, and respond to it, changes from early to late stages of the life cycle. Happe *et al.* (1998) reported that *theory-of-mind* performance was superior in the elderly. This view is in contrast to that of Maylor *et al.* (2002) who report a decline in *theory-of-mind* abilities with advancing years. Sullivan and Ruffman (2004) used two new tasks; identifying emotions from still photos and identifying emotions and cognitions from video clips to investigate this cognitive function. The authors found a decline in social understanding in the elderly.

THE ORIGINS OF SOCIAL ANXIETY

An insight into the linkage between anxiety and exclusion from social groups in the early years is provided by Gazelle and Ladd (2003). In studying 388 children, equal numbers of boys and girls, the authors observed social behaviour, peer exclusion and emotional adjustment at kindergarten (primary school). Observations, primarily by the teacher, were made at entry and every spring thereafter through the fourth year. These observations indicated that soon after joining the primary school, anxiety (due to solitude) and peer exclusion co-occur in the children. Anxious solitude became more entrenched in those anxious solitary children who were excluded early on, in comparison with their nonexcluded anxious solitary counterparts. The *diathesis–stress* model proposed by the authors indicated that the joint forces of individual vulnerability (anxious solitude) and interpersonal adversity (peer exclusion) were strongly associated with symptoms of depression, noted in the children over time.

The role of stress and anxiety in mental health will be explored in Chapter 5, but in view of the role of developmental stressors in children and their impact on later life mental health, a brief review of social anxiety and the links between anxiety and the physiological events in mother–infant relationships will be given here.

Anxiety might be related to fear of physical injury or attack, as it is in other animals, it might also be generated by social anxiety, for instance fear of evaluation by others. This is an interesting issue and probably relates to the need to appear attractive to others, in the case of human courtship or to make friends and become a member of a social group. It is an interesting question as to why, when people wish to appear attractive to others do some people become so overwhelmed with anxiety that they behave fearfully and submissively, behaviours which might be interpreted as avoidant or unattractive.

Gilbert (2001) suggests that the adaptive behaviour of 'attractiveness', in order to impress others, has evolved in humans as a competitive feature of human social behaviour. These behaviours, in turn, are thought to have physiological regulating effects and increase inclusive (genetic) fitness. In terms of social hierarchies in social groups, a low social rank, perceived or real, or being ostracised is associated with negative consequences for controlling social resources and physiological regulation. Social anxiety, like shame, can be adaptive to the extent that it helps people to 'stay on track' with what is socially acceptable and thus avoid social sanction and exclusion. Dysfunctional social anxiety appears to be the result of activation of basic defensive mechanisms associated with threat detection and response (e.g. inhibition, eye-gaze avoidance, flight or submission) that can be generated rapidly in response to immediate threats, override conscious wishes and interfere with being seen as a 'useful associate'.

Gilbert (2001) also suggests that socially anxious people readily elicit approval and investment from others but that they perceive themselves to have an inferior (i.e. low-rank) position and, because of this, activate submissive defences when attempting to present themselves as confident, able and attractive to others. These submissive defences, which evolved to inhibit animals in low-rank positions from making claims on resources or up-rank bids, interfere with confident performance, leading to a cycle of repeated failures.

ANXIETY, FEAR AND EARLY DEVELOPMENT

Various studies indicate that fearful children are at a high risk for later emotional distress. Kagan and colleagues (1983) have shown that a child who is profoundly shy at the age of two years is more likely to suffer from anxiety and depression later in life than a less inhibited child. Children who become severely inhibited in unfamiliar places produce high levels of stress hormones, including cortisol from the adrenal gland.

Cortisol is produced at elevated levels at times of crisis and is part of the 'fight or flight' reaction, which includes maximising energy for use by the muscles. Cortisol results in a number of other physiological changes occurring at times of 'fight or flight', however, long-term elevations of this stress hormone may contribute to gastric ulcers, cardiovascular disease and neurotoxicity, see Chapter 5. Fearful children enter a vicious circle leading through isolation and lowered self-esteem, underachievement possibly leading to anxiety and depression.

There is some evidence that unusually fearful children are prone to physical illness, for example fearful children and their families are more likely to suffer from allergic disorders. In animal studies persistent elevation of cortisol increases vulnerability of neurons in the hippocampus to damage by other substances. This region is involved in memory, motivation and emotion and so fear-related responses involving chronic elevated levels of cortisol are thought to have a negative effect on brain function.

This idea cannot be studied in children due to ethical reasons; however, Kalin *et al.* (1991) have studied these phenomena in rhesus monkeys. The comparative developmental stages in monkeys and children are similar, and can be studied, for instance in relation to the age at which selective defensive behaviours develop: At *two months of age* infant rhesus monkeys are able to make choices and are generally permitted to move away from parents and mix with peers. At *10 weeks:* the young monkeys are able to make emotional responses specific to expressions on the faces of other monkeys, an indication that some of the innate wiring or learned skills needed to discriminate threatening cues are in place.

The brain regions that regulate fearfulness are thought to develop at 9–12 weeks. A brief description of the limbic system is presented in Chapter 2. This system is linked to the *prefrontal cortex*, which is an area of the brain concerned with cognitive and emotional responses, brought about by the interpretation of sensory stimuli. This is possibly the site where potential danger is assessed. The *amygdala*, part of the limbic system, is involved in generating fear, which is expressed via the *hypothalamus* which secretes cortico-releasing hormone (CRH) stimulating the pituitary to produce adrenocorticotropic hormone (ACTH), which in turns causes the adrenal gland to release cortisol and prepares the body to defend itself, see Figure 5.2.

In human maturation, when an infant reaches 12 months of age the *prefrontal cortex* increases in activity and enables the child to distinguish between threatening cues. During this developmental stage, when monkeys respond selectively, children begin to show marked fear of strangers and become skilled at social referencing. They regulate their level of fear based on interpretation of the expressions they observe on a parent's face.

At this relative time in development of monkeys and young humans, the hypothalamus also appears to develop, suggesting that monkeys are good models of human emotional behaviour. Animals have been used to explore mother–infant relations, and the effects of maternal deprivation (Bowlby 1977). However, the work by Kagan (1983) provides an important insight into the physiological mechanisms that underpin mother–infant bonding, and anxiety produced by disruption of the bond as a result of maternal separation. In these experiments, stress, induced by separation from the mother, was related to the activity of the brain pathways which contain opiate receptors. Injected morphine decreased the amount of *cooing* displayed in *alone* and *stare* conditions, indicators of stress. Conversely the alarm signal of *cooing* was increased by naloxone, a compound which binds to opiate receptors and blocks effects of morphine and endogenous opiates (i.e. an opiate antagonist). The conclusion from these studies is that *opiate-using neural pathways* regulate affiliative (mother–infant) behaviours. Injected morphine had no effect on frequency of *stare-induced barking* and other hostile behaviours, which are elicited in the presence of potential predators. However *benzodiazepines* were effective in reducing stress in this situation, indicating that these drugs are primarily involved in response to direct threats.

In summary, when a young monkey is separated from its mother, *opiate-releasing* and *opiate-sensitive* mechanisms become inhibited. This gives rise to yearning for the mother and a generalised vulnerability and resulting vocalisations. This reduction of activity in *opiate-sensitive* systems enables motor systems in the brain to produce *cooing*. When a potential predator appears, neurons that secrete endogenous benzodiazepine become suppressed to some degree. This leads to elevated anxiety and the appearance of behaviours and hormones that accompany fear. As a sense of alarm grows the system prepares for *fight or flight*. The benzodiazepines thus alter opiate systems, which results in *cooing* behaviour during threatening situations. The therapeutic implications of this work include the possibility of administering benzodiazepines to adults and children who exhibit elevated electrical activity in the right prefrontal cortex. Caution needs to be exercised here in relation to the addictive properties of benzodiazepines, however, controlled use of these drugs at critical periods of brain development might be effective. A further intervention might be the use of behavioural training to teach extremely uninhibited children to regulate benzodiazepine-sensitive systems without the use of medication.

This insight into the relative contributions of various brain systems, which respond to fear in humans, suggests that specific signalling pathways that are disrupted in a particular child, might be important in setting the stage for later life mental health problems. These include vulnerability to depression and substance misuse. A theoretical explanation for opiate dependency is that self-medication on natural and synthetic opioids is a compensatory behaviour directed at restoring imbalanced *opiate-using neural pathways*. It is not surprising, therefore, that morphine-like opiates and benzodiazepines are powerful drugs of abuse, in view of the existence of endogenous receptors for these compounds in humans and other animals. This discovery has

important implications for the interventions used in drug-dependent individuals, particularly with respect to the developmental events resulting from
the complex interaction of developmental factors leading to social inclusion or exclusion. Social deprivation in the early years, therefore, increases
behavioural maladaption and vulnerability to mental and physical problems in later life. These early events lay down the trajectories which lead
into successful ageing or premature ageing and the related quality-of-life
experiences.

REFERENCES

Bartfai, T. and M. Schultzberg (1993). Cytokines in neuronal cell types. *Neurochem-
istry International*, **22**, 435.
Blakemore, S. J. and U. Frith (2005). *The Learning Brain: Lessons for Education*. Oxford:
Blackwell Publishing.
Bowlby, J. (1977). The making and breaking of affectional bonds. I. Aetiology and
psychopathology in the light of attachment theory. An expanded version of the
Fiftieth Maudsley Lecture, delivered before the Royal College of Psychiatrists, 19
November 1976. *British Journal of Psychiatry*, **130**, 201–10.
Davies-Netzley, S., M. S. Hurlburt and R. L. Hough (1996). Childhood abuse as
a precursor to homelessness for homeless women with severe mental illness.
Violence and Victims, **11**(2), 129–42.
de Magalhaes, J. P. and A. Sandberg (2005). Cognitive aging as an extension of brain
development: a model linking learning, brain plasticity, and neurodegeneration.
Mechanisms of Ageing and Development, **126**(10), 1026–33.
DeMallie, D. A., C. S. North and E. M. Smith (1997). Psychiatric disorders among the
homeless: a comparison of older and younger groups. *Gerontologist*, **37**(1), 61–6.
Edelman, G. M. (1987). *Neural Darwinism*. New York: Basic Books.
Farrington, D. P. (1993). Childhood origins of teenage antisocial behaviour and adult
social dysfunction. *Journal of the Royal Society of Medicine*, **86**(1), 13–17.
Fierman, A. H., B. P. Dreyer, L. Quinn, S. Shulman, C. D. Courtlandt and R. Guzzo
(1991). Growth delay in homeless children. *Pediatrics*, **88**(5), 918–25.
Gazelle, H. and G. W. Ladd (2003). Anxious solitude and peer exclusion: a
diathesis-stress model of internalizing trajectories in childhood. *Child Development*,
74(1), 257–78.
Gilbert, P. (2001). Evolution and social anxiety. The role of attraction, social compe-
tition, and social hierarchies. *Psychiatric Clinics of North America*, **24**(4), 723–51.
Guerri, C. (2005). Ethanol toxicity in the developing brain. *Alcohol and Alcoholism*, **40**.
Halliday, G., K. Baker and C. Harper (1995). Serotonin and alcohol-related brain
damage. *Metabolic Brain Disease*, **10**(1), 25–30.
Happe, F. G., E. Winner and H. Brownell (1998). The getting of wisdom: theory of
mind in old age. *Developmental Psychology*, **34**(2), 358–62.
Hedden, T. and J. D. Gabrieli (2005). Healthy and pathological processes in adult
development: new evidence from neuroimaging of the aging brain. *Current
Opinion in Neurology*, **18**(6), 740–7.
Holzman, C., N. Paneth, R. Little and J. Pinto-Martin (1995). Perinatal brain injury
in premature infants born to mothers using alcohol in pregnancy. Neonatal Brain
Hemorrhage Study Team. *Pediatrics*, **95**, 66.
Kagan, J. (1983). Stress, coping in early development. In: N. Garmezy and
M. L. Rutter (eds), *Stress, Coping, and Development in Children*. New York: McGraw-
Hill.

Kalin, N. H. (1993). The neurobiology of fear. *Scientific American*, **268**, 94.

Kalin, N. H., S. E. Shelton and L. K. Takahashi (1991). Defensive behaviors in infant rhesus monkeys: ontogeny and context-dependent selective expression. *Child Development*, **62**(5), 1175–83.

Kettinger, L. A., P. Nair and M. E. Schuler (2000). Exposure to environmental risk factors and parenting attitudes among substance-abusing women. *American Journal of Drug and Alcohol Abuse*, **26**(1), 1–11.

Krebs, H. (1980). The effects of alcohol on metabolic processes. In: Richter, D. (ed.), *Addiction and Brain Damage*. Baltimore: Croom Helm, p. 11.

Lahti, J., K. Raikkonen, J. Ekelund, L. Peltonen, O. T. Raitakari and L. Keltikangas-Jarvinen (2005). Novelty seeking: interaction between parental alcohol use and dopamine D4 receptor gene exon III polymorphism over 17 years. *Psychiatric Genetics*, **15**(2), 133–9.

Maden, M. (2001). Vitamin A and the developing embryo. *Postgraduate Medical Journal*, **77**, 489–91.

Maylor, E. A., J. M. Moulson, A. M. Muncer and L. A. Taylor (2002). Does performance on theory of mind tasks decline in old age? *British Journal of Psychology*, **93**(Pt 4), 465–85.

Michaelis, E. K. (1990). Fetal alcohol exposure: cellular toxicity and molecular events involved in toxicity. *Alcoholism: Clinical and Experimental Research*, **14**, 819.

Okada, T., N. Yamada and K. Tsuzuki (2003). Long-term potentiation in the hippocampal CA1 area and dentate gyrus play different roles in spatial learning. *European Journal of Neuroscience*, **17**, 341.

Phillips, L. H., R. D. MacLean and R. Allen (2002). Age and the understanding of emotions: neuropsychological and sociocognitive perspectives. *Journals of Gerontology Series B Psychological Sciences and Social Sciences*, **57**(6), P526–30.

Pietrini, P., E. Ricciardi, M. Panicucci, M. Furey and M. Guazzelli (2005). Brain metabolic correlates of mental activity during physiological and pathological aging in human subjects. *Alcohol and Alcoholism*, **40**(Supplement 1), i 17.

Randall, C. L., U. Ekblad and R. F. Anton (1990). Perspectives on the pathophysiology of fetal alcohol syndrome. *Alcoholism: Clinical and Experimental Research*, **14**, 897.

Rubin, D. H., C. J. Erickson, M. San Agustin, S. D. Cleary, J. K. Allen and P. Cohen (1996). Cognitive and academic functioning of homeless children compared with housed children. *Pediatrics*, **97**(3), 289–94.

Seear, M., G. Lockitch and B. Jacobson (1992). Thiamine, riboflavin, and pyridoxine deficiencies in a population of critically ill children. *Journal of Pediatrics*, **121**, 533.

Serretti, A., L. Mandelli, C. Lorenzi, S. Landoni, R. Calati, C. Insacco, *et al.* (2005). Temperament and character in mood disorders: influence of DRD4, SERTPR, TPH and MAO-A polymorphisms. *Neuropsychobiology*, **53**(1), 9–16.

Sokol, R. J. (1981). Alcohol and abnormal outcomes of pregnancy. *CMA Journal*, **125**, 143.

Spinrad, T. L., N. Eisenberg, E. Harris, L. Hanish, R. A. Fabes, K. Kupanoff, *et al.* (2004). The relation of children's everyday nonsocial peer play behavior to their emotionality, regulation, and social functioning. *Development Psychology*, **40**(1), 67–80.

Sullivan, S. and T. Ruffman (2004). Social understanding: how does it fare with advancing years? *British Journal of Psychology*, **95**(Pt 1), 1–18.

Teicher, M. H. (2002). Scars that won't heal: the neurobiology of child abuse. *Scientific American*, **286**, 68.

van den Bree, M. B. M. (2005). Risk factors predicting development of alcohol problem use over time: longitudinal analyses in a large population-based sample of adolescents. *Alcohol and Alcoholism*, **40**(1), S09.

Weinreb, L., C. Wehler, J. Perloff, R. Scott, D. Hosmer, L. Sagor, *et al.* (2002). Hunger: its impact on children's health and mental health. *Pediatrics*, **110**(4), e41.

West, J. R., W. J. Chen and N. J. Pantazis (1994). Fetal alcohol syndrome: the vulnerability of the developing brain and possible mechanisms of damage. *Metabolic Brain Disease*, **9**, 291.

Zhang, L., J. L. Barker, G. Xing, O. Giorgi, W. Ma, Y. H. Chang, *et al.* (1997). 5-HT1A receptor mRNA expressions differ in the embryonic spinal cord of male and female rats. *Neuroscience Letters*, **237**(1), 41–4.

Part II

Health and Illness in Social Groups

CHAPTER 4

PHYSICAL HEALTH

THE CHANGING CONCEPT OF HEALTH

Health is a wide concept that originated from the West German word *xaillpa* (OED 1973), meaning 'wholeness', pertaining to soundness of body, and includes physical, mental, moral and spiritual welfare. According to the *Oxford English Dictionary*, 'healthy living' is characterised by the promotion of bodily and spiritual health, and earlier definitions included intellectual and moral soundness. 'Healthless' is rarely used nowadays, but in 1568 the word was used to describe the destitution of bodily, mental and spiritual health. The World Health Organisation (WHO) definition of health (1946) – entered into force in 1948, not amended since that date – is 'a state of complete physical, mental and social well-being and not merely the absences of disease or infirmity'.

A historical consideration of the concept of *health* is helpful when considering social exclusion, as the contemporary philosophical views, at any period, have determined the responses of the community in dealing with those who were not supported within the mainstream of society. This is seen in the provision of asylums for the insane in the eighteenth century, which used to contain not only those who we would consider to have mental health problems, but also those considered to be morally weak including women having children out of wedlock and others considered to be socially deviant. A brief review of services and institutions designed for the socially excluded will be included in Part III of this book, however, it should be noted that the health and social provisions, which gradually became available within the developing British society, depended on the contemporary view of an individual's social and health needs matched, and often overshadowed by, the community protection issues and the political environment at that time. In other words, health is not a unitary concept and it should be considered within a community context. Community responses to health will therefore be influenced by the availability of self-help, community resources available and accessible for those in need, professional services reflected by the relative influences of the various health professional groups and the political motivation to allocate resources. These community drivers are underpinned by the coercive or voluntary strategies adopted locally.

It is interesting to note that the term *destitute* is now rarely used in descriptions of the socially excluded. 'Destitute' was used in 1530 to describe those who were forsaken, had been abandoned and were in want of necessities of life such as food and clothing, and were 'entirely lacking'. This change in the use of language is a reflection that in modern society people are no longer abandoned to the extent that they lack the basic necessities of life, however, values have changed and health and wholeness in the twenty-first century depend on a range of factors which are denied to some in this highly complex post-industrial society.

A biomedical perspective has predominated health policy in the western world during the last three centuries. This biomedical model was criticised in the late 1970s because of its somatic reductionism. This critique of the traditional biomedical concept of health has been accompanied by the adoption of a biopsychosocial concept of health among medical researchers in the last two decades. In reviewing articles in *The Lancet* between 1978–82 and 1996–2000 Alonso (2004) found that none of the 52 examined included a replicable definition of 'health' or 'healthy status'. Psychological or both psychological and social dimensions were used in the seven 'health' papers, but only three studies include psychological dimensions in their measures of 'healthy status'.

The reviewer points out that although a more holistic concept of health is evident in academic and related organisations over the last few decades, no similar change has occurred in the medical literature. Possible reasons are discussed, especially the difficulty of applying the biopsychosocial model in medical care and the difficulty of competing with the traditional biomedical concept of health, which has proved fruitful and dominant in medicine over the past three centuries. The problem of providing evidence-based outcomes from the biopsychosocial model is cited as one of the reasons why the change towards a more holistic concept of health appears not to be evident in the medical literature. In view of the importance of social class and poverty as key determinants of disease (Benach and Amable 2004) it is clear that a narrow biomedical view is inappropriate when tacking health dimensions of social exclusion.

HOMELESSNESS AND ILL HEALTH

The homeless population in the UK is increasing and consists of three main subpopulations: (i) rough sleepers and hostel dwellers, mainly the single homeless; (ii) homeless families; and (iii) individuals who involuntarily live in shared or inadequate accommodation. While some data is available relating to accommodation and health status of the first two groups, information on the third group is sparse. Ill health is often considered to be a consequence of social exclusion, however, it can also be the cause.

Chronic illness can result in social exclusion (Bosma *et al.* 2005). Diseases such as rheumatism, multiple sclerosis, pulmonary emphysema and the duration of these primary diseases and comorbidity have all been associated with increased social exclusion. The extent of exclusion has been demonstrated to be related to educational level, whether or not the patient was employed or engaged in volunteer work, whether or not the patient lived together with a partner. Bosma *et al.* (2005) measured social exclusion by means of 'Autonomy outside the home' subscale of the 'Impact on participation and autonomy' questionnaire. This study of social exclusion of chronically ill patients showed that exclusion was significantly linked to income and the inability of the individuals to organise their own care. Social status and the level of communication between the health-service providers are important components of the biopsychosocial approach to health care (Davidson *et al.* 2006). The Royal College of Physicians (Connelly and Crown 1994) has reported that physical, mental health and obstetric problems are significantly higher in homeless families and people in inadequate accommodation. These problems also have been found in single homeless people. All of these groups have problems in accessing appropriate healthcare services. The Royal College of Physicians called for a coordinated approach to community care and housing policy to prevent vulnerable people from becoming homeless. Particular attention is drawn to the need for primary care, accident and emergency services, community care and discharge services to become more aware and coordinated in their response to the homeless.

Health demographics

Griffiths (2002), in reviewing the single homeless rough sleeper population, has estimated that 30–50 % of homeless people have mental health problems, 70 % misuse drugs, and homeless people have high rates of tuberculosis, respiratory problems and skin diseases and have a life expectancy of 42 years.

Significantly more health problems occur in homeless families than the general population. Street homeless people are 40 times more likely than the general public not to be registered with a general practitioner (CRISIS, 2002). Vostanis *et al.* (1996) have found that homeless children have a doubled risk of being admitted to hospital for accidents and infectious diseases, they have significantly higher behavioural problems, and mental health problems are significantly higher among homeless mothers and children. In a study of the adult homeless population of Dublin, Holohan (2000) found that this subpopulation consisted of 80 % smokers, 30 % problem drinkers and 30 % illegal drug users, half of the population perceived their health as poor. At least one physical or psychiatric problem was reported by 60 % of the interviewees, 41 % of whom had chronic disease. This study found that homeless people, in comparison to the general population, have increased risks for illness and suffer similar, but more prevalent, health problems, which varied with demographic and behavioural factors, such as gender and age.

HEALTH, POVERTY, EMPLOYMENT AND COMMUNITY DEVELOPMENT

Health inequalities in the community have been found to be highly corre- lated with social class and poverty. In Europe, in 2006, communities are still characterised by the existence of social classes and social stratification in which a predominance of high levels of unemployment and precar- ious jobs are found in the lower classes, and where poverty is endemic, social problems are much worse than the EU average (Benach and Amable 2004). Poverty and health status are inversely correlated. In Europe 15 % of people live in poverty; however, estimates for the elderly who live in poverty are much higher (Del Rey Calero 2004). Social capital is the social structure that promotes the activities of individuals, stimulates produc- tion and allows for success. Social exclusion does not allow individuals to participate in society and poverty results in a wide range of basic and unmet needs such as food, health and independence, and leads to reduced social cohesion. Macintyre and Ellaway (2000) found that health prob- lems were more common in deprived areas in Scotland, where poorer mental health in the community was associated with low levels of social cohesion.

It is generally acknowledged that social cohesion will be improved by the promotion of social participation, empowerment, self-esteem and personal achievement. However, a very significant factor in social participation is the involvement of community members in both voluntary and paid work. This is discussed more fully in chapter 14.

In the UK social deprivation and concurrent health problems are often found in regions of economic decline, due to the reduced availability of jobs. Some of the most deprived areas are found in Scotland and Wales (Pritchard and Puzey 2004), where large-scale industrial areas have been run down, with resulting high levels of unemployment in local areas. In these areas increased numbers of people become homeless, with the resulting health needs related to poor living conditions. Links between accommo- dation problems and mental and physical ill health are well established. Regrettably a vicious cycle of unemployment, homelessness and poor health is found in these economically deprived areas. There have been many studies on the individual and the psychological consequences of unem- ployment and consistent relationships are found between unemployment and minor psychological disorders. A more limited number of studies have included pathological effects of unemployment but there is some evidence that increased physiological illness does occur, especially among unemployed girls.

Unemployment appears to be a risk indicator for increasing alcohol consumption, particularly in young men, as well as increased tobacco consumption and increased use of illicit drugs. These negative health behaviours result in deteriorating health giving mortality rates significantly higher among unemployed young men and women, especially in suicides and accidents. Social support and high employment rates have been found to have a protective effect on health (Hammarstrom 1994).

An appraisal of the potential for health improvements by means of the development of macroeconomic global policies has been produced by the Commission on Macroeconomics and Health (the Sachs report). However, this has been criticised on the basis of its narrow medico-technical solutions to public health problems and its omission of other, non-economic, root causes of both poor health and poverty. The Sachs report promotes the role of charity while 'preserving the status quo of a deeply unjust and irrational international economic order. The ultimate source of poor health status and miserable living conditions is the extreme concentration of power, nationally and internationally, in the hands of the few' (Katz 2005).

HEALTH STATUS

A wide range of inherited and environmental factors interact to determine the health of any one individual, which will change during the course of the lifetime (see Chapter 3). The impact of socio-economic factors have been briefly reviewed above, however, the physical environmental factors in the person's home and working environment should not be overlooked. These factors include the environmental pollutants that are more likely to be found in areas inhabited by the poorest people. In the UK there is a heightened awareness of these environmental threats since the discovery of the link between high levels of the atmospheric metallic lead in high traffic density areas such as the motorway interconnections north of Birmingham, called 'spaghetti junction', and the intellectual development of children living in this area. This discovery resulted in the removal of lead from petrol. Manual workers are potentially at risk due to the high levels of environmental pollutants in the workplace, however, people vary in their susceptibility to the environmental threats to which they are exposed. These differences have a genetic basis, genetic polymorphisms tending to be more variable within a race than between races.

With advances in molecular genetics, differences in disease susceptibility can now be studied by various laboratory tools and databases that can be used to help identify the genetic variations in environmental response that play a major role in human susceptibility to environmental agents (Olden and White 2005). Poor people have a similar genetic makeup as those who are more fortunate, but they are more at risk as a result of living and working in environments containing multiple and high levels of carcinogens or other toxicants capable of interacting with susceptibility genes to cause disease. Most of our understanding of the problems of environmental toxins has been obtained from studies of single agents. In the real world health disparities result from multiple agents. Despite this highly complex interaction of inherited and environmental factors the health of those in the lower levels of society might be greatly improved by greater collaboration of social, environmental and genetic scientists, by the development of new innovative ways to address the health of disadvantaged communities.

Health problems become greater with age and older people now constitute the majority of those with health problems in developed countries. Socio-economic indicators, in particular markers of poverty such as receipt of income support, are consistently associated with increased poor health outcomes. Social resources such as marital status and social support have a significant effect on the indicators of psychological health, as measured by the General Health Questionnaire (GHQ). In particular smoking is more strongly associated with these indicators than with self-rated health. Grundy and Sloggett (2003) analysed variations in the health of adults, in England, aged 65–84 by indicators of *personal capital*. This was characterised by attributes acquired in childhood and young adulthood, and by current social resources and current socio-economic circumstances. This approach demonstrated that self-rated health may provide a holistic indicator of health in the sense of well-being, in contrast to more biomedical specific issues measured by, for example the amount and frequency of prescribed medications which may be more indicative of specific morbidities. This study emphasises again the need to consider both socio-economic and socio-psychological influences on later life health (Grundy and Sloggett 2003).

Older homeless individuals have a much greater disease burden than the young adult homeless population. Garibaldi *et al.* found that across Philadelphia homeless individuals over 50 years of age were almost 4 times more likely to have a chronic medical condition, 2.8 times more likely not to have health insurance and 2.4 times more likely to be heroin dependent compared with those younger than 50 years. However, this group was also more likely to use shelter-based clinics as its source of usual care and were less likely to report a need for substance misuse treatment (Garibaldi *et al.* 2005).

MORTALITY AND MORBIDITY

The death rates of homeless and socially excluded people are significantly higher than that in the general public. This is due to a number of factors including poor health status, the concomitant risk related to abuse of alcohol and other drugs, and suicide. Anxiety and homelessness were found to be important predictors of increased mortality by Gossop *et al.* (2002). In this work deaths among 1075 drug misusers, involved in 54 treatment programmes during a four-year period, were critically examined. Information was collected at intake interviews conducted with clients, death certificates and post-mortem examinations. In this study the annual mortality rate was 1.2 %, about six times higher than that for a general, age-matched population. Of these deaths, 14 % were due to self-inflicted injuries, accidents or violence and 18 % were due to medical causes. The majority of deaths (68 %) were linked to drug overdoses. Post-mortem examinations revealed that opiates were the drugs most commonly used but in the majority of cases more than one drug was detected. High risk factors for mortality included polydrug use and, specifically, heavy drinking, and use of benzodiazepines and amphetamines were frequently found.

There are significant gender differences in mortality and morbidity. This is particularly the case in the young and middle-aged groups (Moller-Leimkuhler 2003). Explanations for this gender difference include increased vulnerability in males who have maladaptive coping strategies such as emotional unexpressiveness, reluctance to seek help or alcohol abuse. Psychosocial stress is increased in different societal conditions, which include changes in male gender role, the changing self-image resulting from postmodern individualism and rapid social changes as have occurred in Eastern Europe and Russia during recent years. These changes have been paralleled by increases in rates of offending behaviour, conduct disorders, suicide and depression, particularly in men, and might be the result of a perceived reduction in social role opportunities leading to social exclusion.

The underlying mental health status of males and females who are vulnerable to premature death is not completely clear due to a variety of methodological reasons. In a critical review of the literature Jenkins (1985) found measurement and study design problems and conflicting findings. Frequently in the literature social factors related to the aetiology of minor affective disorder were studied without adequate exclusion of biomedical and psychological factors. In such studies life events, chronic social stress and inadequate social supports in the aetiology of minor affective disorder have been found but the significance of these factors is small, suggesting the greater importance of biological and psychological factors. The evidence for a genetic contribution to these mental health problems is limited, but there is some evidence that changes in sex hormone profiles in women are linked to mood changes. In a carefully controlled cohort study of executive officers in the Home Office women did report significantly more somatic symptoms than men. However, this study provided only partial support for the notion that there is a substantial sex difference in the self-perception of illness, illness behaviour and sickness absence in individuals with minor psychiatric morbidity in this homogeneous group of men and women.

INFECTIONS

Infections are more likely in individuals who have a poor life style due to a range of issues related to their environment, poor immune status and life-style factors such as promiscuous sexual behaviour. There is concern about the increasing rise of tuberculosis (TB) in homeless populations. Tuber-culosis is a major health problem around the world and its incidence is growing 0.4 % each year (Marques Gomes 2004). In 2004 there were 2 billion people infected, and 8.4 million new cases each year. The major causes of this global health concern appear to be the increasing number of patients resistant to several drugs, increased mobility of people, poverty, wars, social exclusion and the lack of accessible health care.

To address this problem of epidemic proportions new innovative diag-nostic methods are being investigated which are more rapid and specific. An example of the use of molecular biology techniques is described by Diel *et al.* (2002). In a cluster analysis of 398 cases of diagnosed TB in Hamburg from 1997 to 1999 Diel found 135 (33.9 %) cases were classified into 35 clusters ranging from 2–23 patients. Using sophisticated molecular biology and epidemiological techniques, alcohol abuse appeared to be the strongest predictor for recent transmission, followed by a history of previous contact and unemployment. Homelessness, foreign ethnicity, sex, drug addiction and HIV positivity were not assessed to be independent risk factors. The authors conclude that recent transmission of TB in Hamburg was highly associated with alcohol abuse. In this study the use of modern molecular techniques including the restriction fragment length polymorphism (RFLP), for the detection of transmission chains, is effective in tracing contacts in comparison with conventional contact tracing.

In a US study in which Kimerling *et al.* (1998) also used RFLP, the most important risk associated with TB was homelessness (odds ratio 8.9; $P < 0.001$). Here homelessness accounted for 29 % (51/175) of new cases diagnosed during the study period. Further analysis of this homeless group showed the most predominant were younger ($P < 0.001$), of male gender ($P < 0.001$), black race ($P = 0.002$), and were heavy alcohol consumers ($P < 0.001$) and non-injection drug users. In contrast to these studies are the findings of Solsona *et al.* studying the homeless population in Barcelona evaluated using chest x-ray, tuberculin tests and sputum smears in 447 subjects. Of the sample population 75 % were infected with Mycobacterium tuberculosis. Active TB was present in 1.11 % and 13.8 % showed radiographic evidence of inactive pulmonary TB. However, although infection was associated with age and smoking, no associations were found with alcohol abuse or sex (Solsona *et al.* 2001). It is important that treatment of TB in the homeless population is appropriate to their living circumstances, however, it is often difficult to directly monitor treatment and follow up cases, an important public health priority. Treatment should include education about the disease (Poinsignon *et al.* 1998).

The association between infectious diseases, lifestyle and heavy alcohol consumption may accelerate the progression of hepatitis C (HCV) related liver disease and/or limit efforts at an anti-viral treatment. Injection drug use is currently the primary transmission route for HCV. In Canada where HCV is a major health burden, the majority of injecting drug users (IDUs) are HCV positive. IDUs were traditionally excluded from HCV treatment unless they abstained from drug use; recently, however, research has suggested significant benefits can be obtained in HCV treatment even when the patient is still injecting drugs, although there are some questions over side effects and motivation of the IDU to take medication. Fischer *et al.* have concluded that treatment of HCV-infected illicit drug users is now possible and is necessary to reduce transmission rates (Fischer *et al.* 2004). In a sample of 884 homeless and impoverished individuals in Los Angeles 22% were HCV positive. People most likely to be infected were lifetime IDUs, and recent daily users of crack cocaine. Among the non-injection drug users the individuals who reported lifetime alcohol abuse were more likely to be HCV positive. After statistical analysis, Nyamathi *et al.* (2002) reported that IDUs have over 25 times greater chance of having HCV than those who did not inject. Other predictors of HCV include older age, living by oneself before 18 years old and chronic alcohol abuse. Men also had a 1.5 times greater risk of HCV infection than women. Binge drinking is a significant cause of acute risk for HCV in people receiving opioid maintenance therapy at an inner city hospital (Watson 2005).

SEXUAL TRANSMISSION

The relationship between drug abuse and issues that influence risk and vulnerability to HIV was investigated by Surratt *et al.* (2005) in which 254 men and women from the US Virgin Isles who were chronic alcohol or drug users were interviewed. Crack cocaine use was particularly high in women compared to men (84.7% vs 48.8%). Women reported higher numbers of sexual partners, more occasions of unprotected sex and self-reported levels of HIV infection were also higher in the females. It is thought that women partake in 'survival sex' to support their drug and/or alcohol dependence thus aiding the spread of sexually transmitted infections (STIs) in this particular region.

In another study in Miami (Surratt and Inciardi 2004), 485 homeless female sex workers were recruited into an HIV prevention programme. Compared to non-homeless sex workers, the homeless sample were daily alcohol and crack users. This group also reported more oral and vaginal acts, unprotected sex and many other sexual activities while 'high' on drugs. Homeless women appeared to encounter more customers who refused protected sex, however, there was no major difference between HIV seropositivity between homeless and non-homeless. The highest risks for HIV are found in men who have sex with men (MSM) and injecting drug users (IDUs). Until work by Beckett *et al.*, little was known about substance use after HIV infection. In a national sample of HIV patients, the prevalence of substance abuse between the two groups (mentioned above) and also heterosexual men and women were investigated in an attempt to find the association between substance use and sexual behaviours. Marijuana, alcohol and hard drug use were most strongly associated with being sexually active among MSM. Whereas substance use predicted high-risk sex, there were few differences among exposure groups in these associations (Beckett *et al.* 2003).

There is a strong correlation between the frequency of depression and suicidal ideas in homeless people who display behaviours which could increase the risk of STI transmission. Rohde *et al.* (2001), in a sample of 523 homeless adolescents, found 12.2 % had a DSM-IV diagnosis of major depression, 6.5 % had dysthymia (chronic low-grade depression). Depression preceded (rather than followed) homelessness and was associated with STIs, lack of condom use, homosexual orientation (in older participants) and lifetime homosexual experience. Suicidal thoughts and hopelessness were associated with higher rates of intravenous drug use but lower rates of multiple sex partners and, in young homeless women, less sexual coercion. The results of this investigation therefore concluded that depression is frequent in homeless older adolescents and appears to have a complex association with STI-related behaviours.

The link between mental ill health and sexually acquired infections is reinforced by Ladd and Petry (2003), who studied 174 treatment-seeking cocaine abusers with antisocial personality disorder (ASP). ASP can be associated with increased severity of psychosocial problems and risks of HIV infection. Patients with ASP reported greater participation in lifetime sexual risk behaviours, including number of casual sexual partners, inconsistent protected sex and frequency of anal sex.

In conclusion, socially excluded people have a complex range of health risks often exacerbated by lack of or inadequate accommodation and employment. The risks related to poor physical conditions, nutrition, low levels of health education and access to services, increased vulnerability to problematic alcohol and drug use, all increase risks of infection, pathological problems and death. A holistic concept of health and relevant methods of study are required to understand these multifactorial problems. The role of stress further reduces resilience as discussed in the next chapter.

REFERENCES

Alonso, Y. (2004). The biopsychosocial model in medical research: the evolution of the health concept over the last two decades. *Patient Education and Counselling*, **53**(2), 239–44.

Beckett, M., A. Burnam, R. L. Collins, D. E. Kanouse and R. Beckman (2003). Substance use and high-risk sex among people with HIV: a comparison across exposure groups. *AIDS and Behaviour*, **7**(2), 209–19.

Benach, J. and M. Amable (2004). Social classes and poverty. *Gaceta Sanitaria*, **18**(Supplement 1), 16–23.

Bosma, H., J. P. Diederiks, H. M. van Santen and J. T. van Eijk (2005). More social exclusion of chronically ill patients with lower incomes. *Nederlandse Tijdschrift voor Geneeskunde*, **149**(34), 1898–902.

Connelly, J. and J. Crown (1994). *Homelessness and Ill Health: Report of a Working Party of the Royal College of Physicians.* London: Royal College of Physicians.

CRISIS (2002). *Critical Condition: Vulnerable Single Homeless people and Access to GPs.* London: CRISIS.

Davidson, R., J. Kitzinger and K. Hunt (2006). The wealthy get healthy, the poor get poorly? Lay perceptions of health inequalities. *Social Science and Medicine*, **62**(9), 2172–82.

Del Rey Calero, J. (2004). Poverty, social exclusion, social capital and health. *Anales de la Real Academia Nacional de Medicina (Madrid)*, **121**(1), 57–72.

Diel, R., S. Schneider, K. Meywald-Walter, C. M. Ruf, S. Rusch-Gerdes and S. Niemann (2002). Epidemiology of tuberculosis in Hamburg, Germany: long-term population-based analysis applying classical and molecular epidemiological techniques. *Journal of Clinical Microbiology*, **40**(2), 532–9.

Fischer, B., E. Haydon, J. Rehm, M. Krajden and J. Reimer (2004). Injection drug use and the hepatitis C virus: considerations for a targeted treatment approach – the case study of Canada. *Journal of Urban Health*, **81**(3), 428–47.

Garibaldi, B., A. Conde-Martel and T. P. O'Toole (2005). Self-reported comorbidities, perceived needs, and sources for usual care for older and younger homeless adults. *Journal of General Internal Medicine*, **20**(8), 726–30.

Gossop, M., D. Stewart, S. Treacy and J. Marsden (2002). A prospective study of mortality among drug misusers during a 4-year period after seeking treatment. *Addiction*, **97**(1), 39–47.

Griffiths, S. (2002). *Assessing the Needs of the Rough Sleepers.* London: Homeless Directorate, ODPM.

Grundy, E. and A. Sloggett (2003). Health inequalities in the older population: the role of personal capital, social resources and socio-economic circumstances. *Social Sciences and Medicine*, **56**(5), 935–47.

Hammarstrom, A. (1994). Health consequences of youth unemployment – review from a gender perspective. *Social Sciences and Medicine*, **38**(5), 699–709.

Holohan, T. W. (2000). Health and homelessness in Dublin. *Irish Medical Journal*, **93**(2), 41–3.

Jenkins, R. (1985). Sex differences in minor psychiatric morbidity. *Psychological Medicine. Monograph Supplement*, **7**, 1–53.

Katz, A. (2005). The Sachs report: investing in health for economic development – or increasing the size of the crumbs from the rich man's table? Part II. *International Journal of Health Services*, **35**(1), 171–88.

Ladd, G. T. and N. M. Petry (2003). Antisocial personality in treatment-seeking cocaine abusers: psychosocial functioning and HIV risk. *Journal of Substance Abuse Treatment*, **24**(4), 323–30.

Macintyre, S. and A. Ellaway (2000). Neighbourhood cohesion and health in socially contrasting neighbourhoods: implications for the social exclusion and public health agendas. *Health Bulletin (Edinburgh)*, **58**(6), 450–6.

Marques Gomes, M. J. (2004). Tuberculosis. Future perspectives. *Revista Portuguesa de Pneumologia*, **10**(2), 135–44.

Moller-Leimkuhler, A. M. (2003). The gender gap in suicide and premature death or: why are men so vulnerable? *European Archives of Psychiatry and Clinical Neuroscience*, **253**(1), 1–8.

Nyamathi, A. M., E. L. Dixon, W. Robbins, C. Smith, D. Wiley, B. Leake, *et al.* (2002). Risk factors for hepatitis C virus infection among homeless adults. *Journal of General Internal Medicine*, **17**(2), 134–43.

Olden, K. and S. L. White (2005). Health-related disparities: influence of environmental factors. *Medicine Clinics of North America*, **89**(4), 721–38.

OED (1973). *The Shorter Oxford English Dictionary.* Oxford: Clarendon Press.

Poinsignon, Y., Z. Marjanovic, P. Bordon, C. Georges and D. Farge (1998). Re-emergence of tuberculosis and socioeconomic uncertainty. *Revue de Medicine Interne,* **19**(9), 649–57.

Pritchard, J. W. and J. W. Puzey (2004). Homelessness – on the health agenda in Wales? *Review of Environmental Health*, **19**(3–4), 363–79.

Rohde, P., J. Noell, L. Ochs and J. R. Seeley (2001). Depression, suicidal ideation and STD-related risk in homeless older adolescents. *Journal of Adolescence*, **24**(4), 447–60.

Solsona, J., J. A. Cayla, J. Nadal, M. Bedia, C. Mata, J. Brau, *et al.* (2001). Screening for tuberculosis upon admission to shelters and free-meal services. *European Journal of Epidemiology*, **17**(2), 123–8.

Surratt, H. L. and J. A. Inciardi (2004). HIV risk, seropositivity and predictors of infection among homeless and non-homeless women sex workers in Miami, Florida, USA. *AIDS Care*, **16**(5), 594–604.

Surratt, H. L., J. A. Inciardi, J. C. Weaver and V. M. Falu (2005). Emerging linkages between substance abuse and HIV infection in St. Croix, US Virgin Islands. *AIDS Care*, **17**(Supplement 1), S26–35.

Vostanis, P., C. Feehan, E. Grattan and W. L. Bickerton (1996). A randomised controlled outpatient trial of cognitive-behavioural treatment for children and adolescents with depression: 9-month follow-up. *Journal of Affective Disorders*, **40**(1–2), 105–16.

Watson, B., P. S. Haber, K. M. Conigrave, J. B. Whitfield, C. Wallace, J. Lauer, W. Weinmann and F. M. Wurst (2005). Alcohol consumption patterns amongst hepatitis C positive people receiving opioid maintenance treatment. *Alcohol and Alcoholism*, **40**(1), P 065.

WHO (1946). *Preamble to the Constitution of the World Health Organisation as Adopted by the International Health Conference,* New York: WHO.

CHAPTER 5

STRESS AND SOCIALLY EXCLUDED GROUPS

STRESS AND HEALTH

During recent years advanced societies have begun to recognise the links between stress and social exclusion in the development of health policies. In the process of creating, implementing and evaluating the European health policy on behalf of the World Health Organisation (WHO 1946), Holcik and Koupilova (2001) highlighted the main social determinants of health. These include social gradient, stress, early life experiences, social exclusion, job control at work, unemployment, social support, addiction, food and transport. Concern for socially excluded individuals is in part motivated by the health policy agenda but strongly driven by criminal justice agendas (see Chapter 12). Community safety is a high-level political initiative. From both health policy and criminal justice perspectives there is increasing interest in children and families, with an intention to understand the nature, origins and developmental course of social exclusion, which involves a continuous transition from one stressful situation to the next. A greater appreciation of this process will hopefully lead to more effective interventions for those with the related problems of criminal activity, substance misuse and mental illness.

Evidence relating stress with illness has emerged from a variety of experimental, clinical and epidemiological research strategies. This work has indicated the interlinking of biological and psychological factors resulting in a stress response elicited by an imbalance between external demands and personal resources. A range of factors relevant to this cause and effect have been identified, these include the length of time and the predictability of the challenge, the extent to which the events may be controlled by the individual, the psychological coping responses and the availability of social supports. Although several distinct cognitive-behavioural and psychophysiological mediating processes have been suggested to account for the various acute and chronic influences on health, mechanisms through which stress responses may increase risk of illness are poorly understood. Frequently the expression 'biological predisposition' is used to account for individual differences in susceptibility to disease or variations in clinical course (Steptoe 2002). A direct correlation between the number of major life events experienced over the previous six months and skin problems has been reported by Gupta and Gupta (2004). The scalp was found to be most frequently affected and significantly correlated with the number of major life events experienced over the previous six months. In this study the number of major life events experienced over the previous six months was measured using the Social Readjustment Rating Scale (SRRS) of Holmes and Rahe, in addition to the frequency and severity of a range of cutaneous symptoms ('burning', 'crawling sensation', 'tingling', 'pricking' or 'pins and needles', 'pain', 'tenderness of skin', 'numbness', 'moderate to severe itching' and 'easy bruising') that the subject may have experienced over the previous month.

Evidence for the significant role of stress in predisposing individuals to poor physical health was documented by DeLongis *et al.* (1988) who assessed the daily stresses of married couples over a six-month period. She found that concurrent health problems such as flu, sore throat, headaches and backaches were related to daily stress. However, the relationship of daily stress to mood disturbance was more complex. Mood effects were limited to a single day with positive mood scores being achieved on a day following a negatively rated day.

In this study, subjects with poor unsupportive social relationships and with low self-esteem were more prone to experience an increase in psychological and physical problems both on and following stressful days than were participants high in self-esteem and social support. The implications of this study are that individuals with limited psychosocial resources are more vulnerable to illness and mood disturbance when exposed to stressful events.

The relationship between stress and mental health involves a wide range of affective (emotional) behaviours. Conflict with family and friends has been shown (Bassuk *et al.* 2002) to be a good predictor of adverse mental health and strongly predicts outcomes of psychosocial interventions. In this study sibling conflict was a stronger predictor of mental health than parent conflict. This work suggests that an understanding of stress and the ways in which people cope with it may be useful for understanding a fundamental aspect of social exclusion and homelessness. Although homelessness of families has become a growing social problem, we have a very limited understanding of daily survival strategies that are used by such families. From narratives of a group of 64 mothers, living in temporary emergency shelters with their children, Banyard (1995) found that a range of coping responses to daily stressful events were employed by the women, these included the use of direct actions and more palliative strategies.

Unemployment may affect health either due to poor standards of living and material conditions of life. Unemployment is stressful and may result in social isolation and long-term illness. Conversely chronic ill health can lead to unemployment, therefore studies must be carried out carefully to conclude unemployment is the cause of poor health. Unemployed people have more illnesses, have higher blood pressure, increased mortality and reduced psychological health (Jin 1995; Montgomery *et al.* 1999).

Chronic stress associated with work environments has a negative impact on health and was demonstrated by a 2–6 times increase in the risk of sudden heart disease (Bosma *et al.* 1998; Siegrist *et al.* 1990). The *demand–control* model of stress suggest that jobs combining high psychological demands with low levels of control lead to stress and can increase the risk of diseases such as coronary heart disease (CHD). This work involved a large longitudinal study of British civil servants and compared organisation of their work with health outcomes (Marmot and Theorell 1988). Significant differences in health were found to be related to occupational grade. Those in the lowest grade showed three times higher mortality rates than those in the highest grade. This work indicated that a lack of freedom to make decisions at work is linked to at-risk behaviours such as smoking, physiological factors such as high blood pressure and health outcomes such as CHD. This suggests that jobs combining much effort but with little reward either financial, emotional, career advancement or job security, lead to emotional distress, job strain and illness.

SOCIAL SUPPORT

Durkheim (1933) was one of the first observers to draw attention to the link between social environment and health. He reviewed suicide rates across different subpopulations and discovered that the differences in rates have persisted over time and across cultures. He explained the occurrence of high suicide rates in people who were poorly integrated into society, the process of integrating individuals into the community, resulting in either encouraging or deterring suicide. More recent studies have focused on health and marital status as particularly important social support factors contributing to well-being. Single, widowed and divorced people have a higher mortality rate than those who are married, men having a significantly higher rate of mortality than women. These differences first noted in the mid-nineteenth century have been consistent over time and across cultures. Explanations for this observation include the view that married people tend to be happier, more satisfied with life, less likely to be socially isolated and have more social ties than unmarried people. This has been substantiated by Berkman and Syme (1979) who followed a random sample of adults for nine years. Analysis of the data from this longitudinal study indicated that the socially isolated groups had a 2–3 times higher risk of mortality. Patrick and Holloway (1990) performed a two-year follow-up study of people with disabilities, and found that people with fewer social contacts were more likely to deteriorate physically and psychosocially, than people with high social contact. The most significant difference between those with and without social support was seen among those who reported an adverse life event during the study.

Social support is a broad term that includes financial help, advice, practical assistance and psychological support. Social support has been shown to act as a buffer against events which may otherwise result in health-damaging effects. However, social support was found to be protective only within the context of a severe life event (Brown and Harris 1978). It is possible that social support also influences coping with stresses through psychological, hormonal and neurophysiological pathways. The benefits of social support and links with health-related issues have been reviewed by Uchino *et al.* (1996).

WHAT IS STRESS?

Our understanding of stress has become more sophisticated during the last four decades from concepts based on engineering models in the 1960s, in which an individual's stress response was likened to machine systems. These ideas suggested that a stress-producing strain was a direct reflection of the strain generated by external forces. This approach focused on the characteristics of the external stimulus and the change in performance of the individual under unusual loading conditions. Concepts such as system capacity, introduced from *human factors* research, were concerned with activities in the workplace but had limited utility in the wider areas of social behaviour.

Studies by physiological psychologists at the same time were significantly influenced by the work of Hans Selye (1936–55), who described the stress response as a homeostatic process in which the body responded to traumatic inputs by *specific* source-related stress and *non-specific* responses involving generalised neuronal and hormonal changes. This idea was expressed as the *General Adaptation Syndrome* (GAS) (Seltzer 1952), which highlighted the role of the pituitary–adrenal reaction. If the stressor was unabated for a long period *diseases of adaptation* would develop producing pathological damage which included gastric ulcers, thymus involution, adrenal atrophy and ultimately exhaustion and death. This simple explanation was later elaborated with additional information collected from studies into brain washing in the 1960s (at the time of the cold war), impact of isolation on cognition (in relation to Antarctic and space exploration); and other reflections of scientific and technological progress in society are reflected in the literature. Trends in stress research can be summarised as follows:

- 1927–60: stress, conflict, emotion, tension, danger, disaster;

- 1961–5: anxiety, fear, frustration;

- 1966–8: (sensory) deprivation;

- 1972–: environmental, occupational, physiological, social;

- 1980–: post-traumatic stress.

In consideration of the emerging information on stress-related phenomena, Selye (1973) drew attention to pathological changes in nervous,
immune and endocrine systems and commented that the objective of
adaptation was not to remove stress from an individual's life, as 'complete
freedom from stress is death' (Selye 1973).

Our contemporary understanding of the nature of stress has emerged
from the work of Baum; Singer and Baum; Lazarus; Cox and Mackay, as
reviewed by Appley and Turnbull (1986). Cox and Mackay described stress
as a set of linked processes which involve:

1. Demand: load or input or environmental stressors acting on the individual.

2. Reception: cognitive appraisal, perception/subjective recognition of
demand which might be conscious or unconscious.

3. Response(s) to the perception of the stressor: physiological, psychological,
behavioural and/or social.

4. Perceived consequences of response for the individual or his/her environment.

Feedback occurs at each of the above stages. This model is presented in
Figure 5.1.

This transactional perspective of stress takes account of a range of cognitive processes involved in the stress response, inherited vulnerabilities,
the development of coping skills, previous traumatic events (life events),

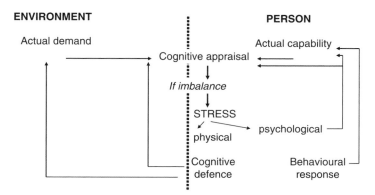

Figure 5.1 Interactional model of stress, showing the dynamic system of transaction
between the individual and the environment. Based on text from Cox and Mackay,
1981 (cited in Appley and Turnbull, 1986).

personalities characteristics (e.g. Type A and B) and pathological risk. Emphasis here is placed on individual vulnerabilities and the cognitive processes, which are integrated with biological, psychological and sociological processes, each with its own subsystems. Temporal factors affecting the stress response include the mediating influences of circadian (about a day), monthly and annual biological rhythms.

An example of these chronobiological influences includes the seasonal changes seen in the occurrence of mental illness, in particular the marked seasonality of suicide. The distinction between short-acting, acute and long-term chronic stress is important. Acute stress involves the 'fight or flight' response, which is an evolutionary adaptation mechanism providing the individual with a physiological and behavioural response mechanism to an immediate threat by the mobilisation of appropriate body resources. Long-term exposure to stressors will result in pathological changes caused by the overproduction of corticosteroids, which have a damaging effect on the body's tissues including the brain and reduce the effectiveness of the immune system.

The study of psychoneuroimmunology is an emerging discipline which attempts to provide an insight into the influences of social and psychological factors on biological pathways of health and disease. Stress causes many changes in the body by interfering with neuroendocrine, immune and autonomic metabolic systems leading to an increase in heart rate, respiration, dilation of blood vessels to the muscles and alterations in gastrointestinal (GI) function. These changes are thought to either directly cause disease or make the individual more prone to it (Brunner *et al.* 1993). This complex interaction between environment, life style and behaviours has a major influence on health, and is particularly important in people who live in poverty, are homeless and not part of a supportive community (Najman 1980).

MEASURING STRESS

Life events are implicated in the mechanisms leading to physical disorders, as noted above. These pathological consequences include diabetes and other clinical problems found in homeless and other vulnerable groups. Life experiences or life events include the loss of accommodation, bereavement and unemployment and can be measured by the *Social Readjustment Rating Scale* (SRRS). The SRRS provides an estimate of the amount of life change experienced in a defined period, measured using a list of 42 events involving a degree of change or loss of some kind. Each event is scored depending on how much life change it involves. Criticisms of the SRRS include the significance of events to individuals, for instance death of a mother may be more upsetting to a child who has a strong relationship with her than a child who has had poor maternal support.

This problem has been addressed by Brown and Harris who added a modification to this approach by accounting for the meaning of life events from an individual perspective.

The *Hassles Scale* was designed to address another criticism of the SSRS, which does not take account of smaller life events. The measurement of 'daily hassles' is claimed to provide a more accurate predictor of changes in physiological and psychological health than major life events (Reich *et al.* 1988). The link between social and economic circumstances and the onset of depression in women has been investigated (Lora and Fava 1992). Here a highly significant relationship was found between life events with long-term implications and the onset of depression. Events with short-term implications showed little impact on depression. Vulnerability to depression was attributed to loss of mother before 11 years of age, absence of a close relationship with spouse/other person, three or more children under 15 living at home and lack of employment outside the home. The more of these factors experienced by a woman, the more increased her vulnerability to depression.

STRESS IN CHILDREN AND FAMILIES

Stress in adults is thought to have its origins in early childhood experiences. Various studies indicate that fearful children are at a high risk for later emotional distress, Kagan and colleagues, for instance, have shown that a child who is profoundly shy at the age of two years is more likely to suffer from anxiety and depression later in life than a less inhibited child. A vicious circle leading through isolation and lowered self-esteem and underachievement is thought to lead to anxiety and depression with the possibility that early experience will lead to physical illness in fearful children. Children who become severely inhibited in unfamiliar places produce high levels of stress hormones, including cortisol from the adrenal gland.

Cortisol is produced at elevated levels at times of crisis and is part of the 'fight or flight' response, as described in Figure 5.2. Adverse experiences can occur both pre- and perinatally. Peacock *et al.* (1995) have observed that lower social class, less education, single marital status, low income, trouble with 'nerves' and depression, help from professional agencies and little contact with neighbours were all significantly associated with an increased risk of preterm birth. In this study of 1513 women, no apparent effects of smoking, alcohol or caffeine were found on the length of gestation overall, although there was an association between smoking and delivery before 32 weeks. Analysis of the data indicated three subgroups of women delivering preterm: two predominantly of low social status and a third of older women

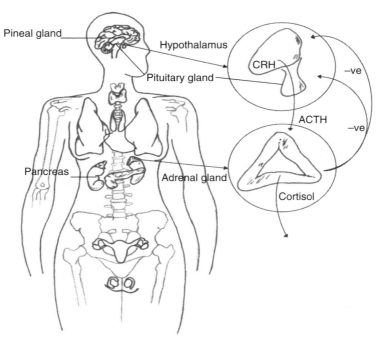

Figure 5.2   The hypothalamus–pituitary–adrenal (HPA) axis showing the production of cortico-releasing hormone (CRH) from the hypothalamus causing the production of adrenocorticotrophic hormone from the pituitary gland. This neuro-endocrine activation stimulates the adrenal cortex to produce the stress hormone cortisol. The synthesis of cortisol is controlled by a negative feedback system, indicated by –ve in the diagram.
Source: Image produced by Gemma Evans.

with higher social status who did not smoke. Mean gestational age was highest in the third group suggesting that adverse social circumstances are associated with very early births.

Chronic stress and ethnic differences in levels of infection have been observed in inner city areas measured in individuals and in communities with the use of interviews and analysing administrative records. In a study by Culhane *et al.* (2002), black women had significantly higher rates of bacterial vaginosis (64 %) compared with white women (35 %). Exposure to chronic stressors varied in individuals from different races, for example 32 % of the black women reported threats to personal safety compared with 13 % of white women. There were significant racial differences in exposure to stress in the community, for example 63 % of the black women lived in neighbourhoods with aggravated assault rates that were above the mean values of 25 % reported by the white women.

Postnatally homeless children are confronted by serious threats to their ability to succeed and their future well-being. Of particular concern are health problems, hunger, poor nutrition, developmental delays, anxiety, depression, behavioural problems and educational underachievement. The needs of these children have been identified in a number of studies directed at informing public policy. Factors that have been identified, which may mediate the observed outcomes, include inadequate housing conditions, instability in accommodation, inadequate services and barriers to accessing services that are available (Rafferty and Shinn 1991).

Data from the British National Survey of Psychiatric Morbidity indicates that lone mothers are increasing in numbers as marital stability declines. Using rating scales for psychiatric symptoms and ICD-10 diagnoses of 5281 women, established by lay interviewers using the CIS-R, their high rates of material disadvantage and of depressive disorder may have considerable implications for psychiatric and social policy. Targosz *et al.* (2003) found that lone mothers had prevalence rates of depressive episodes of 7%, approximately three times higher than any other group, with increased frequencies of less severe mixed anxiety/depression. Homelessness has been associated with levels of stress beyond the normal strain of living in poverty. For mothers who are homeless, support from their social networks may provide a buffer from some of the stresses associated with being homeless. In reviewing 12 research articles, which compare social support among low-income housed mothers and homeless mothers, Meadows-Oliver (2005) found four significant attributes of social support used by housed and homeless mothers. These are:

- size of the social support network;

- composition of the social support network;

- contacts with members of the social support network;

- perceived support from members of the social support network.

The problems of a lone parent and her offspring are exacerbated when the mother is separated from her newborn. As might be expected, separating a mother and her newborn during the first week of the child's life involves much emotional strain for the mother. In a study by Nystrom and Axelsson (2002), women's narratives revealed their perceptions of despair, powerlessness, homelessness, disappointment, and lack of control including emotional instability, threat, guilt and insecurity.

A review of the formative influences of stress-related and other intrinsic and extrinsic factors in the process of human development is provided in Chapter 3. The main conclusion from this expanding literature is the growing awareness of the vulnerability of the children for later life ill health and psychopathology. Another vulnerable group, which is less identified with stress-related problems, is that of the elderly. Here a different set of factors produce stress and anxiety and should be considered as potential antecedents of mental ill health.

STRESS IN THE ELDERLY

The ageing process includes a range of biological changes which include reduced efficiency of the sensory and motor systems resulting in problems of hearing, seeing and increasing difficulties in locomotion. These changes are reflected in increasing social isolation and often concurrent increases in psychopathology related to anxiety as individuals adapt or fail to adapt to their changing social status. Some individuals have increased problems associated with personal characteristics such as shyness, loneliness and high levels of external control. This has been demonstrated by Fletcher and Hansson (1991) who used the *Social Components of Retirement Anxiety Scale* (SCRAS), to assess retirement anxiety. In studying 308 men and 384 women aged 25–76, higher scores were found in people who had reduced mobility and social skills, were shy, lonely or expected to have little personal control over their lives after retirement. Major social transitions were more difficult for these people. The onset of disability in the elderly has been associated with a range of factors such as cognitive impairment, depression, comorbidities, increased and decreased body mass index, poor functioning of the lower limbs, low frequency of social contacts, low level of physical activity, no alcohol use compared to moderate use, poor self-perceived health, smoking and vision impairment (Stuck *et al.* 1999).

An awareness of these key factors is useful in preventing disability among the elderly. For instance anxiety in the elderly increases with reduced mobility. When a person can no longer drive or is less able to use public transport he/she becomes less independent and restricted in their ability to socially interact. These problems are perceived differently by males and females (Yoshimoto and Kawata 1996). Elderly people become more anxious with increasing age, which can significantly reduce their functioning and the ability to perform activities of daily living. Impairment of social function appears to be more affected by anxiety, more so than the effects of depression and cognitive decline (Schultz *et al.* 2004) The process of ageing is accompanied by increased mental and physical frailty which increases the elderly person's susceptibility to physical and psychological stress.

As discussed above stress is vital in modulating the immune system. In the young the effects of stress can be buffered by an optimal immune response. However, in the elderly a decline in immune system function can lead to a chronic pro-inflammatory state. The immunological response in ageing has been associated with reduced T-cell responses and increased pro-inflammatory cytokines (tumor necrosis factor alpha and interleukin 6), which is reflected in elevated ratio of *cortisol/sulphated dehydroepiandrosterone (DHEA) ratio* (Stephen and Butcher 2004).

Luz *et al.* (2003) showed that the elderly were more stressed, depressed and anxious than the young subjects, when the emotional status of each participant was assessed by monitoring salivary cortisol and serum DHEA. In the elderly the stress hormone cortisol was elevated in contrast to DHEA levels which were significantly reduced. Positive correlations were found between psychological tests and evening cortisol levels and negatively correlated to morning DHEA levels. No significant effects in pro-inflammatory cytokines were found. This psychoneuroimmunology approach suggests that significant distress and activation of the hypothalamic–pituitary–adrenal axis occurs in healthy ageing, and complex changes in pro-inflammation state (monitored by cytokine production) occur during the ageing process (Luz *et al.* 2003).

Major life events occur in the elderly when they move from their established family home into retirement accommodation, residential home and perhaps a nursing care home, sometimes involving occasional or long-term admission into hospital. Hospitalisation can be a very stressful time, resulting in a poorer night sleep pattern. Carvalhaes-Neto *et al.* (2003) found no significant change in cortisol measurements. However, relocation of elderly subjects to a new nursing home resulted in significantly elevated cortisol levels a week after the move. This stress hormone level declined four weeks after the move which was concurrent with lower anxiety and depression ratings than those waiting to move (Hodgson *et al.* 2004).

Bereavement is a major life event and will be expected to have significant influence on the mental health of the remaining partner. Brown *et al.* (1996) investigated the changes in social rhythm stability and sleep in bereaved elderly spouses and in non-bereaved elderly controls. A lower social rhythm stability or activity level in the presence of a major depressive episode was observed in the case of bereavement of a spouse (Bennett and Stevens 1997). As women have a greater life expectancy than men, bereavement of a spouse in later life is likely to occur. Mental health and morale are affected and continue to have an impact several years following the loss. However, physical health and social participation appear to be unchanged in females following death of their spouses (Bennett and Stevens 1997). In contrast to women, mental health and morale is affected in men by widowhood. Men have reduced participation in social activities following bereavement, in contrast to the evidence supporting the stability of functioning among bereaved women (Bennett 1998). Bennett found that men who had recently become widowed showed greater declines in mental health, morale and social functioning.

Although many *frail elderly* maintain their independence and remain socially active, the problems of cognitive decline reduce sociability. This is particularly the case in dementia. The pathophysiology of brain ageing may be a direct result of the dissociation of adrenocortical secretion which occurs with age. Changes of adrenocortical secretion occurring with ageing appear to be primarily dependent on the ageing process, however, pathological conditions may amplify these changes. The ratio between cortisol and DHEA is a good marker of neuroendocrine features in the old, reflecting the opposing effects of cortisol and DHEA on the central nervous system. A decline of DHEA secretion is found in healthy centenarians. This metabolite is more reduced in old depressed patients and an even greater decrease in DHEA is found in those who are demented. A reduction of biological rhythmicity is indicated by the flattening of the circadian patterns of serum cortisol in elderly subjects (Ferrari *et al.* 2001).

These biopsychosocial findings are important for assisting in the planning of medical and social services for relocating the elderly. The elderly should be prepared for initial stressors before the stressful period. Attention should be paid to the first four weeks after a change in accommodation or health care as behavioural assessments are unlikely to give a true representation of the individual's needs.

ANXIETY, SOCIALISATION AND MENTAL HEALTH

In Chapter 3 and in the earlier part of this chapter (see 'Stress in Children and Families') the link between fearfulness in children and a high risk for later emotional distress was described (Kalin 1993). In summary, *opiate-using neural pathways* appear to regulate affiliative behaviours (e.g. stress induced by separation from the mother), and *benzodiazepines* seem to be primarily involved in response to direct threats (e.g. threats from predators). This reduction of activity in *opiate-sensitive systems* enables motor systems in the brain to elicit alarm signals and communication aimed at restoring the mother–child bond. Childhood events that involved disruption of this critical relationship have, for some time, been linked to increased vulnerability to later life drug dependence (see Chapter 8). Additionally, poor parenting and economic deprivation are associated with teenage antisocial behaviour and adult social dysfunction.

Farrington (1993) studied 411 males, in London, from 8 years to 32 years. He found that childhood nervousness, antisocial family background and hyperactivity-impulsivity-attention deficit were the most significant predictors of teenage antisocial behaviour and adult social dysfunction. These animal-based and human studies give an insight into the psychobiological basis of anxiety and stress.

From a sociobiological perspective, Gilbert (2001) has reviewed the social significance of human social anxiety and suggests that the evolution of competition for attractiveness is associated with *inclusive fitness* (see Dawkins' explanation of *inclusive fitness* in *The Selfish Gene* (1976)). Low social ranked individuals, or those who have been ostracised, have many negative consequences for controlling social resources and physiological regulation. 'Social anxiety', like shame, can be adaptive to the extent that it helps people to 'stay on track' with what is socially acceptable and what is not but could result in social sanction and exclusion. However, dysfunctional social anxiety is the result of activation of basic defensive mechanisms for threat detection and response (e.g. inhibition, eye-gaze avoidance, flight or submission) that can be recruited rapidly for dealing with immediate threats, override conscious wishes and interfere with being seen as a 'useful associate'. Panksepp (2005) suggests that the role of 'social pain' may be greater than personal anger and anxiety, and underpins aspects of social exclusion and abandonment, such as jealousy, shame and guilt.

These observations suggest that the apparent increase in personal and social anxiety and consequential psychopathologies in contemporary society may be explained by increased competition for social prestige, attractiveness and material resources. The next chapter will provide an introduction to mental illness, which, in part, is associated with anxiety and stress. Schizophrenia, for example, is considered to be a 'stress-reactive' disease, the onset of which is associated with environmentally produced stress. Socially stressful situations, for instance leaving the family home or becoming homeless, are thought to contribute to psychotic illness, as proposed in the *vulnerability-stress model of schizophrenic episodes* by Nuechterlein *et al.* (1986).

REFERENCES

Appley, M. and Turnbull R. eds. (1986). *Dynamics of Stress*. New York: Plenum.

Banyard, V. L. (1995). 'Taking another route': daily survival narratives from mothers who are homeless. *American Journal of Community Psychology*, **23**(6), 871–91.

Bassuk, E. L., K. D. Mickelson, H. D. Bissell and J. N. Perloff (2002). Role of kin and nonkin support in the mental health of low-income women. *American Journal of Orthopsychiatry*, **72**(1), 39–49.

Bennett, K. M. (1998). Longitudinal changes in mental and physical health among elderly, recently widowed men. *Mortality*, **3**(3), 265–73.

Bennett, K. M. and R. Stevens (1997). Widowhood in elderly women: the medium- and long-term effects on mental and physical health. *Mortality*, **2**(2), 137–48.

Berkman, L. F. and S. L. Syme (1979). Social networks, host resistance, and mortality: a nine-year follow-up study of Alameda County residents. *American Journal of Epidemiology*, **109**(2), 186–204.

Bosma, H., S. A. Stansfeld and M. G. Marmot (1998). Job control, personal characteristics, and heart disease. *Journal of Occupational Health Psychology*, **3**(4), 402–9.

Brown, G. W. and T. Harris (1978). *Social Origins of Depression: A Study of Psychiatric Disorders in Women*. London: Tavistock.

Brown, L. F., C. F. Reynolds, T. H. Monk, H. G. Prigerson, M. A. Dew, P. R. Houck, S. Mazumdar, D. J. Buysse, C. C. Hoch and D. J. Kupfer (1996). Social rhythm stability following late-life spousal bereavement: associations with depression and sleep impairment. *Psychiatry Research*, **62**(2), 161–9.

Brunner, E. J., M. Marmot, I. R. White and J. R. O'Brien (1993). Gender and employment grade differences in blood cholesterol, apolipoproteins and haemostatic factors in the Whitehall II study. *Atherosclerosis*, **102**, 195–207.

Carvalhaes-Neto, N., L. R. Ramos, D. Suchecki, S. Tufik and M. K. Huayllas (2003). The effect of hospitalization on the sleep pattern and on cortisol secretion of healthy elderly. *Experimental Aging Research*, **29**(4), 425–36.

Culhane, J. F., V. Rauh, K. F. McCollum, I. T. Elo and V. Hogan (2002). Exposure to chronic stress and ethnic differences in rates of bacterial vaginosis among pregnant women. *American Journal of Obstetrics Gynecology*, **187**(5), 1272–6.

Dawkins, R. (1976). *The Selfish Gene*. Oxford: Oxford University Press.

DeLongis, A., S. Folkman and R. S. Lazarus (1988). The impact of daily stress on health and mood: psychological and social resources as mediators. *Journal of Personality and Social Psychology*, **54**(3), 486–95.

Durkheim, E. (1933). *The Division of Labour in Society (translated with an introduction by G. Simpson)*. New York: Free Press.

Farrington, D. P. (1993). Childhood origins of teenage antisocial behaviour and adult social dysfunction *Journal of the Royal Society of Medicine*, **86**(1), 13–17.

Ferrari, E., D. Casarotti, B. Muzzoni, N. Albertelli, L. Cravello, M. Fioravanti, *et al.* (2001). Age-related changes of the adrenal secretory pattern: possible role in pathological brain aging. *Brain Research Review*, **37**(1), 294–300.

Fletcher, W. L. and R. O. Hansson (1991). Assessing the social components of retirement anxiety. *Psychology and Aging*, **6**(1), 76–85.

Gilbert, P. (2001). Evolution and social anxiety. The role of attraction, social competition, and social hierarchies. *Psychiatric Clinics of North America*, **24**(4), 723–51.

Gupta, M. A. and A. K. Gupta (2004). Stressful major life events are associated with a higher frequency of cutaneous sensory symptoms: an empirical study of non-clinical subjects. *Journal of the European Academy of Dermatology and Venereology*, **18**(5), 560–5.

Hodgson, N., V. A. Freedman, A. Douglas, D. A. Granger and A. Erno (2004). Biobehavioral correlates of relocation in the frail elderly: salivary cortisol, affect, and cognitive function. *Journal of the American Geriatrics Society*, **52**(11), 1856–62.

Holcik, J. and I. Koupilova (2001). Social determinants of health. Basic facts and recommendations for practice within the context of the Health City Program. *Casopis Lekaru Ceskych*, **140**(1), 3–7.

Jin, R. L. (1995). Effect of unemployment on health: acknowledgement. *Canadian Medical Association Journal*, **153**(11), 1567–8.

Kalin, N. H. (1993). The neurobiology of fear. *Scientific American*, **268**, 94.

Lora, A. and E. Fava (1992). Provoking agents, vulnerability factors and depression in an Italian setting: a replication of Brown and Harris's model. *Journal of Affective Disorders*, **24**(4), 227–35.

Luz, C., F. Dornelles, T. Preissler, D. Collaziol, I. M. da Cruz and M. E. Bauer (2003). Impact of psychological and endocrine factors on cytokine production of healthy elderly people. *Mechanisms of Ageing and Development*, **124**(8), 887–95.

Marmot, M. and T. Theorell (1988). Social class and cardiovascular disease: the contribution of work. *International Journal of Health Services*, **18**, 657–74.

Meadows-Oliver, M. (2005). Social support among homeless and housed mothers: an integrative review. *Journal of Psychosocial Nursing and Mental Health Services*, **43**(2), 40–7.

Montgomery, S. M., D. G. Cook, M. J. Bartley and M. E. Wadsworth (1999). Unemployment pre-dates symptoms of depression and anxiety resulting in medical consultation in young men. *International Journal of Epidemiology*, 28(1), 95–100.

Najman, J. M. (1980). Theories of disease causation and the concept of a general susceptibility: a review. *Social Science and Medicine*, **14A**(3), 231–7.

Nuechterlein, K. H., M. E. Dawson, M. Gitlin, J. Vemtura, M. J. C. Goldstein, K. S. Snyder, *et al.* (1986). A heuristic vulnerability/stress model of schizophrenia. *Schizophrenia Bulletin*, 10, 300–12.

Nystrom, K. and K. Axelsson (2002). Mothers' experience of being separated from their newborns. *Journal of Obstetrics and Gynecology and Neonatal Nursing*, **31**(3), 275–82.

Panksepp, J. (2005). Why does separation distress hurt? Comment on MacDonald and Leary (2005). *Psychological Bulletin*, **131**(2), 237–40.

Patrick, M. and F. Holloway (1990). A two-year follow-up of new long-stay patients in an inner city district general hospital. *International Journal of Social Psychiatry*, **36**(3), 207–15.

Peacock, J. L., J. M. Bland and H. R. Anderson (1995). Preterm delivery: effects of socioeconomic factors, psychological stress, smoking, alcohol, and caffeine. *British Medical Journal*, **311**(7004), 531–5.

Rafferty, Y. and M. Shinn (1991). The impact of homelessness on children. *American Journal of Psychology*, **46**(11), 1170–9.

Reich, W. P., D. P. Parrella and W. J. Filstead (1988). Unconfounding the Hassles Scale: external sources versus internal responses to stress. *Journal of Behavioral Medicine*, **11**(3), 239–49.

Schultz, S., A. Hoth and K. Buckwalter (2004). Anxiety and impaired social function in the elderly. *Annals of Clinical Psychiatry*, **16**(1), 47–51.

Seltzer, J. G. (1952). Stress and the general adaptation syndrome or the theories and concepts of Hans Selye. *Journal of the Florida Medical Association*, **38**(7), 481–5.

Selye, H. (1973). The evolution of the stress concept. *American Journal of Science*, **61**(6), 692–9.

Siegrist, J., R. Peter, A. Junge, P. Cremer and D. Seidel (1990). Low status control, high effort at work and ischemic heart disease: prospective evidence from blue-collar men. *Social Science and Medicine*, **31**(10), 1127–34.

Stephen, K. and J. M. Butcher (2004). Stress responses and innate immunity: aging as a contributory factor. *Aging Cell*, **3**(4), 151–60.

Steptoe A. (2002). Invited review. The links between stress and illness. *Journal of Psychosomatic Research*, **35**(6), 633–44.

Stuck, A. E., J. M. Walthert, T. Nikolaus, C. J. Bula, C. Hohmann and J. C. Beck (1999). Risk factors for functional status decline in community-living elderly people: a systematic literature review. *Social Science and Medicine*, **48**(4), 445–69.

Targosz, S., P. Bebbington, G. Lewis, T. Brugha, R. Jenkins, M. Farrell, *et al.* (2003). Lone mothers, social exclusion and depression. *Psychological Medicine*, **33**(4), 715–22.

Uchino, B. N., J. T. Cacioppob and J. K. Kiecolt-Glaserc (1996). The relationship between social support and physiological processes: a review with emphasis on underlying mechanisms and implications for health. *Psychological Bulletin*, **119**(3), 488–531.

WHO (1946). *Preamble to the Constitution of the World Health Organisation as Adopted by the International Health Conference.* New York: WHO.

Yoshimoto, T. and C. Kawata (1996). Travel outside the home and perceived problems with such travel, among elderly people in a small town. *Nippon Ronen Igakkai Zasshi*, **33**(6), 430–9.

CHAPTER 6

MENTAL ILLNESS

UNDERSTANDING AND RESPONDING TO MENTAL ILLNESS

> Millions of people suffer from mental health conditions some time in their lives. For a minority, these can be severe or long lasting. Even now, with welcome new attitudes in society, those suffering mental distress still find themselves excluded from many aspects of life that the rest of us take for granted – from jobs, family support, proper health care and community life (Tony Blair 2004).

A common feature found in socially excluded people is that they have complex needs, often involving mental health and related substance misuse problems, compounded by accommodation and employment problems. Mental health problems have been evident in human populations since recorded history and have been frequently associated with spiritual phenomena. Hippocrates (460 BC), in referring to the 'The sacred disease' stated that 'madness was no more sacred than any other disease and has a natural cause from which it originates like other afflictions'. The Ancient Greeks believed that mental illness was the result of an imbalance of body 'humours', called *phlegm* and *bile*, a concept which led eventually to the foundations of neurochemistry and endocrinology. Galen, in *De Locis Affect* (200 AD), described black bile as 'Arising in some people in large quantity either because of their original humoral constitution or by their customary diet which is transformed into this humor by digestion in the blood vessels. Like the thick phlegm, this heavy atrabilious blood obstructs the passage through the middle or posterior cavity of the brain and sometimes causes epilepsy. When its excess pervades the brain matter, it causes melancholy'.

In more recent times considerable progress in our understanding of mental illness has depended on research developments in the biological basis of a complex range of problems. Clinicians were initially concerned with morbidity and mortality of psychiatric patients, but significant progress in the first half of the twentieth century was made in the treatment of *general paralysis of the insane (GPI)*. Developments of *electroconvulsive therapy* led to a dramatic impact on the lives of thousands of otherwise institutionalised patients. These major developments were overshadowed by psychological theories of mental health at the turn of the century, leading to the psychoanalytic movement, which became synonymous with psychiatry. This psychodynamic approach then obscured the main traditions of medical and neuropathological-based approaches, which had existed for 2000 years. Developments in psychopharmacology in the 1950s began with the production of chlorpromazine, which was developed as a surgical anaesthetic. This compound also appeared to alleviate the symptoms of both schizophrenia and mania. It was adopted as the first antipsychotic drug. Chlorpromazine was used as a model for the synthesis of imipramine, specifically intended as an antipsychotic, but also found to be very effective in the treatment of depression. Lithium was introduced for the treatment of manic depressive illness in 1949.

These developments of psychopharmacology in the 1950s provided an increasing range of pharmacological tools for use in the experimental exploration of brain function in animals and humans. Although preclinical studies were promoted in the search for new and more specific medications, the emerging discipline of psychopharmacology began to give an important insight into the mechanisms of brain function in health and disease. Psychopharmacological developments were followed by the use of computer-based imaging techniques in the 1980s, which have provided more information on brain function and led to new treatments, and a greater understanding of the neurobiological basis of behaviour.

Despite the proven efficiency of biological treatment these approaches were not without much criticism due to side effects of the medications, such as *tardive dyskinesia*. Nevertheless it is too easy to forget the many thousands of patients who, until recently, have been institutionalised in large Victorian asylums. Before the UK government policy of *Care in the Community* (1990, see Chapter 12) these large institutions were frequently found on the periphery of urban conurbations, such as London where psychiatric hospitals housing many thousands of patients had been built approximately 15 miles (i.e. a stage coach journey) from the centre of London. These included asylums at Banstead, Epsom, Warley, Netherne and Frien Barnet, all of which had developed into psychiatric hospitals prior to the *Care in the Community Act*. After 1990 people who had previously been patients in these institutions were moved into the community, which contributed to the homeless and socially excluded populations in urban areas. A further demographic change was the *Rough Sleepers Initiative* (Griffiths 2002), which significantly reduced the number of people with mental health problems on the streets of the UK. However, there was a concomitant rise in numbers of people with mental health problems living in hostel and temporary accommodation, which is now being investigated (van den Bree *et al.* in preparation).

MENTAL HEALTH PROBLEMS IN THE COMMUNITY

Estimates of psychiatric morbidity within the homeless population vary from 30% to 50% (Parkin 1971; Scott 1993). However, this figure probably represents an underestimation due to significant methodological problems in ascertaining the real picture relating to accessing these difficult-to-reach populations (Susser *et al.* 1989), lack of standardisation of screening and assessment tools as discussed by Luscombe and Brook (2005). Other ascertainment problems include the transient nature of the population and the use of self-report screening instruments used by researchers with no previous knowledge of the participants, some of whom would have been overcautious in their response to researchers in view of the personal nature of the survey (Timms and Fry 1989).

Various assessment tools have been used such as the *Diagnostic Interview Schedule* (DIS). This was used by Fichter and Quadflieg (1999) in studying 146 men and 32 women who were homeless in Germany. These researchers found a very high prevalence of lifetime mental illness, 91.8% with substance abuse disorder, 82.9% with alcohol dependence, 41.8% had an affective disorder, 22.6% had an anxiety disorder and 12.4% suffered from schizophrenia. The homeless men in this study were on the average 43 years of age; most of them unmarried or divorced, had a relatively low degree of school education and a relatively long duration of homelessness. These results are in line with studies from other countries but, using the same methodology, rates of mental illness among homeless individuals were higher in Germany than in Los Angeles.

The presence and number of symptoms of schizophrenia, antisocial personality and earlier onset of major depression and conduct disorder have been found to be associated with alcohol use disorder and earlier age of onset of drug use disorder, all of which are related to the length of time that an individual had been homeless.

These studies highlight the role of personal vulnerability factors in the onset and chronicity of homelessness and associated mental illness. Important vulnerability factors include gender, family stability, maternal psychiatric illness, housing, employment and experience in the armed forces. North *et al.* (1998) carried out a detailed statistical analysis of

the data, which showed that more education, but not family background problems, was associated with shorter lifetime duration of
homelessness.

In studying German homeless women Torchalla *et al.* (2004) found
that early onset of homelessness and the reticence in seeking help were
predominant features, which were frequently linked to escape from
violence in the family home. In this study of 22 homeless women,
the prevalence of diagnosed psychiatric disorders was 71%; with 43%
of the women diagnosed with substance abuse/dependence, followed
by anxiety disorders (35%) and schizophrenia (12%). Females have
been reported to have less self-esteem and family support, as well as
more self-blame and parental blame, than did their male counterparts
(Kingree 1995). An important conclusion from gender-focused studies
is that the situation giving rise to being homeless, need for help and
help-seeking pattern appear to be quite different in men and women.
The most frequently reported needs of the homeless were for improved
social relations, employment, accommodation and money (Gelberg and
Linn 1988).

In the UK, the Office of Population Censuses and Surveys (OPCS) (Gill
et al. 1996) collected data from a range of people who did not have adequate
shelter including residents in hostels and people sleeping rough. The results
of this survey showed that around 38% of hostel residents displayed
symptoms of neurotic disorders and 8% displayed psychotic symptoms.
Of hostel residents 16% were found to be alcohol dependent and 6%
were dependent on other drugs. Other earlier surveys undertaken by the
Centre for Housing Policy, British Household Panel Survey (ONS 1991)
and reviewed by Bines (1994) and Anderson *et al.* (1993), highlighted the
health problems of homeless people. These surveys found that mental
health problems were higher among single homeless people compared to
the general population: 28% of hostel and bed and breakfast (B&B) residents reported mental health problems; 36% of day centre users and 40%
of soup run users, compared to just 5% of the general population. In
accounting for the effects of age and gender, mental health problems were
found to be eight times as high among people in hostels and B&Bs and
eleven times as high among people sleeping rough compared to the general
population. A high proportion of single homeless people also reported
heavy drinking or alcohol-related problems and many homeless people
had multiple issues of mental health problems and alcohol-related problems (30% of those in hostels and almost 50% of those sleeping rough).
Physical health problems were also reported to be more prevalent in the
single homeless population.

Children in homeless families have a high risk of physical and mental
illness. In comparison to the other children, Cumella *et al.* (1998) found
that homeless children in Birmingham had delayed communication, higher

scores for mental health problems, histories of abuse and were also more likely to have stopped attending school or nursery since becoming homeless. Few of these homeless families were engaged with specialist child and adolescent mental health services.

CLASSIFICATION AND PROBLEM IDENTIFICATION

Early attempts to classify the various forms of mental illness (Kreplin 1855–1926) focused on *functional* and *organic psychosis*, providing descriptions of *dementia praecox*, *manic depression*, *paranoid*, *catatonic*, *hebephrenic* and *simple schizophrenia*. More recent perspectives distinguish between *neurosis*, where less severe symptoms are expressed and the individual has normal experience of life but the emotions or *affect* are disturbed to a greater degree than normal. These conditions are in contrast to *psychosis*, where a greater severity of illness occurs, and the person has an inability to distinguish between subjective experience and reality. Disorders of the *affect* are emotional problems and include anxiety states, depressive neurosis, manic depressive psychosis and involutional melancholia. A helpful review of mental health classification has recently been published (Neel 2006).

Depression is commonly found in socially excluded and homeless people. Such individuals have reduced vital potency, depressed mood, retardation of psychic processes and generally have decreased drive and general activity. Biological symptoms of depression include loss of appetite, weight disturbance, gastrointestinal tract disturbance, sleep disturbance, early morning waking, loss of libido and diurnal variations in mood. A range of environmental factors contribute to the onset and repeated episodes of depression. These include: previous mental health status; social stressors; perceived lack of social support; frequency of social interaction and isolation; exclusion; social roles and attachments; physical health status; developmental experience; family/cultural background belief/faith and links with social networks (church, community groups). These psychological and behavioural problems mitigate against the development of *social capital* (see Chapter 14). Although depression is the most therapeutically accessible psychiatric state pharmacology must be used with care in consideration of the complex interaction of biological, psychological and social factors. Long-term problems of depression in women appear to be more serious than those that occur in men. This is seen as earlier age of onset, greater family history of affective disorders, greater symptom reporting, poorer social adjustment and poorer quality of life (Kornstein *et al.* 2000). In providing treatment and support for those with mental health problems a combination of psychodynamic, behaviour and biological approaches can be used, depending on the severity of the illness, as shown in Table 6.1.

Table 6.1   A comparison of psychodynamic, behavioural and biological approaches to mental illness.

Emphasis	Psychodynamic (Mind)	Behavioural	Biological (Brain)
Cause	Disturbed dynamics Childhood experiences	Learned habits	Biological imbalances
Methods of study	Introspection (free association, dream analysis)	Conditioning experiments	Neurosciences
Types of illness	Mild (neuroses, personality disorders)	Mild to severe (neuroses, personality disorders, addictive behaviour)	Moderate to severe (depression, mania, schizophrenia)
Method of treatment	Psychotherapy	Behavioural modification	Medication

THE AETIOLOGY OF DEPRESSION

Socially excluded people exhibit a range of co-morbid conditions, many of which are linked to substance misuse (see Chapter 8). The problems of *dual diagnosis* present major issues in the provision of health and social support for those presenting with complex needs. The most common mental health problem presenting in these groups, in particular the homeless, is depression. The underlying mechanisms of this range of exogenous and endogenous problems are complex but some insight into the development of effective interventions can be derived by considering some important contemporary ideas.

During the last three decades a greater understanding of the biological basis of depression has resulted from observations that certain medications, which improve or worsen mood, do so via specific neurotransmitters in the brain (see Chapter 7). In the 1960s mental illness was originally thought to result from changes in the functioning of neurotransmitter receptors, problems in the regulation of neurotransmitter systems and interactions of the monoamine and cholinergic neurotransmitter systems. New insights have emerged from the observations of disordered neuroendocrine functioning in depression. Although there are methodological and clinical problems in the development of biological markers, improvements in standardised EEG methodology have identified sleep abnormalities in depression, and contemporary advances in molecular genetics are increasing our understanding of the inheritance and biochemistry of depression (Rothschild 1988). With reference to Table 6.1, socially excluded people generally have more profound and resistant mental health problems, due to significant deficiencies in adequate nutrition, shelter and health status. These needs should be addressed before behavioural and social dimensions of care and support are provided. In view of these more severe mental health problems, it is appropriate to review the biological basis of depression. A number of models have been suggested to provide an insight into potentially useful therapeutic approaches. These include the *amine hypothesis*, the *endocrine hypothesis, biological rhythm disturbance* and the *dysregulation hypothesis.*

The amine hypothesis

In Chapter 7 a brief review of the biological basis of behaviour is presented. From this perspective it is clear that subtle changes in the neurochemistry of the brain have significant effects on the expression of various aspects of human behaviour. These compounds have been studied extensively during the last four decades in attempts to understand the pharmacological basis of depression. Neurochemical studies using laboratory animals have implicated the *biogenic amines* in mental health problems. Their mechanism of action in treating depression has not been fully established. However, the extensive literature on the pharmacology of antidepressant drugs, involving blockade of neuronal uptake systems for some biogenic amines and blockade of many receptors for neurotransmitters can explain some of their adverse effects and certain interactions with other drugs (Richelson 1991). Serotonin abnormalities appear to be related to a variety of psychopathological dimensions such as anxiety, depressed mood, impulsivity, aggression and behavioural disinhibition, suggesting an interrelationship and possibly a common biological basis between these conditions (Apter *et al.* 1990).

Medications that act via various mechanisms to increase synaptic concentrations of monoamines improve the symptoms of depression. The monoamine hypothesis of depression, first proposed 30 years ago, predicts that the underlying pathophysiological basis of depression is depletion in the levels of serotonin, norepinephrine and/or dopamine in the central nervous system. This hypothesis is supported by studies on the mechanism of the action of antidepressants, which elevate the levels of these neurotransmitters in the brain. Amine-based antidepressants have all been shown to be effective in the alleviation of depressive symptoms. However, this multitude of studies has failed to find consistent evidence of a primary dysfunction of a specific monoamine system in patients with major depressive disorders. Methodological problems relating to the absence of direct measurements of monoamines in humans have obscured the link between these neuro-transmitter systems and depression. However, in studies where monoamine depletion is induced in experimental subjects, clinical syndromes can be reproduced, and allow a more direct method for investigating the role of monoamines.

These studies indicate that antidepressant responses are reversed temporarily, with the response being dependent on the class of antide-pressant. Conversely, monoamine depletion does not worsen symptoms in depressed patients not taking medication, nor does it cause depression in healthy volunteers with no depressive illness.

The endocrine hypothesis

Anxiety and other mental health problems have biological and psycholog-ical components (see Chapter 5). The primary action of the endocrine system in producing hormones, long-distance messengers, has been linked to the progression of mental illness. Anxiety is often accompanied by neuroen-docrine and other physiological changes in both psychiatric patients and normal volunteers. Studies of the *hypothalamic–pituitary–adrenal* (HPA) axis (see Figure 5.1, p. 71) and the loss of integrity of the HPA in anxiety and in depression have suggested that a neuroendocrine continuum for anxiety and depression exists, in which anxiety occurs during the early behavioural development contributing to major depressive episodes that occur later. The stress hormone, cortisol, produced in the adrenal glands, is controlled by corticotropin-releasing factor (CRF), from the pituitary and subject to a set of feedback controls with the HPA. A number of studies have shown increased concentrations of CRF in the cerebrospinal fluid in both anxiety and depression. However, the release of other hormones of the HPA or peptides is regulated differently in the two disorders.

Lowered levels of the stress hormone, cortisol, after a dexamethasone test and increased numbers of glucocorticoid receptors have been measured in anxiety. Depression, however is characterised by higher cortisol production and is not suppressed after dexamethasone. Decreased numbers of gluco-corticoid receptors are found in depression. To explain these findings a 'neuroendocrine continuum' model has been suggested by Boyer (2000). This model proposes that general desensitisation of CRF receptors at pitu-itary, limbic (amygdala) and cortical, as well as hippocampal levels, could be secondary to the loss of hippocampal inhibition resulting from hippocampal damage linked to repeated stressing events. The question as to whether the physiological and biochemical disturbances are causes or consequences of the affective disorders still has to be resolved. The role of inherited factors is supported by twin studies, which show very different concordance rates for monozygotic and dizygotic twins, 60–70% and 10–20%, respectively (Rafaelsen 1981).

The relationship between the endocrine and immune systems has been demonstrated by the administration of the cytokines interleukin-2 and interferon-alpha used for the treatment of various disorders, such as hepatitis C and various forms of cancer. These treatments produce side effects with symptoms associated with depression, including loss of appetite, fatigue, increased sleepiness, irritability, as well as cognitive changes. In animal studies administration of pro-inflammatory cytokines induces a pattern of behavioural alterations called 'sickness behaviour' which resembles the vegetative symptoms of depression in humans. Changes in levels of serotonin (5-HT), 5-HT receptors and in the 5-HT precursor, tryptophan, in depressed people support a role for 5-HT in the development of depression. Furthermore, dysregulation of the noradrenergic system and a hyperactive HPA axis in depression have been shown. IL-1, IL-6 and TNF-alpha are found to be potent stimulators of the HPA axis. The conclusion from these studies is that cytokines may induce the symptoms of depression, by their influence on the 5-HT, noradrenergic and HPA system (Wichers and Maes 2002).

This complex range of physiological interactions suggests that depression is not solely related to a change in either the biogenic amines or the HPA axis. Depressed patients have high cortico-steroid levels, particularly due to continued high secretion rates at night, indicating a disturbance of diurnal rhythms (Rafaelsen 1981).

Biological rhythm disturbance

Depressed patients and those with substance misuse problems frequently have disturbed sleep, wake early and have poor sleep quality. Sleep manipulations can alleviate symptoms of depression in some patients; and the majority of antidepressants bring about significant changes in EEG recordings. The link between sleep and depression has been examined by monitoring the influence of antidepressants on sleep in relation to clinical improvements in depressed patients. The roles of rapid eye movement (REM) and non-REM sleep have also been studied. Polygraphic recordings have not produced clear evidence of the involvement of REM sleep or non-REM sleep in the mechanisms underlying clinical change. Different biological dysfunctions appear to underlie particular neuroendocrine and sleep EEG disturbances in major depression (Staner *et al.* 2003). However, the physiological mechanisms of sleep during treatment with antidepressants are still unclear and more fundamental sleep research is necessary (van Bemmel 1997).

Other information on biological rhythm disturbances comes from seasonal and non-seasonal mood disorders. Many research reports suggest that abnormalities in circadian rhythms are involved in the aetiology of seasonal affective disorder (SAD), a syndrome in which depression develops during autumn or winter and remits the following spring or summer. Several lines of evidence suggest that changes in the circadian system are also involved in the development of non-seasonal mood disorders, such as major depression and bipolar disorder.

The possibility that some people are more vulnerable to these conditions comes from studies that have been designed to address the influence of alcohol exposure during development. Alcohol adversely influences the developing brain. During periods of rapid brain growth alcohol causes cell loss, alters connections between brain regions and reduces the production of neurotransmitters. Alcohol adversely effects a wide range of brain structures including the development of the *suprachiasmatic nuclei* (SCN), the master circadian pacemaker. Abnormal development of the SCN will result in subtle abnormalities in circadian rhythms that may contribute to the development of seasonal and non-seasonal mood disorders. Circadian rhythms are affected by pharmacological, psychological and light treatments. Neurotransmitters, receptors, enzymes and the second messenger system in the brain have circadian rhythms which will influence the effectiveness of psychotropic medications, depending on the time of administration in relation to the body's clock (Sher 2004). The fact that lithium and other antidepressant drugs cause alterations in circadian rhythms point to the effect of light impacting on the retina and subsequent influences on the HPA (see earlier section in this chapter and Figure 5.1, p. 71). These antidepressants cause changes in both the intrinsic rhythm of circadian oscillators and in the sensitivity of the retina to light. Circadian entrainment in humans is principally via photoreceptors in the retina. The *retinal–hypothalamic–pineal axis* is the main pathway for neuronal entrainment of rhythms which use light as a phase cue. The hormone melatonin, produced in the pineal gland, is thought to regulate the sensitivity of the retina to light (Steiner *et al.* 1987).

Dysregulation hypothesis

The previous sections indicate that although depression is associated with changes in the neurotransmitters, hormones and disruptions in biological rhythms, no one system can solely account for the pathophysiology of effective disorders. Siever and Davis (Steiner *et al.* 1987) have suggested that:

> . . . the activity of neurotransmitter systems in the affective disorders and related psychiatric syndromes may be better understood as a reflection of a relative failure in their regulation, rather than as simple increases or decreases in their activity.

This concept of 'dysregulation' suggests that persistent impairment in one or more neurotransmitter homeostatic regulatory mechanisms provides a trait vulnerability to unstable or erratic neurotransmitter production. Dysregulation of the *hypothalamic–pituitary–adrenal axis*, as well as the endocrine control of the reproductive system, have been found in depressed patients, furthermore abnormalities of the hormone melatonin occur in patients with affective disorders. It is likely that the production of mela-tonin influences the *retinal–hypothalamic–pineal axis* and thereby increases the possible expression of affective disorders (Steiner *et al.* 1987).

The dysregulation hypothesis provides an explanation for the failure of regulation of one or more of the above-described physiological systems. As a result of significant changes in brain chemistry and hormonal balance it might be expected that adverse effects on cognition would occur. The chronic production of neurotoxic compounds such as the corticosteroids and the kynurenines (see Chapter 7) would exacerbate brain dysfunction. The therapeutic implications of these physiological and behavioural phenomena have been discussed by Thase *et al.* (1996). In their study, patients with increased HPA function were shown to be less responsive to psychotherapy leading the authors to the conclusion that this group would benefit from biomedical interventions prior to psychological treatment.

POST-TRAUMATIC STRESS DISORDER

In addition to depression, post-traumatic stress disorder (PTSD) is thought to occur in a significant number of socially excluded people. Although there is a controversy regarding the diagnosis of PTSD, it is generally regarded as an anxiety disorder that develops following exposure to an extremely traumatic stress, which is perceived to be exceptionally threatening or catas-trophic in nature (Turnbull 1998). The characteristics of PTSD include a re-experiencing of the dramatic event, persistent avoidance of stimuli associ-ated with trauma, numbing of general responsiveness and persistent symp-toms of hyperarousal. PTSD may exist with major depressive disorder and may persist as a combination of the above symptoms and typical grief.

The link between PTSD and alcohol misuse has been explained by the self-medication hypothesis (Khantzian 1990). Early substance misuse increases the likelihood of exposure to potentially traumatising events, and hence the likelihood of developing PTSD. Individuals who begin using alcohol at an early stage are at particular risk because they have relied on alcohol as a way of combating stress and failed to develop more effective stress reduction strategies. There is a high association between PTSD and alcohol misuse in this group, associated with higher incidence of childhood phys-ical and sexual abuse. A history of childhood sexual abuse has been shown to increase the risk of later alcohol problems by a factor of three (Winfield *et al.* 1990), women being at a greater risk of developing PTSD following dramatic events if they had early experiences of physical and sexual abuse (Breslau *et al.* 1999). From interviews with 130 women, working as pros-titutes in San Francisco, Farley and Barkan (1998) found that 50% had been sexually assaulted as children and 49 % reported that they had been physically assaulted as children. As adults in prostitution, 82 % had been physically assaulted; 83 % had been threatened with a weapon; 68 % had been raped while working as prostitutes; and 84 % reported current or past homelessness. Of the 130 people interviewed, 68 % met DSM III-R criteria for a diagnosis of PTSD. Of these respondents 88 % stated that they wanted to leave prostitution.

In a population of 600 homeless men and 300 homeless women in St Louis, the onset of PTSD had preceded the onset of homelessness. PTSD was estimated using a revised *Diagnostic Interview Schedule* that includes a module for assessment of post-traumatic stress disorder (PTSD). In both sexes childhood histories of abuse and family fighting were predictive of both traumatic events and PTSD. Symptomology of PTSD appeared long before the onset of homelessness (North and Smith 1992). In a later report the same authors highlight the role of substance misuse and major depression in the episodes of violence in the lives of those diagnosed with PTSD. The violence was often received through victimisation and expressed by specific violent traumatic events. The majority of men and a substantial proportion of women also had a history of physically aggressive behaviours, often beginning in childhood. These studies reflect the level of violence in the lives of the homeless, a major risk factor experienced by the homeless (North *et al.* 1994).

War veterans are frequently identified in homeless populations, or presenting as socially excluded people in community homeless services. A significant number of war veterans have significant alcohol abuse problems and associated PTSD as a result of experience in war situations or due to earlier traumatic events in their lives before joining the services. Vulnerability to and severity of PTSD have been linked to childhood experiences, underlying mental instability and social exclusion (Kasprow and Rosenheck 2000). Post-combat stress has a significant impact on quality of life (Clark and Kirisci 1996) and it has been estimated that in excess of 50 % of PTSD suffers have drinking problems which relate to pre-war and combat experiences (Gruden *et al.* 1999). Stress can result in long-term damage to the specific brain areas such as the hippocampus, the area involved in learning and memory, with associated memory deficits. In combat veterans, size of the hippocampus has been shown to be correlated with deficits in verbal memory on neuropsychological testing (Bremner *et al.* 1999). These structural problems are accompanied by functional problems in information processing related to specific brain neurochemical systems, in particular those involving the neuromodulator serotonin (5-HT). An understanding of these mechanisms in the *prefrontal cortex* provides an explanation for the link between PTSD and alcohol abuse (Bonin *et al.* 2000).

Genetic factors have been implicated in stress-related conditions in relation to the basis of reward-mediated behaviour (Comings and Blum 2000;

Young *et al.* 2001) and the metabolism of serotonin (Maes *et al.* 1999). There is clear evidence for the use of effective pharmacotherapy in treating PTSD (Albucher and Liberzon 2002), however, a pharmacological approach is not advised for individuals who are at risk of developing addictive behaviours, as reviewed by Bonner and Waterhouse (1996). Whatever approach is used in providing support for those suffering from PTSD, with or without concurrent alcohol problems, it is clearly important to determine the clients' needs and provide ongoing monitoring of their progress.

Surprisingly low basal levels of the stress hormone, cortisol, have been reported in individuals with PTSD. There is evidence for enhanced negative feedback sensitivity of the HPA axis in PTSD, which could account for this observation. Kanter *et al.* (2001) suggest that decreased adrenocortical responsiveness may be an additional or alternative mechanism accounting for low cortisol in PTSD, see Figure 5.2.

In conclusion, the complex needs of homeless and socially excluded people often centre around a range of mental health problems, frequently associated with high-risk life styles, including violence. Risky health behaviours, including substance misuse, are often accompanied by mental health problems, as expanded in Chapter 8. An insight into the common underlying physiological basis of these co-occurring problems suggests functional maladaptation of the neurotransmitter and endocrine systems. Inadequate regulatory control by the feedback systems, which maintain the optimal operation of these systems, results in sleep problems and a general lack of physiological homeostasis, which is concurrent with chaotic life styles. In view of such significant perturbations in these biological systems, it would seem sensible to increase our understanding of these systems, the expression of which has a fundamental influence on individual and social behaviours and the ability of individuals to function in the community.

REFERENCES

Albucher, R. C. and I. Liberzon (2002). Psychopharmacological treatment in PTSD: a critical review. *Journal of Psychiatric Research*, **36**(6), 355–67.

Anderson, I. K., P. A. Kemp and Quilgars, D. (1993). *Single Homeless People.* London: HMSO.

Apter, A., H. M. van Praag, R. Plutchik, S. Sevy, M. Korn and S. L. Brown (1990). Interrelationships among anxiety, aggression, impulsivity, and mood: a serotonergically linked cluster? *Psychiatry Research*, **32**(2), 191–9.

Bines, W. (1994). *The Health of Single Homeless People: Centre for Housing Policy.* London: Joseph Rowntree Foundation.

Blair, T. (2004). *Mental Health and Social Exclusion: Foreword.* London: Office of the Deputy Prime Minister.

Bonin, M., G. R. Norton, I. Frombach and G. J. Asmundson (2000). PTSD in different treatment settings: a preliminary investigation of PTSD symptomatology in substance abuse and chronic pain patients. *Depression and Anxiety*, **11**(3), 131–3.

Bonner, A. and J. Waterhouse (eds) (1996). *Addictive Behaviour. Molecules to Mankind.* Basingstoke: Macmillan.

Boyer, P. (2000). Do anxiety and depression have a common pathophysiological mechanism? *Acta Psychiatrica Scandinavica*, **406**, 24–9.

Bremner, J. D., L. H. Staib, D. Kaloupek, S. M. Southwick, R. Soufer and D. S. Charney (1999). Neural correlates of exposure to traumatic pictures and sound in Vietnam combat veterans with and without posttraumatic stress disorder: a positron emission tomography study. *Biological Psychiatry*, **45**(7), 806–16.

Breslau, N., H. D. Chilcoat, R. C. Kessler and G. C. Davis (1999). Previous exposure to trauma and PTSD effects of subsequent trauma: results from the Detroit Area Survey of Trauma. *American Journal of Psychiatry*, **156**(6), 902–7.

Clark, D. B. and L. Kirisci (1996). Posttraumatic stress disorder, depression, alcohol use disorders and quality of life in adolescents. *Anxiety*, **2**(5), 226–33.

Comings, D. E. and K. Blum (2000). Reward deficiency syndrome: genetic aspects of behavioral disorders. *Progress in Brain Research*, **126**, 325–41.

Cumella, S., E. Grattan and P. Vostanis (1998). The mental health of children in homeless families and their contact with health, education and social services. *Health and Social Care in the Community*, **6**(5), 331–42.

Delgado, P. L. (2000). Depression: the case for a monoamine deficiency. *Journal of Clinical Psychiatry*, **61**(Supplement 6), 7–11.

Farley, M. and H. Barkan (1998). Prostitution, violence, and posttraumatic stress disorder. *Women's Health*, **27**(3), 37–49.

Fichter, M. and N. Quadflieg (1999). Alcoholism in homeless men in the mid-nineties: results from the Bavarian Public Health Study on homelessness. *European Archives of Psychiatry and Clinical Neuroscience*, **249**(1), 34–44.

Galen (200 AD). *De Locis Affect* (reviewed in *The Anatomy of Melancholy*). Vol. 8 (ed. Burton, R.). Psyplexus, http://www.psyplexus.com/burton/12.htm.

Gelberg, L. and L. S. Linn (1988). Social and physical health of homeless adults previously treated for mental health problems. *Hospital and Community Psychiatry*, **39**(5), 510–16.

Gill, B., H. Meltzer, K. Hinds and M. Pettigrew (1996). *Psychiatric Morbidity among Homeless People*. London: Office for National Statistics Social Survey Division.

Griffiths, S. (2002). *Assessing the Needs of the Rough Sleepers*. London: Homeless Directorate, ODPM.

Gruden, V., V. Gruden, Jr. and Z. Gruden (1999). PTSD and alcoholism. *Collegium Antropologicum*, **23**(2), 607–10.

Hirschfeld, R. M. (2000). History and evolution of the monoamine hypothesis of depression. *Journal of Clinical Psychiatry*, **61**(Supplement 6), 4–6.

Kanter, E. D., C. W. Wilkinson, A. D. Radant, E. C. Petrie, D. J. Dobie, M. E. McFall, *et al.* (2001). Glucocorticoid feedback sensitivity and adrenocortical responsiveness in posttraumatic stress disorder. *Biological Psychiatry*, **50**(4), 238–45.

Kasprow, W. J. and R. Rosenheck (2000). Mortality among homeless and nonhomeless mentally ill veterans. *Journal of Nervous Mental Disorders*, **188**(3), 141–7.

Khantzian, E. J. (1990). Self-regulation and self-medication factors in alcoholism and the addictions. Similarities and differences. *Recent Developments in Alcoholism*, **8**, 255–71.

Kingree, J. B. (1995). Understanding gender differences in psychosocial functioning and treatment retention. *American Journal of Drug and Alcohol Abuse*, **21**(2), 267–81.

Kornstein, S. G., A. F. Schatzberg, M. E. Thase, K. A. Yonkers, J. P. McCullough, G. I. Keitner, *et al.* (2000). Gender differences in chronic major and double depression. *Journal of Affective Disorders*, **60**(1), 1–11.

Luscombe, C. and A. Brook (2005). Prevalence of alcohol abuse in homeless populations: the use of holistic assessments in the non-statutory sector. *Alcohol and Alcoholism*, **40**(Supplement 1), S02–4.

Maes, M., A. H. Lin, R. Verkerk, L. Delmeire, A. Van Gastel, M. Van der Planken, *et al.* (1999). Serotonergic and noradrenergic markers of post-traumatic stress disorder with and without major depression. *Neuropsychopharmacology*, **20**(2), 188–97.

Neel, L. B. (2006). *Psychiatry*. Oxford: Blackwell Publishing.

North, C. S., D. E. Pollio, E. M. Smith and E. L. Spitznagel (1998). Correlates of early onset and chronicity of homelessness in a large urban homeless population. *Journal of Nervous Mental Disorders*, **186**(7), 393–400.

North, C. S. and E. M. Smith (1992). Posttraumatic stress disorder among homeless men and women. *Hospital and Community Psychiatry*, **43**(10), 1010–16.

North, C. S., E. M. Smith and E. L. Spitznagel (1994). Violence and the homeless: an epidemiologic study of victimization and aggression. *Journal of Trauma and Stress*, **7**(1), 95–110.

ONS (1991). *British household panel survey*. London: Office for National Statistics (ONS).

Parkin, F. (1971). *Class Inequality and Political Order, Social Stratification in Capitalist and Communist Societies*. London: MacGibbon and Kee.

Rafaelsen, O. J. (1981). Biological perturbations in affective disorders in man. *Encephale*, **7**(Supplement 4), 413–19.

Richelson, E. (1991). Biological basis of depression and therapeutic relevance. *Journal of Clinical Psychiatry*, **52**(Supplement), 4–10.

Rothschild, A. J. (1988). Biology of depression. *Medicine Clinics of North America*, **72**(4), 765–90.

Scott, J. (1993). Homelessness and mental illness. *British Journal of Psychiatry*, **162**, 314–24.

Sher, L. (2004). Etiology, pathogenesis, and treatment of seasonal and non-seasonal mood disorders: possible role of circadian rhythm abnormalities related to developmental alcohol exposure. *Medical Hypotheses*, **62**(5), 797–801.

Staner, L., F. Duval, J. Haba, M. C. Mokrani and J. P. Macher (2003). Disturbances in hypothalamic pituitary adrenal and thyroid axis identify different sleep EEG patterns in major depressed patients. *Journal of Psychiatric Research*, **37**(1), 1–8.

Steiner, M., E. S. Werstiuk and J. Seggie (1987). Dysregulation of neuroendocrine crossroads: depression, circadian rhythms and the retina – a hypothesis. *Progress in Neuropsychopharmacology and Biological Psychiatry*, **11**(2–3), 267–78.

Susser, E., S. Conover and E. L. Struening (1989). Problems of epidemiologic method in assessing the type and extent of mental illness among homeless adults. *Hospital and Community Psychiatry*, **40**(3), 261–5.

Thase, M. E., S. Dube, K. Bowler, R. H. Howland, J. E. Myers, E. Friedman, *et al.* (1996). Hypothalamic–pituitary–adrenocortical activity and response to cognitive behavior therapy in unmedicated, hospitalized depressed patients. *American Journal of Psychiatry*, **153**(7), 886–91.

Timms, P. W. and A. H. Fry (1989). Homelessness and mental illness. *Health Trends*, **21**(3), 70–1.

Torchalla, I., F. Albrecht, G. Buchkremer and G. Langle (2004). Homeless women with psychiatric disorders – a field study. *Psychiatrische Praxis*, **31**(5), 228–35.

Turnbull, G. J. (1998). A review of post-traumatic stress disorder. Part I: Historical development and classification. *Injury*, **29**(2), 87–91.

van Bemmel, A. L. (1997). The link between sleep and depression: the effects of antidepressants on EEG sleep. *Journal of Psychosomatic Research*, **42**(6), 555–64.

van den Bree, M. B. M., A. B. Bonner, R. Dowling and C. Luscombe (2007). Study of prevalence and severity of mental health problems and related problems within the homeless population. *In preparation*.

Wichers, M. and M. Maes (2002). The psychoneuroimmuno-pathophysiology of cytokine-induced depression in humans. *International Journal of Neuropsychopharmacology*, **5**(4), 375–88.

Winfield, I., L. K. George, M. Swartz and D. G. Blazer (1990). Sexual assault and psychiatric disorders among a community sample of women. *American Journal of Psychiatry*, **147**(3), 335–41.

Young, L. J., M. M. Lim, B. Gingrich and T. R. Insel (2001). Cellular mechanisms of social attachment. *Hormones and Behavior*, **40**(2), 133–8.

CHAPTER 7

THE NEUROBIOLOGICAL BASIS OF MALADAPTIVE BEHAVIOURS

BIOLOGICAL PERSPECTIVES

Socially excluded people are vulnerable to a wide range of challenges due to life style and lack of adequate physical and psychological supports. This chapter will consider the various biological aspects of brain function, which underpin an individual's response to these challenges. Nutritional deficits, infectious disease, substance misuse and dependency and pathological features such as premature ageing, are conspicuous features of the street-dwelling homeless people. However, less obvious features including neurocognitive dysfunction and mental illness, present to varying degrees of severity in these subpopulations. To understand the aetiology and progression of these problems, a review of the key biological systems will be presented here.

In Chapter 3 (Figure 3.1) the biopsychosocial model was introduced to provide an explanation of the complex linkages between the major biological, psychological and social systems. Each of these systems consists of a number of subsystems, which are the subject of a number of academic disciplines. Within the biological sciences these include the studies into genetics, pathology, neurophysiology, neuropsychology, biochemistry, psychopharmacology, immunology, neuropsychoimmunology, chronobiology and others. Each of these areas of study has its own set of methodologies, expanding literature and terminology. With the rapid development in these areas of study and advances in technologies, the various disciplines are becoming less accessible to researchers in other disciplines. To provide an example of this inaccessibility, consider human genetics. The study of inheritance has been developing during the last 200 years but an increasing rate of progress has occurred since the discovery and breaking of the genetic code in the 1950s. The study of molecular genetics requires a good understanding of biochemistry, supported by statistical and laboratory skills and is virtually unintelligible to other biologists let alone social scientists and non-academics.

However, the benefits emerging from these technologically complex methodologies include a greater insight into human physical and mental illness, innovative interventions in pharmacology and molecular medicine and advances in the availability of biological markers contributing to assessments and outcome monitoring. There are significant commercial interests in these developments providing a 'double-edged sword' in that these contemporary advances involve expensive laboratory procedures, often funded by commercial sponsors; conversely, the therapeutic interventions can be expensive, and are not always available to the economically disadvantaged. Furthermore these therapeutic interventions are not always the most suitable approaches to addressing the complex needs of the socially excluded.

In an attempt to facilitate communication across the disciplines and subdisciplines, which could potentially contribute to the support of the socially excluded, the following sections will provide an introduction to the main biological components that should be considered in integrative biopsychosocial approaches to social exclusion.

Genes, proteins and behaviour

Information, to be used in the development of the single cell as it matures into foetus and then an embryo, is chemically coded via the 30 000 genes that are inherited from the parents. The chemical coding of this inherited information is achieved by DNA (deoxyribonucleic acid). An understanding of the relationship between molecular and cellular events and human behaviour can be gained by following the development of an embryonic cell, which develops into a neuron within the brain. Inside the embryonic cell, destined to become a neuron, the nucleus contains 23 pairs of chromosomes. The 23 chromosomes vary greatly in size from the large chromosome 1, which contains several thousand genes, to chromosome 4 which has a smaller number of genes and has been associated with schizophrenia; an additional chromosome 21 results in Down's syndrome. The 23rd pair can either consist of a medium-sized X chromosome plus a small Y chromosome, in the case of a male; or of a pair of medium-sized X chromosomes as found in females.

The infrastructure of chromosomes is not only important for containing the DNA, acting as a vehicle for its transmission from one cell generation to the next, but also it is a component of the regulatory process whereby genes can be active or quiescent in particular cell types. For instance, the gene for facilitating the production of the contractile protein *myoglobin* is active (i.e. 'expressed') in muscle cells. This regulatory process is important in development, for instance when the genes controlling secondary sexual characteristics become active during adolescence, and in day-to-day maintenance of physiological functioning such as when hormones have an inhibiting or activating influence on gene activity, as in the case of stress hormones (see Chapter 5). It is generally understood that human behaviours, associated with for instance schizophrenia or alcohol dependency, involve a complex interaction between genetic and environmental factors. This process of gene expression is achieved by the production of proteins, the vast array of which form the structural basis of our bodies, regulate our metabolic processes and are essential to the body's system of defence.

Protein synthesis

Information pertaining to the development and maintenance of the individual and his/her physiology and behaviour is coded within individual cells, which constitute the organ systems and structure of the human body. This information is contained within the genetic coding of the DNA; the integrity of this large molecule is maintained by the chromosome structures as briefly described in the previous section. Genes function by controlling the cellular production of one of a vast range of proteins, which provide the main structural components of the body. For instance a specific gene controls the formation of keratin, the main constituent of nails and hair, enzymes (biochemical catalysts) facilitate each stage of our metabolism, for example *alcohol dehydrogenase*, which metabolises alcohol (see Figure 7.2), is controlled by the *alcohol dehydrogenase* gene. The synthesis of some hormones, for example insulin, is regulated in a similar way. Figure 7.1 provides a summary of the processes by which genes, contained in the nucleus of a neuron, control the production of proteins required for cellular

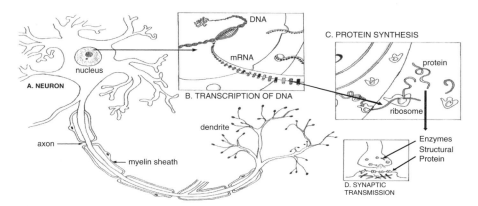

Figure 7.1 Flow diagram showing: (A) The neuron, with axon and dendritic projections, and a nucleus which contains the genetic material, DNA. (B) In the nucleus the DNA is transcribed (copied) into mRNA which leaves the nucleus and provides a template for the production of proteins (translation) (C) facilitated by ribosomes and the availability of amino acids (the building blocks of proteins). The synthesised proteins, specified by particular genes, may be used as (D) cellular structures (e.g. cellular membranes, neurotransmitter receptors) or as enzymes to catalyse particular metabolic pathways, such as the formation of the neurotransmitters inside the neuron. *Source*: Image produced by Gemma Evans.

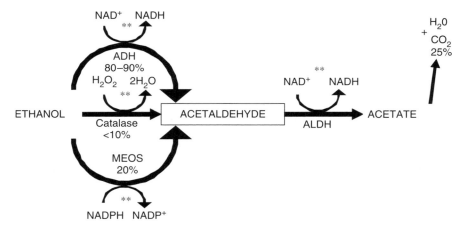

Figure 7.2 Metabolic conversion of alcohol (ethanol) into acetaldehyde, acetate and finally carbon dioxide and water. The liver-based enzymes *alcohol dehydrogenase* (ADH) and *acetaldehyde hydrogenase* (ALDH) control this degradation from toxic to harmless compounds, but in doing so free radicals (∗∗) are produced. These short-lived particles contribute to tissue damage, including those found in foetal alcohol syndrome. Polymorphic forms of the enzyme ALDH result in individuals with varying sensitivities to alcohol (see section on 'Polymorphims').

maintenance and function. By this means genes responsible for the production of the receptor proteins used in synaptic transmission, and other genes, produce the enzymes underpinning the production and regulation of neurotransmitters (see later section on 'Neurotransmission and information management', p. 104).

Although these are complex biochemical processes, a basic understanding of these mechanisms is helpful in providing an insight into individual vulnerability, for instance by understanding the genetic mechanisms which increase the risk of psychopathology, or environmental influences which adversely affect the expression of the genes. Environmental influences include dietary restrictions in the availability of *amino acids* and cofactors, such as vitamins, required for the synthesis of essential proteins, or the presence of cytotoxic compounds such as alcohol and its metabolites, which might interfere with protein synthesis (see Chapter 8). These two examples are typically found in the homeless who are potentially nutritionally challenged, a situation often exacerbated by the abuse of alcohol.

Polymorphisms

A simple explanation for human individuality is that each person inherits a unique collection of genes from their parents and the expression of these genes is modulated by environmental influences, such as nutritional and toxic factors plus a wide range of experiences which contribute to the process of learning. For many years the realisation that a gene can have various forms has been explored in studies of the genetics of plants and animals. An example of this is the existence of polymorphic forms of the gene, *acetaldehyde dehydrogenase*, one of a number of polymorphic genes that control the metabolism of alcohol (see Figure 7.2). Acetaldehyde dehydrogenase occurs in various polymorphic forms, one of which is found in 'flushers', people who are highly sensitive to small amounts of alcohol (Sobue *et al.* 2002).

Another polymorphism is found in the genes that determine the structure of the protein receptor for dopamine. This dopamine receptor–neurotransmitter activity is found in the central mechanism of reward, as discussed in Chapter 3. There are at least nine different forms of the dopamine receptor gene. The DRD4 polymorphism has been associated with high levels of novelty-seeking behaviour and linked to a number of clinical phenomena (Aguirre-Samudio and Nicolini 2005; Saxon *et al.* 2005). The classification of alcoholic-dependent individuals by Cloninger into type I and type II groups has been linked to the presence of the DRD4 gene in type II alcoholics (Serretti *et al.* 2006). Such individuals have serious drinking problems before 25 years of age, and display antisocial behaviour.

Sexual differentiation

Sexual differentiation begins in the developing foetus as a consequence of the presence of two X chromosomes or one X and one Y chromosome, in females and males, respectively. The foetus develops the characteristics of *maleness* due to the influence of the *HY antigen* gene found on the Y chromosome. The hormonal influences of this gene causes the *androgenisation* of the hypothalamus in the brain, and the gender differentiation resulting from gene–environmental interactions. Female brains tend to be smaller than male brains and there are a number of physiological differences that suggest that males and females should be treated differently in some therapeutic settings. These include depression, schizophrenia, post-traumatic stress and addictive behaviours. This suggestion is based on the differences in cognition and behaviour, which are well established. Information to support this idea includes the frontal cortex, involved in cognitive functions, which is larger in females than in males. On the other hand space perception, processed by the parietal cortex, is relatively larger in males than females.

An important sex difference is found in reaction to stressful events. The amygdala is larger in males than females. Goldstein *et al.* (1999) has suggested that this provides an explanation for the ways in which males and females react differently to stress. In preclinical studies, chronic stress has been shown to cause more pathological harm in males than females (Conrad *et al.* 2004). Sex differences have been reported in PTSD, where beta blockers reduce memory of traumatic events in females but not males (Schelling *et al.* 2004).

With regard to mental illness, the higher levels of depression in women have been associated with 52 % lower levels of the neurotransmitter, serotonin, in women compared to men. Additionally, the greater susceptibility of females to stimulants, such as cocaine, is thought to be related to differences in dopamine metabolism. These neurochemical differences help to explain why women are more vulnerable to drugs of abuse and progress more rapidly into dependence, than men. Schizophrenia will be reviewed later in this chapter, but here it should be noted that women have a significantly larger orbitofrontal-to-amygdala ratio than found in men. A review of the links between brain function and sex differences in behaviour has been published by Cahill (2005).

NEUROTRANSMISSION AND INFORMATION MANAGEMENT

Neurotransmitters and neuromodulatory systems provide the psychopharmacological substrate through which behaviours, including those related to problems of alcohol and other drug dependencies, are expressed. Behavioural individuality results from the chemically coded information which is transmitted from generation to generation and emerges in an individual as a result of their specific environmental context. The uniqueness of individuals resulting from the interplay between genetics, environment and learned experiences is seen in the development of the nervous system which consists of the brain, the spinal cord and the multitude of nerve cells, which are responsible for managing information on a temporal basis.

The reception and processing of information from the senses (such as the eyes, ears, taste receptors) and the behavioural response to environmental stimuli are facilitated by the nerve cells called *neurons*. The distribution of neurons in the brain and rest of the body is determined by the genetic coding, which influences the path taken by developing neurons during embryonic development. During development the chemical coding at the tips of the extending of the axons' neurons ensure that appropriate connections between neurons are established in the developing brain. Information is transmitted through this highly complex neural network by means of electrical impulses, generated by the movement of sodium and potassium ions across the outer membrane of the nerve cells. However, the nerve cells are not in direct physical contact with each other. The flow of electrical impulses is broken at the ends of each neuron by means of a *synapse*. The chemical signalling via this small gap, between adjacent neurons, is important in the management of neural information, achieved by the controlled release of *neurotransmitter* molecules from one neuron and the reception of these molecular messengers on an adjacent neuron, see Figure 7.3.

In quantitative terms, the predominant neurotransmitters controlling the *excitation* of the brain, are the amino acids glutamate and aspartate, and *inhibition* of localised brain activity is influenced by the amino acid GABA. There are a number of neurochemicals, which occur at much lower concentrations than the *excitatory* and *inhibitor transmitters*. These *neuro-modulators* include the catecholamines (dopamine and noradrenaline) and indoleamines (primarily serotonin), sometimes referred to as the *biogenic amines*.

The neuromodulators transmit neuronal impulses (messages within the brain) to neurons some distance from the 'transmitting' neuron to neurons in distant regions of the brain. This is the case with serotonin (5-HT) and

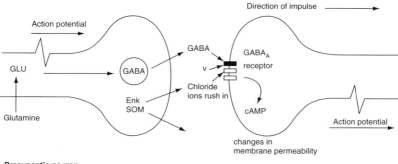

Figure 7.3 Diagrammatic view of ends of two adjacent neurons, separated by a *synaptic gap*. In this example, the neurotransmitter, gamma amino butyric acid (GABA), is synthesised in the neuron from glutamine (derived from the metabolism of glucose). GABA is contained in vesicles, which move towards the distal end of the presynaptic neuron. When the presynaptic neuron is electrically stimulated (an action potential), GABA molecules are released into the synaptic gap. Interaction between GABA molecules and the receptors on the postsynaptic neurone initiate an electrical transmission (action potential) in this neuron. The slowing down of neuron information at synaptic junctions, provides a mechanism for modulating the flow of information, and is the site of action of most drugs of abuse.

Source: From Bonner, A.B. and J. Waterhouse (eds) (1996). *Addictive Behaviour: Molecules to Mankind*. Macmillan. Reproduced with permission of Palgrave Macmillan.

opiates, such as the endorphins, both of which have modulating influence on the activity of particular brain regions. Although 5-HT and endorphins are sometimes described as neurotransmitters, they actually function as *neuromodulators*. As with other biogenic amines (dopamine, noradrenaline and adrenaline) 5-HT is synthesised within the neurons, in the case of 5-HT, from the dietary amino acid tryptophan. The amino acid tyrosine is the dietary precursor of dopamine, noradrenaline and adrenaline. The synthesis of these neuromodulators and neurotransmitters, within the neurons, is catalysed by specific enzymes, which are produced when specific genes are expressed (see p. 101). As mentioned at the beginning of this chapter, all cells, with one or two exceptions, contain the complete set of genes inherited from the individual's parents. However, fewer than 1% of these genes will be active in any single cell. In the case of neurons in for example, the *mesolimbic reward system*, active genes can be *transcribed* and *translated* into the protein enzymes required for the production of dopamine. The activities of the dopamine genes are modulated by 5-HT activity, an interaction which has been proposed to contribute to vulnerability to a spectrum of linked disorders, see Figure 7.4 (Comings 1991).

Dopamine/Serotonin interactions

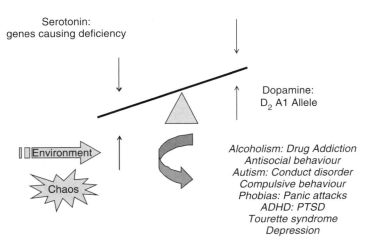

Figure 7.4 The modulating effect of serotonin on the activities of the dopamine-mediated reward system has been proposed by Comings (1991) to underpin the spectrum of related disorders shown in the diagram.

NEUROTRANSMISSION AND MALADAPTIVE BEHAVIOURS

In Chapter 6 it was clear that depression and other mental health problems are underpinned, if not initiated by biological influences such as inherited factors and other aspects of a person's physiology. Evidence for a biological basis of depression comes from drug therapy, light therapy, animal models, genetic studies and postmortem studies. Increasing our understanding of the biological foundations of mental illness has already and will continue to provide important advances in rehabilitation programmes (Dincin 2001).

It is perhaps not surprising that these same physiological systems which are affected in mental illness are also affected by excessive alcohol consumption and other drugs. Alcohol and its metabolites cause disruption of neurotransmitter, hormonal and body clock systems, which possibly contributes to the severity of these chronic relapsing conditions characterised by neurobiological changes that lead to a compulsion to take alcohol and drugs with loss of control over intake. In the brain, neurotransmitter systems are involved in the transition from drug use to the compulsive use of these addictive substances. An increased understanding of these mechanisms is leading to the development of pharmacological therapies to treat addictive behaviours. The midbrain and forebrain neural regions are involved in the positive reinforcing effects of misused substances; and the neural elements involved in the negative reinforcement associated with drug addiction have been studied. Disruption of the neurotransmitters dopamine, opioid peptides, 5-HT, GABA and glutamate occurs as a result of the reinforcing effects of drugs of abuse. The brain structures involved in these behavioural changes include the basal forebrain called the extended amygdala, which contains parts of the nucleus accumbens and amygdala (Koob 2000).

Subjective symptoms of negative affect, such as dysphoria, depression, irritability and anxiety and dysregulation of brain reward systems, occur in the withdrawal from drugs of abuse. Reinforcement and the strengthening of learned cues are key aspects in the process of learning, as described in Chapter 2 (see 'Learning and memory', p. 26). The cellular mechanism of learning and memory is shown in Figure 7.5. These specialised cells, found in the hippocampus, utilise glutamate as a neurotransmitter and have the properties permitting *retrograde transmission*. This unique neurotransmission involves NMDA receptors and a cellular signalling system utilising nitric oxide, which enables the priming of the postsynaptic neuron such that a subsequent impulse will be strengthened in its intensity, as indicated in Figure 7.5. These events involve some of the same neurochemical systems implicated in the acute reinforcing effects of drugs of abuse. In addition, acute withdrawal is accompanied by the activity of corticotropin-releasing

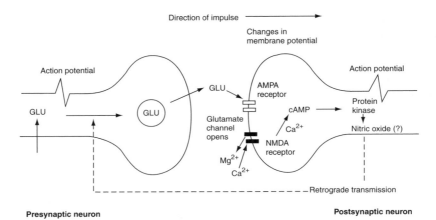

Figure 7.5 Synaptic mechanism involved in the cellular basis of learning. A similar process as in Figure 7.3 results in the stimulation of the postsynaptic neuron. In this case stimulation of NMDA receptors on the postsynaptic membrane result in a cascade of reactions leading to the production of nitric acid which acts a retrograde transmitter which primes the presynaptic neuron. In this way neuronal impulses have a greater effect, and this strengthening of response (termed long-term potentiation, LTP) forms the basis of learning at a cellular level. This NMDA-mediated LTP occurs in specialised cells in the hippocampus, located within the limbic system (see Figure 2.2).

Source: From Bonner, A.B. and J. Waterhouse (eds) (1996). *Addictive Behaviour: Molecules to Mankind*. Macmillan. Reproduced with permission of Palgrave Macmillan.

factor, the brain's stress neurotransmitter system (see Chapter 5). Craving is thought to involve not only conditioning but also continued dysregulation of the central nervous system increasing vulnerability to relapse.

Neurotransmitters and behavioural modulation

Changes in serotonin (5-HT) neurotransmission are implicated in psychiatric disorders. There is a large amount of evidence suggesting that affective disorders and schizophrenia are linked to abnormalities in specific 5-HT receptors. With regard to polymorphism of the serotonin receptor, there is a debate as to the precise mechanisms of action. Alterations in 5-HT(1A), 5-HT(1B) and 5-HT(2A) receptor subtypes have been found in the brains of subjects with both mood disorders and schizophrenia, but there is growing support for the hypothesis of dysregulation of the serotonergic system in these psychiatric disorders (Lopez-Figueroa and Norton 2004).

As well as work on neurotransmitter receptors, the *transporter systems* of dopamine, serotonin and norepinephrine have also been studied. These transporters are plasma membrane proteins, which are essential for the re-uptake and control synaptic neurotransmitters at the synapses. Neuro-logical disorders such as depression, schizophrenia and Parkinson's disease have been associated with abnormal transporter molecules and these have been targeted for therapeutic medications. The 5-HT transporter gene is responsible for the expression of membrane-bound proteins, which transport 5-HT molecules into neurons. Research into this system is beginning to give an insight into the interactions of psychosocial, situational and hereditary factors, which underpin delinquency, violence or drug abuse. The presence of the short variant of the 5-HTTLPR has previously been associated with an increased risk of psychosocial disturbances both in human and non-human primates (Lesch 2001). Adolescents with this polymorphism (see p. 102) have a 12–14-fold increased risk for high intoxication frequency (Oreland *et al.* 2005).

The modulation of behaviour by serotonin

Homeless and socially excluded people frequently suffer from eating disor-ders and sleep problems, which are associated with concurrent mental health problems. Feeding disturbances, depression and suicide, impulsivity and violence, anxiety and harm avoidance, obsessive-compulsive features, seasonal variation of symptoms, as well as disturbances in neuroendocrine and vascular tissues, occur in patients with eating disorders. These clinical features indicate the involvement of serotonin (5-HT) and its dysregula-tion, as well as other neurochemical systems linked to 5-HT. Brewerton (1995) found altered postsynaptic, hypothalamic 5-HT receptor sensitivity in bulimia nervosa, leading to impaired postingestive satiety, associated with reduced hypothalamic serotonergic responsiveness. The control of food intake has been linked with behavioural impulsivity and mood. Recent studies lend support to the hypothesis that concurrent or sequential periods of binge eating, behavioural impulsivity and depression in patients with eating disorders are determined by the modulation of the central nervous system by serotonin (Jimerson and Lesem 1990).

In addition to disruption of eating behaviour, homelessness and other chaotic life styles would be expected to have significant effect on biolog-ical rhythms. Circadian rhythms (oscillations of 'about a day') are intrinsic endogenous rhythms which approximate to 25 hours in an environment without time cues. In a minority of experiments, overt rhythms of different behavioural and physiological variables are not synchronised but inter-nally desynchronised in the steady state. This results in a fluctuating body temperature, with a period of about 25 hours, and a sleep–wake rhythm free running (i.e. in the absence of time cues) for longer or shorter than 25 hours.

A tendency toward the spontaneous occurrence of internal desynchronisa-tion does not depend only on personality data (e.g., neuroticism or age) but also on the external conditions. In constant light, in the normal range of arti-ficial illumination (intensities between 0 and 1500 lux), free-running circa-dian rhythms are not affected. Under constant bright light (intensity greater than 3000 lux) the rhythms of body temperature and melatonin excretion become desynchronised. This also occurs as a result of social behaviour or behavioural stress. In contrast to this effect on the circadian rhythms, physical workload does not affect free-running rhythms (Wever 1986).

The link between mental health problems and disrupted rhythms is well established and sleep deprivation is reported to have beneficial therapeutic effects in depressive illness. These responses reflect neurotransmitter func-tion in pathophysiological states such as affective disorders (Joffe 1984). It is interesting to note that hormonal control of the sleep–wake cycle and other biological rhythms is mediated by melatonin, a metabolite of serotonin (see Figure 7.6).

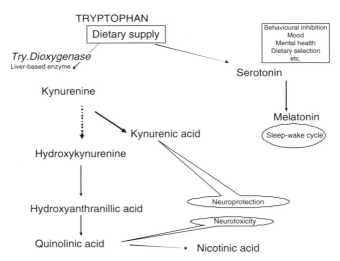

Figure 7.6   The metabolism of the dietary amino acid tryptophan. Tryptophan may be converted into serotonin, a neurotransmitter that has wide ranging influences on brain and behavioural activities. In darkness, serotonin is converted into mela-tonin (produced in the pineal gland, see Figure 2.1), a hormone that regulates the sleep–wake cycle and is an effective free radical scavenger. When induced by cortisol (a stress hormone, see Figure 5.2), oestrogen or tryptophan, the enzyme *tryptophan dioxygenase* (sometimes called *Trp pyrrolase*) converts up to 80% of circu-lating tryptophan into kynurenine and related metabolites. One of these, quinolinic acid, has been implicated in a range of neurotoxic effects, causing neurological damage. Conversely, kynurenic acid provides neuronal protection. These agonistic and antagonistic effects are related to the properties of the NMDA receptors (see Figure 7.4).

Tryptophan and brain functioning

The role of serotonin in eating behaviour and the sleep–wake cycle, as reviewed above, indicates the extent to which 5-HT is involved in a wide range of neuropsychiatric and related conditions including: depression, insomnia, hypertension, behavioural disinhibition (Badawy 1996b; LeMarquand *et al.* (1999); (Muller *et al.* 2002); pathological and suicidal aggression (Pihl *et al.* 1995); delirium (Freese *et al.* 1990; Cleare and Bond 1995); and the control of mood and cognitive performance (Altman and Normile 1988; Maes *et al.* 1999). Brain 5-HT is dependent on the availability of the amino acid precursor tryptophan (Trp), which is derived from the diet, and competes with other large neutral amino acids (LNAAs) for transport into the brain via the blood–brain barrier (Fernstrom *et al.* 1977). Mental performance is significantly affected by changes in the Trp/LNAA ratio (Rosenthal *et al.* 1989; Bellisle *et al.* 1998; Markus *et al.* 2002). This ratio is decreased following consumption of ethanol over a 2–3 hour time period (Badawy *et al.* 1995). Figure 7.6 shows that, in addition to being a precursor for serotonin and melatonin, dietary tryptophan also can be metabolised into kynurenine and other related compounds, a number of which have significant influences on the brain. The kynurenine pathway is the major route for tryptophan metabolism and has been implicated in brain dysfunction in Alzheimer's disease, Huntingdon's disease and acquired immunodeficiency syndrome (AIDS)-dementia complex (Stone and Darlington 2002).

The enzyme tryptophan dioxygenase (TDO) is formed in the liver and its synthesis is controlled by cortisol, the stress-related hormone, oestrogen and circulating tryptophan. Following the induction of TDO enzyme circulating tryptophan will be diverted into the kynurenine pathway with a subsequent reduction in the availability of tryptophan for synthesis into 5-HT in the brain. This reduction of brain 5-HT synthesis will be exacerbated by the competition between kynurenine and Trp for the same transporters through the blood–brain barrier (Young 1981). The consequences of reduced brain 5-HT have been outlined above. Furthermore, cortisol activation of this metabolic pathway may be an important biological determinant of the ethanol withdrawal syndrome (Badawy *et al.* 1998). High concentrations of the kynurenines are excreted in the urine of patients with rheumatoid arthritis, tuberculosis, leukaemia, Hodgkin's disease and bladder tumours.

The kynurenine metabolite quinolinic acid has been implicated in neurological diseases and neurodegeneration including Huntingdon's disease, temporal lobe epilepsy, glutaric aciduria, hepatic encephalopathy and coma (Freese *et al.* 1990). Quinolinic acid (QA) destroys neuronal cell bodies; cortical cells with NMDA receptors are particularly sensitive to QA. NMDA receptors mediate the actions of many of the excitatory amino acids such as glutamate. This is central to memory function and learning via *long-term potentiation* (LTP). Quinolinic acid is a selective excitant (agonist) of the NMDA receptor; kynurenic acid is an antagonist (Freese *et al.* 1990), having a neuroprotective role, see Figure 7.5.

Neurotoxicity induced by quinolinic acid primarily occurs in the hippocampus, striatum and neocortex, brain areas particularly affected by the disorders mentioned above. Excitotoxicity results in overstimulation of NMDA receptors in the hippocampus affecting LTP and the cellular basis of learning (see Chapter 2, 'Learning and memory', p. 26). The link with ethanol consumption stems from observation of increased sensitivity of NMDA receptors in alcohol withdrawal (Oretti *et al.* 1996; Nagy and Laszlo 2002) and excitotoxic damage due to neural compensation for sustained alcohol levels and nutritional deficits underlying alcohol-related brain damage. The specific nutritional deficit here is thiamine (Lovinger 1993). Other studies have demonstrated the role of reduced hippocampal glutamate decarboxylase (GAD) in cell death occurring during ethanol dependence (Davidson *et al.* 1993). The development of brain damage in binge drinkers is more likely due to increased vulnerability of the brain to these neurotoxic mechanisms (Hunt 1993).

Tryptophan metabolism and neuroprotection

While one component of the kynurenine pathway (QA) is implicated in neurotoxicity, there is substantial evidence that an alternative pathway, involving kynurenic acid (KA), is important in providing neuroprotection. KA is an antagonist of the excitatory amino acid receptor, NMDA (Perkins and Stone 1982). It can be synthesised in the brain and can also be transported through the blood–brain barrier and taken up by glia cells.

Shifting the balance of kynurenine metabolism from 3-hydroxykynurenine, which leads to quinolinic acid, to KA reduces glutamate receptor activation and excitotoxic or ischaemic neuronal damage (Schwartz *et al.* 1983). Despite extensive work on pharmacologically designed neuroprotectants, to date therapeutic trials have yet to be undertaken on patients with *alcohol-related brain damage*. With regard to the rehabilitation of alcohol misusers, a pharmacological approach is probably not the most appropriate strategy, where the possibility of substitute dependencies might arise. A more realistic way forward is to support behavioural and physiological change, during addiction rehabilitation, by more naturalistic methods such as dietary interventions. The success of this approach will depend on how much and when, during the diurnal cycle, the supplement should be given. The ability of the patient to absorb the nutrients will relate to the degree of malabsorption, i.e. pathological stage of the gut, and determine whether oral or parenteral therapy will be effective (Bonner *et al.* 2003).

THE MALFUNCTIONING BRAIN

A complex relationship exists between brain function, metabolism and dietary factors such as the precursors for the production of neurotrans-mitters, and potentially toxic compounds, which include alcohol and its metabolite acetaldehyde. It is well established that chronic ethanol misuse is associated with impaired nutrition, primarily as a consequence of the disad-vantaged socio-economic life styles, the perturbations in nutrient handling resulting in reduced absorption and metabolism in chronic alcohol abusers. There is substantial evidence that thiamine deficiency plays a central role in the pathological development of brain damage leading, if untreated, to Korsakoff's psychosis (Thomson *et al.* 2002). Normal CNS activity is depen-dent on nicotinic acid, pyridoxine and vitamin B12 and functional deficits may present in the development of brain damage. Brain changes leading to atrophy, due to excessive ingestion of alcohol, include impaired cognitive function, reflected in reduced quality of life with corresponding increases in morbidity and mortality.

Ageing, homelessness and brain damage

An observation of the long-term homeless, especially those with chronic alcohol problems, suggests that such degeneration is not unlike the effects of the ageing process, leading to the possibility that physiological processes associated with a chaotic life style are symptomatic of premature ageing. A range of genetic, environmental and health-related factors are known to modulate the ageing-related processes, sometimes leading to progression into the devastation of Alzheimer's disease. Normal ageing and Alzheimer's disease have many features in common and, in many respects, both condi-tions only differ by the degree of severity of neurocognitive dysfunction. Cognitive and noncognitive symptoms that characterise this devastating illness are linked to anatomical and neurochemical systems (Garand and Buckwalter 2000). Alzheimer's disease is considered to be a metabolic disease involving a number of risk factors which disrupt the homeostasis of the calcium–energy–redox system and reduce the cerebral reserve capacity when subjected to metabolic stress.

The major genetic risk factors include apolipoprotein (E4) and prese-nilin mutations, as found in Down's syndrome. Medically related metabolic risk factors are associated with cerebrovascular diseases including stroke, cardiovascular diseases, hypo- and hypertension. Other persistent metabolic stress results from traumatic brain injury (TBI) and major depression, and the associated chronic stress. These stress-related conditions appear to result from the increased vulnerability of susceptible brain areas affected by endocrine imbalances resulting from dysregulation of the HPA axis (see Chapter 5, Figure 5.2). Life-style factors and socio-cultural factors in the socially excluded include education, physical activity, diet and smoking. These risk factors negatively affect both reserve capacity and vulnerability of the brain. There is controversy regarding the pathophysiological importance of trace metals, including aluminium and iron. The proposition here is that these environmental agents adversely affect cellular defences, and antioxidant competence in particular. In familial Alzheimer's disease, inherited factors are involved giving weight to the argument that Alzheimer's disease results from interactions of genes and environment factors (Heininger 2000).

Ageing is associated with anatomical, chemical and functional changes in the brain. One of the most prominent changes occurs in the neuronal pathways, which use acetyl choline as a neurotransmitter. These cholinergic neurons, receptors and afferent projections become reduced with age, a process which is possibly related to age-associated deficits observed in working memory and other cognitive tasks. The development of *positron emission tomography* (PET) and *functional magnetic resonance imaging* (fMRI) have provided non-invasive methodologies for the *in vivo* functional exploration of the brain. In this way the neural mechanisms of mental function in physiological and psychopathological conditions in humans at different ages can now be studied.

NEUROBIOLOGICAL BASIS OF SUBSTANCE USE AND DEPENDENCE

Drugs of abuse are complex molecules that have distinct protein targets in the brain and other parts of the body, an interaction which causes physiological and behavioural change. Despite the considerable variation in the chemical structure of these compounds, and their diverse target sites, all have common influences. The common feature that drugs of abuse share is that they either affect the reward system or pain systems, or both. These effects cause the drug taker to repeat consumption of the drug. The repeated intake of the drug can lead, in vulnerable individuals, to dependence, a loss of control over drug use. Lack of access to, or withdrawal from, drugs of abuse, normally leads to negative emotional symptoms, and prolonged periods of sensitisation. The processes of dependence, withdrawal and sensitisation involve learning and the establishment of linkages (cues) between the drug-taking behaviour and drug-related environmental cues. These neurobiological adaptations contribute to the intense craving for the drug and relapse, which can persist even after substantial periods of abstinence.

The basic mechanisms involved in substance use and dependence have been reviewed by the World Health Organisation (WHO 2004) and Badawy (1996a). A more detailed review of the action of cocaine, amphetamines and other drugs of abuse has been published by Syad (2000). The role of reward-mediated behaviours was discussed in Chapter 2.

In the case of acute and chronic effects of alcohol, intoxication and with-drawal have been associated with a number of neurotransmitters which condense with acetaldehyde, the primary metabolite of ethanol, to form tetrahydroisoquinolines (TIQs). TIQs have similar properties and function as opioids (Cohen and Collins 1970). Furthermore, opioids and ethanol appear to act on similar receptor systems, providing an explanation for enhanced ethanol drinking in rodents, and the possibility that the opioid-like prop-erties of TIQs compensate for a deficiency in opioid activity. Evidence of this has been obtained from studies of laboratory-bred genetic strains of mice, C57BL and DBA, which are alcohol and water preferring, respec-tively (Badawy 1996a). This suggests a genetic basis to alcohol-seeking behaviour, which is underpinned by an opioid-linked metabolic response to ethanol. Chronic administration of ethanol has been shown to decrease opioid concentrations in the brain and pituitary (Seizinger *et al.* 1984), with 50 % or more decreases in hypothalamic and hippocampal levels of dynor-phin and alpha neo-endorphin. Genazzani *et al.* (1982) found a three-fold reduction of beta-endorphin in the CSF of chronic alcoholics compared to controls. It is interesting to speculate on the relevance of the studies described in Chapter 5. Here the endocrine-related consequences of high levels of stress in children and deficits in the opioid-linked system are corre-lated with dysfunctional mother–infant bonding (Kalin 1993), as discussed in Chapter 5, Stress in Children and Families.

Opioids and ethanol, therefore, appear to have common modes of action by modifying the responsiveness of the mesolimbic–dopamine reward system and other parts of the limbic system, the outcomes of which are expressed in terms of craving and behaviours associated with withdrawal. A molecular explanation for some of these actions has been proposed by Blum and Trachtenburg (1987), with reference to the *reward cascade*. The cascade is thought to be initiated in the hypothalamus, where neurons secrete serotonin (5-HT) causing the activation of methionine enkephalin, an opioid peptide. This peptide, produced in the substantia nigra, by inhibiting GABA receptors, controls the production of dopamine (DA) from the ventral tegmental area (VTA). Increased DA then has both a direct effect on neurons in the nucleus accumbens and an indirect effect on CA_1 cells in the hippocampus. Both of these regions act as target messengers of reward. This homeostatically regulated system could be dysregulated by a dysfunctioning neurotransmitter (e.g. 5-HT) or neuromodulator (e.g. an opioid peptide) resulting in a change in affect (emotional) or overt behaviour. Such perturbations could originate from neuroendocrine stress-related changes, change in immune system status, drug-induced changes, genetically inherited neurotransmitter defects and nutritional imbalances.

The concentration of 5-HT in the brain, therefore, has a significant influ-ence on mental state. Furthermore, in contrast to other neurotransmitters, brain 5-HT is dependent on the availability of its dietary precursor, trypto-phan, as described earlier in this chapter. In summary, the common action of drugs on the brain systems of reward, appears to involve interactions between different neurochemical systems, however, the common molecular pathways are still yet to be elucidated (Nestler 2005).

NEUROBIOLOGICAL BASIS OF MENTAL ILLNESS

Depression

Medications, which act via various mechanisms to increase synaptic concentrations of monoamine neurotransmitter, improve the symptoms of depression. The monoamine hypothesis of depression, first proposed 30 years ago, predicts that the underlying pathophysiological basis of depression is depletion in the levels of serotonin, norepinephrine and/or dopamine in the central nervous system, see p. 89. This hypothesis is supported by studies on the mechanism of action of antidepressants, which elevate the levels of these neurotransmitters in the brain. Amine-based antidepressants have all been shown to be effective in the alleviation of depressive symptoms. However, this multitude of studies has failed to find consistent evidence of a primary dysfunction of a specific monoamine system in patients with major depressive disorders.

Methodological problems relating to the absence of direct measurements of monoamines in humans have obscured the link between these neurotransmitter systems and depression. However, in studies where monoamine depletion is induced in experimental subjects, clinical syndromes can be reproduced, and allow a more direct method for investigating the role of monoamines. These studies indicate that antidepressant responses are reversed temporarily, with the response being dependent on the class of antidepressant. Conversely, monoamine depletion does not worsen symptoms in depressed patients not taking medication, nor does it cause depression in healthy volunteers with no depressive illness. The conclusion from these studies is that an intact monoamine system is not essential for the therapeutic effect of antidepressant medications currently used. The actual role that a deficiency in monoamine system(s) may play in depression remains to be explored (Delgado 2000).

The amine hypothesis has evolved over the years to include, for example, adaptive changes in receptors providing an explanation as to why there is only a gradual clinical response to antidepressant treatment when the increase in availability of monoamines is rapid. The hypothesis does not address key issues such as why antidepressants are also effective in other disorders such as panic disorder, obsessive-compulsive disorder, and bulimia, or why all drugs that enhance serotonergic or noradrenergic transmission are not necessarily effective in depression. Despite these limitations, however, it is clear that the development of the monoamine hypothesis has been of great importance in understanding depression and in the development of safe and effective medications for its treatment (Hirschfeld 2000). The amino hypothesis is discussed in Chapter 6, in relation to other biological perspectives on the nature of depression.

Schizophrenia

Since the late nineteenth century (Clouston 1891) the possibility that mental illness might have a developmental origin has been considered. Some workers considered schizophrenia to have a solely biological condition, or be the consequence of a secondary neurodegenerative resulting from a degenerative process. A more contemporary view is that a range of biological, psychological and social factors contribute to this illness (Javitt and Cyle 2004). Family, twin and adoption studies provide evidence for a robust genetic component in the development of schizophrenia. Some data indicate a heritability score of 0.8, that is genetic factors contribute 80 % to the development of the condition. Molecular genetic researchers are currently searching for candidate genes that contribute to the susceptibility to the condition (Harrison and Owen 2003). Several of the genes reviewed by Harrison and Owen (e.g. NRTG1, DTNBP1, COMT) are possibly involved in neurodevelopment and related to the glutamate neurotransmitter systems (Tsai and Coyle 2002).

Other risk factors include obstetric complication, time of year of birth, infectious agents (e.g. rubella, influenza), smoking, rhesus incompatibility, maternal malnutrition and maternal diabetes. Trauma during conception and paternal death have also been considered as possible causative agents. However, the evidence for the importance of these factors is limited. There is evidence that a range of minor physical anomalies (MPAs) are elevated in schizophrenics in comparison with the normal population, pointing to the role of neurodevelopmental processes in the occurrence of schizophrenia. An explanation for the development/maturational problems that might lead to schizophrenia suggests a problem of synchrony of communication between different brain areas, leading to neurodevelopment dysregulation. The role of myelin, a fatty sheath surrounding neuronal axons (which is essential for efficient neuronal communication, see Figure 7.1), is presently being investigated as a potential weakness in the development and maturation of the schizophrenic's brain (Bartzokis 2002).

Dean *et al.* (2003) have reviewed the relative importance of neurodevelopmental versus neurodegenerative processes in the aetiology of this illness. In reviewing a range of antecedents of schizophrenia, these authors suggest that a combination of these two processes is involved. One aspect of the pathophysiology, which has been considered for some time, is the sensitivity of the mesolimbic system to the neurotransmitter, dopamine, in schizophrenics. Interest in this brain area grew with the discovery that antipsychotics block dopamine receptors, and the mesolimbic system was found to be sensitive to dopamine in schizophrenics, providing *salience* (significance) to internal and external events. Dopamine sensitivity and dopamine-induced abnormal salience provide an explanation for the abuse of particular drugs, in particular psychostimulants. This is particularly relevant presently in view of the debate concerning the legalisation of cannabis. Cannabis intoxification is known to produce acute psychotic episodes, leading to the proposal that cannabis use can contribute to the onset of schizophrenia (Dean *et al.* 2003).

Human brains have been subjected to selective pressures since the dawn of humankind. Brains evolved to be responsive to experience but the degree of tolerance to maltreatment and physiological stressors such as malnutrition must have limits. When these limits are exceeded, behavioural dysfunction and pathological states appear. An insight into these issues is provided by the destabilisation of behavioural and physiological homeostasis brought about by chronic alcohol consumption (Fadda and Rossetti 1998; Teicher 2002). Although, these biological processes are complex and many issues still need to be resolved, an understanding of the neurobiological basis of behaviours expressed by various groups of socially excluded people, should contribute to the development of services to address individual needs.

REFERENCES

Aguirre-Samudio, A. J. and H. Nicolini (2005). DRD4 polymorphism and the association with mental disorders. *Revista de Investigacion Clínica*, **57**(1), 65–75.

Altman, H. J. and H. J. Normile (1988). What is the nature of the role of the serotonergic nervous system in learning and memory: prospects for development of an effective treatment strategy for senile dementia. *Neurobiology of Aging*, **9**(5–6), 627–38.

Badawy, A. A. (1996a). The neurobiological background to the study of addiction. In: Bonner, A. and J. Waterhouse (eds), *Addictive Behaviour: Molecules to Mankind*. Basingstoke: Macmillan.

Badawy, A. A. (1996b). Tryptophan metabolism and disposition in relation to alcohol and alcoholism. *Advances in Experimental Medicine and Biology*, **398**, 75–82.

Badawy, A. A., C. J. Morgan, J. W. Lovett, D. M. Bradley and R. Thomas (1995). Decrease in circulating tryptophan availability to the brain after acute ethanol consumption by normal volunteers: implications for alcohol-induced aggressive behaviour and depression. *Pharmacopsychiatry*, **28**(Supplement 2), 93–7.

Badawy, A. A., H. Rommelspacher, C. J. Morgan, D. M. Bradley, A. Bonner, A. Ehlert, *et al.* (1998). Tryptophan metabolism in alcoholism. Tryptophan but not excitatory amino acid availability to the brain is increased before the appearance of the alcohol-withdrawal syndrome in men. *Alcohol and Alcoholism*, **33**(6), 616–25.

Bartzokis, G. (2002). Schizophrenia: breakdown in the well-regulated lifelong process of brain development and maturation. *Neuropsychopharmacology*, **27**(4), 672–83.

Bellisle, F., J. E. Blundell, L. Dye, M. Fantino, E. Fern, R. J. Fletcher, *et al.* (1998). Functional food science and behaviour and psychological functions. *British Journal of Nutrition*, **80**(Supplement 1), S173–93.

Blum, K. and M.C. Trachtenburg (1987). New insights into the causes of alcoholism. *Professional Counsellor*, March/April, 33–5.

Bonner, A. B., A. D. Thomson and C. H. Cook (2003). Alcohol, nutrition and brain function. In: Watson, R. R., V. R. Preedy and W. R. Watson (eds), *Nutrition and Alcohol*. Boca Raton, Florida: CRC Press.

Brewerton, T. D. (1995). Toward a unified theory of serotonin dysregulation in eating and related disorders. *Psychoneuroendocrinology*, **20**(6), 561–7.

Cahill, L. (2005). His brain, her brain. *Scientific American*, **292**(5), 22–9.

Cleare, A. J. and A. J. Bond (1995). Relationship of plasma tryptophan and blood serotonin to aggression, mood and anxiety in males. *Journal of Serotonin Research*, **2**, 77–84.

Clouston, T. S. (1891). *The Neuroses of Development*. Edinburgh: Oliver and Boyd.

Cohen, G. and M. Collins (1970). Alkaloids from catecholamines in adrenal tissue: possible role in alcoholism. *Science*, **167**(926), 1749–51.

Comings, D. (1991). The genetics of addictive behaviours: the role of childhood disorders. *Addiction and Recovery*, November/December, 13–15.

Conrad, C. D., J. L. Jackson and L. S. Wise (2004). Chronic stress enhances ibotenic acid-induced damage selectively within the hippocampal CA3 region of male, but not female rats. *Neuroscience*, **125**(3), 759–67.

Davidson, M. D., P. Wilce and B. C. Shanley (1993). Increased sensitivity of the hippocampus in ethanol-dependent rats to toxic effect of N-methyl-D-aspartic acid in vivo. *Brain Research*, **606**(1), 5–9.

Dean, K., E. Bramon and R. Murray (2003). The causes of schizophrenia: neurode-velopmental and other risk factors. *Journal of Psychiatric Practice*, **9**(6), 442–54.

Delgado, P. L. (2000). Depression: the case for a monoamine deficiency. *Journal of Clinical Psychiatry*, **61**(Supplement 6), 7–11.

Dincin, J. (2001). The biological basis of mental illness. *New Directions for Mental Health Services*, **91**, 47–56.

Fadda, F. and Z. L. Rossetti (1998). Chronic ethanol consumption: from neuroadap-tation to neurodegeneration. *Progress in Neurobiology*, **56**(4), 385–431.

Fernstrom, J. D., H. N. Munro and R. J. Wurtman (1977). Brain tryptophan in rats on a high fat diet. *Nature*, **265**(5591), 277.

Freese, A., K. J. Swartz, M. J. During and J. B. Martin (1990). Kynurenine metabolites of tryptophan: implications for neurologic diseases. *Neurology*, **40**(4), 691–5.

Garand, L. and K. C. Buckwalter (2000). The biological basis of behavioral symptoms in dementia. *Issues in Mental Health Nursing*, **21**(1), 91–107.

Genazzani, A. R., G. Nappi, F. Facchinetti, G. L. Mazzella, D. Parrini, E. Sinforiani, *et al.* (1982). Central deficiency of beta-endorphin in alcohol addicts. *Journal of Clinical Endocrinology and Metabolism*, **55**(3), 583–6.

Goldstein, J. M., D. N. Kennedy and V. S. Caviness, Jr. (1999). Images in neuroscience. Brain development, XI: sexual dimorphism. *American Journal of Psychiatry*, **156**(3), 352.

Harrison, P. J. and M. J. Owen (2003). Genes for schizophrenia. Recent findings and their pathophysiological implications. *Lancet*, **361**, 417–19.

Heininger, K. (2000). A unifying hypothesis of Alzheimer's disease. III. Risk factors. *Human Psychopharmacology*, **15**(1), 1–70.

Hirschfeld, R. M. (2000). History and evolution of the monoamine hypothesis of depression. *Journal of Clinical Psychiatry*, **61**(Supplement 6), 4–6.

Hunt, W. A. (1993). Are binge drinkers more at risk of developing brain damage? *Alcohol*, **10**(6), 559–61.

Javitt, D. and J. Cyle (2004). Decoding schizophrenia. *Scientific American*, **290**(1), 38–45.

Jimerson, D. C. and M. D. Lesem (1990). Eating disorders and depression: is there a serotonin connection? *Biological Psychiatry*, **28**(5), 443–53.

Joffe, R. T. (1984). Clinical and biological correlates of sleep deprivation in depression. *Canadian Journal of Psychiatry*, **29**(6), 530–6.

Kalin, N. H. (1993). The neurobiology of fear. *Scientific American*, **268**, 94.

Koob, G. F. (2000). Neurobiology of addiction. Toward the development of new therapies. *Annals of the New York Academy of Sciences*, **909**, 170–85.

LeMarquand, D. G., C. Benkelfat, R. O. Pihl, R. M. Palmour and S. N. Young (1999). Behavioural disinhibition induced by tryptophan depletion in nonalcoholic young men with multigeneration families of paternal alcoholism. *American Journal of Psychiatry*, **156**(11), 1771–9.

Lesch, K. (2001). Serotonin transporter: from genomics and knockouts to behavioral traits and psychiatric disorders. In: Briley, M. and F. Sulser (eds), *Molecular Genetics of Mental Disorders*. London: Dunitz.

Lopez-Figueroa, A. L. and C. S. Norton, (2004). Serotonin 5-HT1A, 5-HT1B, and 5-HT2A receptor mRNA expression in subjects with major depression, bipolar disorder, and schizophrenia. *Biological Psychiatry*, **55**(3), 225–33.

Lovinger, D. M. (1993). Excitotoxicity and alcohol-related brain damage. *Alcoholism: Clinical and Experimental Research*, **17**(1), 19–27.

Maes, M., A. H. Lin, R. Verkerk, L. Delmeire, A. Van Gastel, M. Van der Planken, *et al.* (1999). Serotonergic and noradrenergic markers of post-traumatic stress disorder with and without major depression. *Neuropsychopharmacology*, **20**(2), 188–97.

Markus, C. R., B. Olivier and E. H. de Haan (2002). Whey protein rich in alpha-lactalbumin increases the ratio of plasma tryptophan to the sum of the other large neutral amino acids and improves cognitive performance in stress-vulnerable subjects. *American Journal of Clinical Nutrition*, **75**(6), 1051–6.

Muller, D., I. Nikonenko, P. Jourdain and S. Alberi (2002). LTP, memory and structural plasticity. *Current Molecular Medicine*, **2**(7), 605–11.

Nagy, J. and L. Laszlo (2002). Increased sensitivity to NMDA is involved in alcohol-withdrawal induced cytotoxicity observed in primary cultures of cortical neurones chronically pre-treated with ethanol. *Neurochemistry International*, **40**(7), 585–91.

Nestler, E. J. (2005). Is there a common molecular pathway for addiction? *Nature Neuroscience*, **8**(11), 1445–9.

Oreland, L., K. W. Nilsson., R. L. Sjöberg, M. Damberg, P. O. Alm, J. Öhrvik, *et al.* (2005). Significant interaction of the 5HTT promoter polymorphism genotype and family function for adolescent high alcohol intoxication frequency. *Alcoholism: Clinical and Experimental Research*, **29**, 564–70.

Oretti, R., S. Bano, C. J. Morgan, A. A. Badawy, A. Bonner, P. Buckland, *et al.* (1996). Prevention by cycloheximide of the audiogenic seizures and tryptophan metabolic disturbances of ethanol withdrawal in rats. *Alcohol and Alcoholism*, **31**(3), 243–7.

Perkins, M. N. and T. W. Stone (1982). An iontophoretic investigation of the actions of convulsant kynurenines and their interaction with the endogenous excitant quinolinic acid. *Brain Research*, **247**(1), 184–7.

Pihl, R. O., S. N. Young, P. Harden, S. Plotnick, B. Chamberlain and F. R. Ervin (1995). Acute effect of altered tryptophan levels and alcohol on aggression in normal human males. *Psychopharmacology (Berlin)*, **119**(4), 353–60.

Rosenthal, N. E., M. J. Genhart, B. Caballero, F. M. Jacobsen, R.G. Skwerer, R. D. Coursey, *et al.* (1989). Psychobiological effects of carbohydrate- and protein-rich meals in patients with seasonal affective disorder and normal controls. *Biological Psychiatry*, **25**(8), 1029–40.

Saxon, A. J., M. R. Oreskovich and Z. Brkanac (2005). Genetic determinants of addiction to opioids and cocaine. *Harvard Review of Psychiatry*, **13**(4), 218–32.

Schelling, G., E. Kilger, B. Roozendaal, D. J. de Quervain, J. Briegel, A. Dagge, *et al.* (2004). Stress doses of hydrocortisone, traumatic memories, and symptoms of posttraumatic stress disorder in patients after cardiac surgery: a randomized study. *Biological Psychiatry*, **55**(6), 627–33.

Schwartz, R., W. O. J. Whetsell and R. M. Mangano (1983). Quinolinic acid: an endogenous metabolite that produces axon-sparing lesions in rat brain. *Science*, **219**(4582), 316–18.

Seizinger, B. R., V. Hollt and A. Herz (1984). Proenkephalin B (prodynorphin)-derived opioid peptides: evidence for a differential processing in lobes of the pituitary. *Endocrinology*, **115**(2), 662–71.

Serretti, A., L. Mandelli, C. Lorenzi, S. Landoni, R. Calati, C. Insacco, *et al.* (2006). Temperament and character in mood disorders: influence of DRD4, SERTPR, TPH and MAO-A polymorphisms. *Neuropsychobiology*, **53**(1), 9–16.

Sobue, I., T. Takeshita, S. Maruyama and K. Morimoto (2002). The effects of low Km aldehyde dehydrogenase (ALDH2) phenotype on drinking behavior in Japanese university students. *Journal of Studies on Alcohol*, **63**(5), 527–30.

Stone, T. W. and L. G. Darlington (2002). Endogenous kynurenines as targets for drug discovery and development. *Nature Reviews Drug Discovery*, **1**(8), 609–20.

Syad, F., Ali (2000). *Neurobiological Mechanisms of Drug Abuse*. Vol. 914. New York: New York Academy of Sciences.

Teicher, M. H. (2002). Scars that won't heal: the neurobiology of child abuse. *Scientific American*, **286**, 68.

Thomson, A. D., C. C. Cook, R. Touquet and J. A. Henry (2002). The Royal College of Physicians report on alcohol: guidelines for managing Wernicke's encephalopathy in the Accident and Emergency Department. *Alcohol and Alcoholism*, **37**(6), 513–21.

Tsai, G. and J. T. Coyle (2002). Glutaminergic mechanisms in schizophrenia. *Annual Review of Pharmacology and Toxicology*, **42**, 165–79.

Wever, R. A. (1986). Characteristics of circadian rhythms in human functions. *Journal of Neural Transmission*, **21**(supplement), 323–73.

WHO (2004). *Neuroscience of Psychoactive Substance Use and Dependence*. Geneva: World Health Organisation.

Young, S. N. (1981). Mechanism of decline in rat brain 5-hydroxytryptamine after induction of liver tryptophan pyrrolase by hydrocortisone: roles of tryptophan catabolism and kynurenine synthesis. *British Journal of Pharmacology*, **74**(3), 695–700.

CHAPTER 8

ALCOHOL AND DRUG PROBLEMS

SUBSTANCE MISUSE AND SOCIAL EXCLUSION

The principal risk factors for ill health in the homeless populations are smoking, drug and alcohol abuse, malnutrition, obesity and sedentary life style. These health risks are reflected in problems with respiration, skin, digestion, muscular degeneration, mental health and injuries. Alcohol abusers, heroin addicts and smokers are known to have high mortality rates. Some subpopulations are at even greater risk as in the case of crack users. A study of 131 crack-dependent patients admitted to a detoxification centre, studied in Sao Paulo by Ribeiro *et al.* (2004) had a mortality rate, adjusted for age and sex, of 24.92 per thousand, compared with 3.28 per thousand for the general population. The most common cause of death was murder. In a study of socially excluded drug users in 10 cities from nine European countries, March *et al.* (2006) found that cannabis, heroin and cocaine are the most widely used substances. In this sample population, 60.2 % reported injecting drugs during the last year; 45.9 % reported having hepatitis C; 54.9 % have been in prison; 14.2 % are homeless; 11.3 % have a regular job and 35.2 % are involved in illegal activities. The authors found that being imprisoned, homelessness, irregular employment and delinquency were the main factors causing exclusion from society. Those who had been excluded from a drug treatment programme and abandoned by statutory services were at greater risk of injecting drugs than those who have never been engaged in treatment. This work highlighted the need to target specific groups and to consider the importance of engagement processes, disengagement having more negative consequences than no engagement.

Cultural variations

In considering specific target groups the European Monitoring Centre for Drugs and Drug Addiction (EMCDDA) has undertaken a comparative survey of drug use in ethnic minorities. This pan-European study indicated that black minority ethnic groups (BME) were similar to white indigenous populations in their vulnerability to problematic drug use. However, 'minority [BME] drug users could be said to be facing a position of double jeopardy; they carry the stigmata of racial exclusion and of drug use'. Cultural variations do exist as in the case of the Somali community groups in European countries, in which the use of 'qat' (*khat*) is common. Other culturally specific drug use involves 'Marasotu' (literally a grass from Mara, a town in south-west Turkey), a powder chewed, like qat, by some Greek and Turkish Cypriots in the UK, and 'kompot', a pharmaceutical form of morphine used by old Russians newly arriving in Spain (EMCDDA 2002).

The EMCDDA European survey provided a profile for each of the European countries. The report on the UK indicated heavy use of cannabis by black Caribbeans, and cocaine powder and crack cocaine were the most used 'hard drugs'. There was some drug injecting in this group, which was over-represented in the statistics on drug-related arrests. Heroin use and injecting was reported in Indians in the UK. Increasing use of stimulants, ecstasy and other 'designer' drugs were found in this ethnic group. There is a significant link between social exclusion and drug usage in Pakistani and Bangladeshi populations, which involves injecting heroin. Such problems are largely hidden in these communities, however, new initiatives in East London are currently being developed by the local Drug Action Team to address these problems.

In the UK, 80% of rough sleepers have drug problems, and 50% of this hard-to-reach group have serious alcohol problems. 'Young runaways' are five times more likely than their stable peers to have problems with drugs, and 66% of prisoners admit to drug use and alcohol problems in the year before imprisonment (SEU 2001).

The problems of matching the complex needs with availability and appropriateness of services in the community in the UK were discussed by Gossop *et al.* (2002). In the delivery of substance misuse services in Scotland, the following areas of good practice were noted as: staffing; agency environment; support provided; service delivery; and agency aims and objectives. Good practice was found to be associated with 'the qualitative and intangible aspects of service provision, and not just to more easily quantifiable inputs, processes, outputs and outcomes'. The authors argue that the development of 'evaluation frameworks [to] accommodate this complexity' is essential in responding to the current performance management culture in the UK, but also to identify factors linked to social exclusion indicators, such as housing, education and employment, each of which is linked to intravenous drug use (Neale and Kennedy 2002).

Drug use and vulnerable young people

The roots of drug misuse and other complex needs observed in adults are laid down during the early years, as reviewed in Chapter 3. In the development of substance misuse, these problems begin to manifest themselves in adolescence, in some cases leading to social exclusion. Various studies have shown that substance use was a contributory factor in 37 % of 10-year-olds being presented to local authority care services. Drug use by young people in care is higher and starts at a younger age than for children of the same age in the general population (DrugScope 2001). A major Longitudinal Study of Adolescent Health has been undertaken in the US. Data from 1995 to 2001 was collected from a large sample (14 333 subjects) of middle and high school students, assessed for health-related behaviour and attitudes. The most significant risk factors for later life alcohol misuse were involvement with other substances (i.e., cigarettes and illicit drugs) as well as having substance-using peers, delinquency and low religiosity. These risk factors all predicted several of the four problem use development stages (van den Bree 2005).

This work on adolescents in the US has been complemented by a study in the UK to assess the role of specific family factors on early alcohol use. This work supports the hypothesis that the characteristics of the family environment, experienced by children, provide an important perspective on adolescence, which should inform the development of intervention programmes and strategic policy (Harold 2005). Research by the same group, based at Cardiff University, indicates that, from the analysis of twin data, genetic factors accounted for 20 % of the variance in adolescent alcohol-related problems with another 47 % accounted for by familial environmental influences (Lifford et al., 2005). The outcome of high-risk substance misuse exposure in adolescence will depend on a range of factors, one of which is the individual's cognitive approach to coping. The availability of coping resources will impact on drug and alcohol relapse by 'reducing appraised stress in a relapse-risk situation', thereby decreasing the potential for a continuance of problematic substance misuse when active coping strategies are available, see Chapter 5. Additionally, these results highlight the importance of social resources which promote successful intervention outcomes (Myers et al. 1993).

SUBSTANCE MISUSE AND MENTAL HEALTH

Substance abuse and dependence and mental health problems frequently occur in the community, alcohol dependency being detected in 5 % of households and in 7 % of institutional populations. In a study of the homeless Farrell et al. (2003) found that over 21 % were alcohol dependent, and these individuals also had higher rates of tobacco and other drug dependencies. High rates of psychological problems are associated with heavy drinking and alcohol dependence. Psychiatric disorders often manifest before alcohol problems and are clinically independent disorders. Self-medication is another explanation for alcohol being used to alleviate psychiatric symptoms, which are possibly related to intoxication and withdrawal and are substance-induced mental health problems (Farrell *et al.* 2003).

In the Epidemiologic Catchment Area (ECA) study, one of the largest investigations of the prevalence of mental disorders ever conducted, Regier *et al.* (1990) found a high correlation between all mental health diagnoses and alcohol, anxiety and substance misuse. Kessler *et al.* (1994, 1997) carried out a national comorbidity study in the United States and showed that lifetime comorbidity was greater for alcohol dependence than for alcohol abuse, and comorbidity was more likely to occur in women than in men. Alcohol use and comorbidity, defined by DSMIV criteria, was found to co-occur with major psychiatric disorders. This study indicated that such alcohol-related psychiatric problems occur in more than 20 000 people in the US. Furthermore intravenous drug abusers often have comorbidities including Type 1 diabetes. Saunders *et al.* (2004) found that compared to the normal diabetes patients who did not abuse drugs, this group frequently omitted insulin injections, were underweight and often failed to attend outpatient clinics.

There is increasing evidence that participation in alcohol rehabilitation and other services as well as self-help groups was low in homeless alcoholic individuals, particularly those who have associated mental health disorders. In western Europe although the homeless are adequately supplied with food, clothes and shelter, frequently their mental health needs are neglected (Fichter and Quadflieg 1999).

The classification of clinical groups with complex needs is controversial. Hasegawa *et al.* (1991) have identified three clinical groups: primary depression, secondary depression and non-depressive alcoholism. In this study of 136 alcoholic inpatients depression in the present or past history was found in 33.8%; 9.5% were regarded as primary depression and 24% as secondary depression. Four subtypes of psychiatric comorbidity have been identified by Windle and Scheidt (2004), which were described as: mild course, polydrug, negative affect and chronic/antisocial, based on internal and external criteria. Based on external criteria, the polydrug subtype had the highest rate of family criminality, high-risk sexual behaviour and intravenous drug use; the negative affect subtype had the highest rate of childhood sexual abuse, attempted suicide and childhood homelessness; the chronic/antisocial personality (ASP) subtype had the most severe pattern of drinking and antisocial behaviour.

Anxiety and affective disorders were the main contributors to comorbidity in women. The predominant comorbidity disorders among men were substance use disorders, conduct disorder and antisocial personality disorder. In the British psychiatric morbidity survey although major mental illness is over-represented in homeless women, the majority do not suffer from major mental illness. Despite the severity of the stressors these women face, the large numbers escaping psychiatric disorders speak of their resilience and of the likelihood that important factors other than mental illness contribute to their homelessness (Smith *et al.* 1993).

Substance misuse and depression

Individuals with drinking problems frequently experience depression, which is often one of the reasons why they seek treatment. This condition is often linked with family history and is demonstrated by emotional lability. During in-depth interviews they will cry easily, and talk of the hopelessness of their lives. A proportion of problem drinkers have primary depression, which may predispose them to develop alcohol problems causing an exacerbation of the psychiatric condition. In the ECA study 66% of women were shown to have depression, which predated the alcohol abuse or dependence (Helzer and Pryzbeck 1988). Depressive symptoms are common during alcohol withdrawal, and following heavy consumption. Clinically significant levels of depression are found among inpatients with drinking problems during the early stages of admission (Brown and Schuckit 1988; Davidson 1995), but improvement usually occurs after two to three weeks of abstinence. However, depressive symptoms may persist or even emerge during abstinence, symptoms which should be monitored and treated appropriately.

Substance misuse and suicide

The complex association of alcohol dependence with suicidal behaviour is well established. Alcohol dependence is known to increase the risk for suicidal ideation, suicide attempts and completed suicide. However, this risk is modulated by a wide variety of factors including sociodemographic, clinical, treatment-related and life-situational characteristics as well as current drinking status and the effect of inebriation. Alcohol-dependent individuals are 60 to 100 times more likely to commit suicide than the general population. Alcohol dependence is also associated with a higher lifetime risk of suicide (7%) than either affective disorders (6%) or schizophrenia (4%) (Harris and Barraclough 1998). Anxiety disorders, a combination of anxiety and depressive disorders are also associated with a high risk of suicide behaviour. Multiple comorbidity disorders (depression and anxiety or personality disorders) appear to be associated with the greatest risk of suicidal behaviour (Driessen *et al.* 1998). Harmful and hazardous alcohol use is also implicated in suicidal behaviour in particular groups such as male adolescents and young men. In a five-year follow-up study of almost 50 000 Swedish male conscripts, born in 1950 and 1951, an association between alcohol abuse and suicidal behaviour was found in young and middle-aged men (Rossow *et al.* 1999). In this study, men abusing alcohol had an elevated

risk of attempted suicide, as well as completed suicide. This strong association between alcohol abuse and association with parasuicide persisted even
after controlling to psychiatric morbidity.

Pirkola *et al.* (2004) have proposed the following principles in the treatment of and management of alcohol-dependent subjects:

- suicidal threats or communication of alcohol-dependent subjects in emergency and other contacts should be taken seriously;

- other mental disorders should be well evaluated for and consequent treatment plan with follow-up assessed;

- appropriate and updated pharmacological treatment should focus on both
reducing the amount of drinking and treating symptoms of other mental
disorders;

- psychotherapeutic efforts should be focused on emerging symptoms of
both alcohol use and other mental disorders;

- known epidemiological and clinical risk factors, adverse life events in
particular, should be recognised and taken into account.

There are many explanations for the co-occurrence of suicidal behaviours
and alcohol/drug abuse among adolescents. In some cases, similar
precipitating factors (e.g., interpersonal arguments) precede both suicidal
behaviour and substance abuse. Underlying vulnerability factors such as
depression or impulsivity may increase the likelihood of both suicidal
behaviours and alcohol/drug abuse, additionally the consequences of self-
harm and substance-abusing behaviours such as relief from negative mood
state may be similar; the occurrence of either alcohol or suicidal behaviour
could increase the likelihood of the other outcome (Goldston 2004). From a
genetic perspective suicide attempts and alcoholism appear to be unrelated
to family background (Preuss *et al.* 2003).

Substance misuse and schizophrenia

'Dual diagnosis' is frequently used to describe individuals with coexistent
severe mental illness and substance abuse disorders. Regier *et al.* (1990)
reported a 3.8% prevalence of schizophrenia in people with alcohol disorders. Schizophrenics are three times more likely than the general population
to have an alcohol disorder and six times more likely to have another drug
disorder. There appears to be an increase in schizophrenics misusing drugs
over recent years. An explanation for this might be the greater availability
of drugs in the community, and also improved methods of ascertainment.
Substance misuse may increase in schizophrenics as a stress-related coping
mechanism to facilitate social interaction to offset depression, anxiety or
boredom. Psychotic substance users are more likely to be hostile and more

likely to be admitted to hospital as a result of a violent episode and being noncompliant with medication (Menezes *et al.* 1996). In the development of psychiatric disorders such as schizophrenia, alcohol misuse and drug misuse usually precede the onset of psychosis (Andreasson *et al.* 1987). Schizophrenics are more likely to become violent when consuming alcohol, violence being associated with intoxication or withdrawal effects. Personality changes are associated with prolonged use of substances.

Stigmatisation and exclusion are common in people with schizophrenic illnesses. These social responses are not just caused by a lack of information, prejudices and misconceptions, they are deeply rooted in our cultural tradition. Asmus Finzen referred to a 'second illness' caused by stigmatisation, which results from the negative consequences for the treatment and way of life of those affected. The poor social involvement, negative social attitudes and humiliating discrimination can undermine self-esteem, ability to cope and compliance, which can all mitigate against the recovery process and sustain the illness (Meise *et al.* 2001). Substance use disorders occur in approximately 40 to 50% of individuals with schizophrenia. An 'integrative affect–regulation model', proposed by Blanchard, suggests that this psychopathology results from the accumulation of individual differences in traits and responses to stress (Blanchard *et al.* 2000).

Substance misuse and personality disorders

Personality has many dimensions and is constituted by genetic, environmental and cultural factors. Studies of male alcoholics in treatment suggested they are antisocial, rebellious and impulsive individuals who have difficulty delaying gratification (Bates 1993). Often personality disorders either pre-date or follow the development of excessive alcohol use and are not unique to it. Zuckerman (1985) described a *sensational seeking* trait which had an inherited basis, expressed by high reactivity to stimulation. This was developed by Cloninger (1987) who used this aspect of personality, together with reward dependency and reward dependence, to develop a typology for classifying problematic alcohol users. This led to the description of a description of type I and type II alcoholics. Type II individuals began to drink before 25 years and had high levels of antisocial behaviour and criminality. Although this typology is still used there are major problems in applying this classification as reported by Otter *et al.* (1995).

Substance misuse and anxiety

The ECA study (see above) revealed that anxiety disorders affect more than 7% of adults in the US. It is estimated that about one-third of problem drinkers have significant anxiety problems. Alcohol problems can sometimes develop as a result of agoraphobia and social phobia and may reflect attempts at self-medication. This association with panic disorder is less clear, but individuals with alcohol dependence appear to have higher lifetime incidence of panic disorder, generalised anxiety disorders and social and social phobias compared to the general population. Alcohol withdrawal symptoms can mimic anxiety and panic disorder, and it is possible that a common neurochemical process underlies both (George *et al.* 1990). In a study by Johnson *et al.* (1998), individuals with alcohol dependency and anxiety disorder experience more severe alcohol withdrawal symptoms than non-anxious controls, although the two groups had similar drinking histories. Anxiety symptoms diminish in the early stages of abstinence, and continue to improve with prolonged abstinence.

Substance misuse and eating disorders

Loss of weight and general malnutrition, resulting from dietary neglect are frequently found in drinkers; on the other hand, excessive drinking can result in obesity, due to the high calorie content of the alcohol. There is increasing evidence that the specific eating disorders of anorexia nervosa and bulimia nervosa are associated with alcohol problems more than was once thought. Although higher rates of alcoholism have been found in first degree relatives of patients with anorexia and bulimia nervosa compared with relatives of their controls. There is some inconsistency in the literature in that Eckardt *et al.* (1998) found a 6.7% lifetime prevalence of alcohol problems among patients with anorexia and bulimia nervosa. However, in a 10-year follow-up study of the men with anorexia nervosa Halmi *et al.* (1991) found no significant relationship with drinking problems. There is general agreement that about 30% of women with drinking problems experience significant eating disorders. Individuals who overeat and have drinking problems may have a predisposition towards other impulse disorders such as self-mutilation, suicide and misuse of illicit or prescribed drugs and shoplifting (Lacy and Khatain 1993).

SUBSTANCE MISUSE AND NEUROCOGNITIVE DYSFUNCTION

The association between homelessness and cognitive dysfunction is, as might be expected, highly complex. Although there is a limited number of reports on this topic there is growing evidence that homeless people are significantly more impaired than the general population. Executive (global) cognitive impairment, concerned with the planning and control of behaviour, has been studied by Foulks *et al.* (1990), Seidman *et al.* (1997) and others. This aspect of brain function is essential for the cognitive flexibility required to learn new skills, change behaviour and break the cycle of destructive behaviours. There is very little information presently available to suggest that neurocognitive deficiency leads to homelessness or is a consequence of it, however, cognitive decline appears to be related to indices of homelessness. The relationship between homelessness and cognitive dysfunction is confounded by mental health problems, gender, education, stress and other poverty-related issues such as lack of employment and social isolation. However, the more specific influences of substance misuse, particularly alcohol, have been investigated extensively.

The use of stimulants such as cocaine and methamphetamine has been associated with neuropsychological deficits in stimulant abusers and alcoholics. However, it appears that the damaging effects of chronic stimulant abuse are independent and not necessarily additive with those of alcohol abuse. This is supported by the observation that singly addicted stimulant abusers show similar or greater neurocognitive impairments than individuals who abuse alcohol and stimulants concurrently (Lawton-Craddock *et al.* 2003).

Neurobehavioural deficits resulting from cocaine use are found mainly in executive function and impulsivity. These deficits mitigate against the cocaine abuser controlling and working towards discontinuing drug use. Cocaine and alcohol each selectively affect performance on different neurobehavioural tests. Bolla *et al.* (2000) found, in contrast to Lawton-Craddock *et al.* (2003), that the concomitant use of cocaine and alcohol may have additive negative effects on the brain as compared to the use of only one of these two substances. Whether or not alcohol and cocaine act independently or additively has yet to be resolved. However, a possible explanation for this enigmatic interrelationship may be due to alcohol's opposing actions on cerebrovascular effects brought on by stimulant abuse. Research into the mechanism of neuropsychological impairment in chronic abusers of CNS depressants, including alcohol, as well as opiates and possibly cocaine, especially when such substances are combined in a polydrug pattern of abuse, is in its infancy.

Miller (1985) has argued that appropriate assessments aimed at differentiating between acute drug effects and long-term stable deficits are important in care planning and the facilitation of the integration of different cognitive functions for effective problem solving. Drug abuse alone is unlikely to result in strongly focal or lateralised deficit patterns, in contrast to global, executive functioning which is central to the control of drug consumption.

ALCOHOL AND NEUROCOGNITIVE DEVELOPMENT

It is generally recognised that the most significant risk factor linked with neurocognitive deficits in the homeless is alcohol. The impact of this neurotoxic compound is greatly increased in people who are poorly nourished and have chaotic life styles. Alcohol dependence, alcoholic brain damage and related problems frequently begin in some individuals in the early development stages. The effects on the brain of cumulative damage, resulting from a series of insults that include stress-related events, increases an individual's vulnerability to further damage by changing behaviour, memory or encouraging malnutrition. All of these linked issues contribute to the vicious circle of events leading through alcohol misuse to dependence and alcohol-related brain damage (Bonner *et al.* 2003b).

Alcohol is one of the most common and important toxic substances for the developing foetal brain, its consumption during pregnancy can result in neurobehavioural disorders and mental retardation. Foetal alcohol syndrome (FAS) is a defined clinical syndrome which is caused by dysfunctions in the central nervous system, leading to severe and permanent consequence of maternal alcohol consumption, and which may predispose the individual to alcohol misuse/or damage in later life (Sokol 1980). FAS can occur without gross morphological defects normally associated with FAS. Preclinical research suggests that alcohol interferes with many developmental phases of brain growth, affecting essential molecular, neurochemical and cellular events involved in normal formation of the central nervous system. During development ethanol can interfere with cell proliferation, migration, growth and differentiation and may cause cell death. Exposure to ethanol during early embryogenesis can cause a reduction in the number of cells generated, including the neural stem cells (e.g. radial glia), induces abnormal cell migration, and in humans, drinking during this period is associated with a greater incidence of craniofacial defects and mental disabilities. Ethanol exposure causes a decreased proliferation of neural precursor cells *in vitro*, whereas the differentiation process is apparently unchanged, however, ethanol delays proliferation of neural precursor cells *in vitro* (Tabernero *et al.* 2005).

If alcohol exposure occurs later, when cells are differentiating and synapses are establishing, a reduction in the number of synapses formed may occur and cell death will follow. Alterations in both neurotrophic support and in the expression of cell adhesion molecules, which affect glial–neuronal interactions and cell survival are thought to be responsible for these effects. Experimental evidence indicates that alcohol disrupts radial glial and astroglial development leading to alterations in cell migration and neuronal survival and differentiation.

Regional differences in the brain's susceptibility to alcoholic damage have been found in clinical and neuroimaging techniques. Even within a particular region some cell populations are more vulnerable than others. Localised damage involves many systems including disruptions of protein synthesis, prostaglandins, gangliosides, hypoxia and free radical damage (Bonner *et al.* 2003a). The hippocampus, corpus callosum, neocortex and cerebellum are especially susceptible to alcohol and have been associated with the behavioural deficits. These tissue-damaging effects vary in severity depending on nutritional factors and antioxidants (Guerri 2005).

Postnatally the family environment can have significant negative influences on the developing child by inadequate parenting, nutrition, stress and abuse. Chronic stress and abuse, often reported in socially deprived families, result in the production of the stress hormone, cortisol, which can chronically suppress brain development due to damage to the region of the brain concerned with learning and memory (Kalin 1993). Stress in this early period is thought to lead to late life psychiatric problems (Teicher 2002).

Deficits in retrieval of verbal and nonverbal information and in visuospatial functioning are present in young people with histories of heavy drinking during early and middle adolescence. Alcohol-dependent adolescents differed in neuropsychological functioning on several scores in comparison with other adolescents. In tests of learning and discrimination recognition, excessive alcohol use was associated with poorer performance on verbal and nonverbal retention and poor visuospatial functioning was found in adolescents who were withdrawing from alcohol whereas lifetime alcohol withdrawal was associated with poorer retrieval of verbal and nonverbal information (Brown *et al.* 2000).

Recent studies indicate that alcohol exposure during adolescence may convey unique risks for subsequent neurocognitive deficits and problem drinking. Grobin *et al.* (2001) have demonstrated enhanced neurosteroid sensitisation in animals pretreated as adolescents supporting the proposal that adolescence is a period of unique sensitivity to the effects of both acute and chronic consumption of alcohol.

The development of adult social dysfunction is dependent not only on antisocial behaviour such as poor parenting and economic deprivation, but also on childhood nervousness and social isolation and other internalising disorders (Farrington 1993). Attention deficit hyperactivity disorder (ADHD) has frequently been diagnosed in children with FAS and other alcohol-related birth defects, leading to the possibility that alcohol is a priming factor in ADHD. Coles *et al.* (1997) found no clear distinctions on behavioural and neurocognitive measures between children with the physical characteristics associated with prenatal alcohol exposure and those with a diagnosis of ADHD – with those with ADHD performing more poorly on conventional tests sensitive to conduct disorder and attentional problems. These results suggested that the alcohol-affected children do not have the same neurocognitive and behavioural characteristics as children with a primary diagnosis of ADHD.

ALCOHOL AND NEUROCOGNITIVE DYSFUNCTION

In a study of mild to moderately alcohol-dependent high-functioning outpatients, Horner *et al.* (1999) found mild cognitive deficits were related to the amount of recent, but not lifetime, alcohol consumption. In more severely affected alcoholic patients, neurocognitive effects of alcohol consumption may be obscured by other medical or psychosocial factors. This is particularly the case in traumatic brain injury, which is often associated with alcohol-related accidents (Taylor *et al.* 2002). In this clinical group a hypermetabolic state involves a wide range of physiological responses relating to an acute stress response. Cortisol-related stress has a tissue-damaging effect on the brain as described in Chapter 5. This is partly manifested in poorer cognitive performance in patients with alcohol problems. In these patients the number of previous withdrawals, higher levels of alcohol consumption and higher cortisol levels during a recent withdrawal are associated with increased neuropsychological damage.

Cognitive impairment appears to be related to the impact of stress on the regulation of the hypothalamic–pituitary–adrenal axis (Errico *et al.* 2002), see Figure 5.2. Neurological disorders and degeneration are thought to be related to levels of acetaldehyde in the cortex and hippocampus. Acetaldehyde is formed from alcohol (see Figure 7.2) and is more toxic than alcohol and causes tissue damage, due to changes in neurotransmitters and receptors. Alcoholic brain damage is thought to result from oxidative damage to tissues, proteins and DNA, due to the toxic effects of acetaldehyde (Peters and Ward 1988). These molecular events impact on the functional capacity of the brain to process information.

Cognitive dysfunction has been demonstrated in the males, females and abstinent children of alcohol misusers who lack a P300 wave (Begleiter and Porjesz 1999; Hesselbrock *et al.* 2001; Rodriguez Holguin *et al.* 1999). These neuropsychological responses are indicative of frontal lobe problems in the children of alcoholic parents and might be due to genetic factors. Conversely dysfunction may originate from a combination of alcohol, nutritional and hormonal factors, which adversely affect pre-, peri- or postnatal development. Cognitive impairment in alcoholics frequently takes the form of frontal lobe dysfunction and may be relatively subtle, requiring a neuropsychological examination for diagnosis. Signs of cognitive impairment may precede those of alcohol related neurological disorders by more than ten years (Tuck and Jackson 1991).

Abnormalities of the corpus callosum (CC) range from subtle decrements in its size to partial and even complete agenesis, as seen in FAS. Prenatal exposure to alcohol is also known to result in neurocognitive deficits. The amount of CC displacement is correlated with impairment in verbal learning ability (Sowell *et al.* 2001). Both male and female adult alcoholics demonstrate deficits on tests of learning, memory, abstracting, problem solving, perceptual analysis and synthesis, speed of information processing and efficiency. From a clinical neurological perspective these deficits are equivalent to mild to moderate damage. Some recovery of function is found after 16 days and normal function can return after four to five years. In an ^{18}F-FDG PET study Wang *et al.* (1992) found increases in brain function predominantly within 16–30 days after abstinence. The largest increases occurred in the frontal cortex, but increases in function were also in parietal, temporal cortices. In females these structural-imaging studies indicated an increase in ventricular volume, sulcal widening and a reduction in hippocampus, brain volume and corpus callosum. Pathological damage in females was apparent after shorter drinking history than in males, who showed better recovery with abstinence. In neuropsychological assessments females performed worse than males with equivalent drinking histories. Behavioural measures such as depressive symptoms and neurocognitive performance and biological measures (e.g., event-related potentials), assessed at the end of treatment, provide a good indication of relapse in recovering alcoholics (Parsons 1998).

The Wernicke Korsakoff syndrome (WKS), caused by a combination of alcohol misuse and an absolute or relative deficiency of dietary vitamin B_1 (thiamine), is a major cause of brain damage in chronic alcoholism. There are many possible mechanisms responsible for thiamine deficiency-related neuronal cell death, these include impaired brain glucose oxidation, accumulation of brain lactate, mitochondrial dysfunction and region-selective neuronal cell death confined mainly to thalamus and brain stem (Butterworth 2005). A genetic susceptibility in the pathogenesis of WKS has been proposed since the late 1970s – very few genetic studies have been carried out on candidate markers to date. The genes, which are associated with the thiamine transporter proteins or enzymes and require thiamine as a cofactor, are possible candidate genes for WKS. Transketolase activity is reduced in Wernicke Korsakoff patients and a variant of the transketolase enzyme has been proposed to be associated with WKS (Guerrini and Thomson 2005).

Contemporary studies support the hypothesis of a continuum of neurocognitive deficits ranging from the severe deficits found in Korsakoff patients to moderate deficits found in alcoholics and moderate to mild deficits in heavy social drinkers (more than 21 drinks/week). Genetic and environmental influences result in individual differences in neurocognitive deficits, which vary in occurrence and magnitude. A review of nutritional issues in the socially excluded will follow in the next chapter.

REFERENCES

Andreasson, S., P. Allebeck, A. Engstrom and U. Rydberg (1987). Cannabis and schizophrenia. A longitudinal study of Swedish conscripts. *Lancet*, **2**(8574), 1483–6.
Bates, M. E. (1993). Recent developments in alcoholism: psychology. *Recent Developments in Alcohol*, **11**, 45–72.
Begleiter, H. and B. Porjesz (1999). What is inherited in the predisposition toward alcoholism? A proposed model. *Alcoholism – Clinical and Experimental Research*, **23**(7), 1125–35.

Blanchard, J. J., S. A. Brown, W. P. Horan and A. R. Sherwood (2000). Substance use disorders in schizophrenia: review, integration, and a proposed model. *Clinical Psychology Review*, **20**(2), 207–34.

Bolla, K. I., F. R. Funderburk and J. L. Cadet (2000). Differential effects of cocaine and alcohol on neurocognitive performance. *Neurology*, **54**(12), 2285–92.

Bonner, A. B., S. Dalwai, J. S. Marway and V. R. Preedy (2003a). Acute exposure to the nutritional toxin alcohol reduces brain protein synthesis in vivo. *Metabolism*, **52**(4), 389–96.

Bonner, A. B., A. D. Thomson and C. H. Cook (2003b). Alcohol, nutrition and brain function. In: Watson R. R., V. R. Preedy and W. R. Watson (eds), *Nutrition and Alcohol*. Boca Raton, Florida: CRC Press.

Brown, S. A. and M. A. Schuckit (1988). Changes in depression among abstinent alcoholics. *Journal of Studies on Alcohol*, **49**(5), 412–17.

Brown, S. A., S. F. Tapert, E. Granholm and D. C. Delis (2000). Neurocognitive functioning of adolescents: effects of protracted alcohol use. *Alcoholism – Clinical and Experimental Research*, **24**, 164.

Butterworth, R. (2005). Mitochondrial dysfunction, oxidative/nitrosative stress and selective neural cell death due to thiamine deficiency. *Alcohol and Alcoholism*, **40**(Supplement 1), S12.

Cloninger, C. R. (1987). A systematic method for clinical description and classification of personality variants. A proposal. *Archives of General Psychiatry*, **44**(6), 573–88.

Coles, C. D., K. A. Platzman, C. L. Raskind-Hood, R. T. Brown, A. Falek and I. E. Smith (1997). A comparison of children affected by prenatal alcohol exposure and attention deficit, hyperactivity disorder. *Alcoholism – Clinical and Experimental Research*, **21**(1), 150–61.

Davidson, K. M. (1995). Diagnosis of depression in alcohol dependence: changes in prevalence with drinking status. *British Journal of Psychiatry*, **166**(2), 199–204.

Driessen, M., C. Veltrup, J. Weber, U. John, T. Wetterling and H. Dilling (1998). Psychiatric co-morbidity, suicidal behaviour and suicidal ideation in alcoholics seeking treatment. *Addiction*, **93**(6), 889–94.

DrugScope (2001). *Social Exclusion and Reintegration*. London, DrugScope.

Eckardt, M. J., S. E. File, G. L. Gessa, K. A. Grant, C. Guerri, P. L. Hoffman, *et al.* (1998). Effects of moderate alcohol consumption on the central nervous system. *Alcoholism – Clinical and Experimental Research*, **22**(5), 998–1040.

EMCDDA (2002). *Update and Complete Analysis of Drug Use, Consequences and Correlates amongst Minorities*. Volume 1 Synthesis. European Monitoring Centre for Drugs and Drug Addiction (EMCDDA).

Errico, A. L., A. C. King, W. R. Lovallo and O. A. Parsons (2002). Cortisol dysregulation and cognitive impairment in abstinent male alcoholics. *Alcoholism – Clinical and Experimental Research*, **26**(8), 1198–204.

Farrell, M., S. Howes, C. Taylor, G. Lewis, R. Jenkins, P. Bebbington *et al.* (2003). Substance misuse and psychiatric comorbidity: an overview of the OPCS National Psychiatric Morbidity Survey. *International Review of Psychiatry*, **15**(1–2), 43–9.

Farrington, D. P. (1993). Childhood origins of teenage antisocial behaviour and adult social dysfunction. *Journal of the Royal Society of Medicine*, **86**(1), 13–17.

Fichter, M. and N. Quadflieg (1999). Alcoholism in homeless men in the mid-nineties: results from the Bavarian Public Health Study on homelessness. *European Archives of Psychiatry and Clinical Neuroscience*, **249**(1), 34–44.

Foulks, E. F., W. G. McCown, M. Duckworth and P. B. Sutker (1990). Neuropsychological testing of homeless mentally ill veterans. *Hospital and Community Psychiatry*, **41**(6), 672–4.

George, D. T., D. J. Nutt, B. A. Dwyer and M. Linnoila (1990). Alcoholism and panic disorder: is the comorbidity more than coincidence? *Acta Psychiatrica Scandinavica*, **81**(2), 97–107.

Goldston, D. B. (2004). Conceptual issues in understanding the relationship between suicidal behavior and substance use during adolescence. *Drug and Alcohol Dependence*, **76**, Supplement, S79–91.

Gossop, M., D. Stewart, S. Treacy and J. Marsden (2002). A prospective study of mortality among drug misusers during a 4-year period after seeking treatment. *Addiction*, **97**(1), 39–47.

Grobin, A. C., D. B. Matthews and D. Montoya (2001). Age-related differences in neurosteroid potentiation of muscimol-stimulated 36Cl(-) flux following chronic ethanol treatment. *Neuroscience*, **105**, 547.

Guerri, C. (2005). Ethanol toxicity in the developing brain. *Alcohol and Alcoholism*, 40.

Guerrini, I. and A. D. Thomson (2005). The genetic susceptibility to the Wernicke Korsakoff syndrome. *Alcohol and Alcoholism*, **40**(Supplement 1), S12.

Halmi, K. A., E. Eckert, P. Marchi, V. Sampugnaro, R. Apple and J. Cohen (1991). Comorbidity of psychiatric diagnoses in anorexia nervosa. *Archives of General Psychiatry*, **48**(8), 712–18.

Harold, G. (2005). Family factors and early adolescent alcohol use. *Alcohol and Alcoholism*, 40(Supplement 1), S05.

Hasegawa, K., H. Mukasa, Y. Nakazawa, H. Kodama and K. Nakamura (1991). Primary and secondary depression in alcoholism – clinical features and family history. *Drug and Alcohol Dependency*, **27**(3), 275–81.

Harris, E. C. and B. Barraclough (1998). Excess mortality of mental disorder. *British Journal of Psychiatry*, **173**, 11–53.

Helzer, J. E. and T. R. Pryzbeck (1988). The co-occurrence of alcoholism with other psychiatric disorders in the general population and its impact on treatment. *Journal of Studies on Alcohol*, **49**(3), 219–24.

Hesselbrock, V., H. Begleiter, B. Porjesz, S. O'Connor and L. Bauer (2001). P300 event-related potential amplitude as an endophenotype of alcoholism – evidence from the collaborative study on the genetics of alcoholism. *Journal of Biomedical Science*, **8**(1), 77–82.

Horner, M. D., L. R. Waid, D. E. Johnson, P. K. Latham and R. F. Anton (1999). The relationship of cognitive functioning to amount of recent and lifetime alcohol consumption in outpatient alcoholics. *Addictive Behaviors*, **24**(3), 449–53.

Johnson, T. J., J. Wendel and S. Hamilton (1998). Social anxiety, alcohol expectancies, and drinking-game participation. *Addictive Behaviors*, **23**(1), 65–79.

Kalin, N. H. (1993). The neurobiology of fear. *Scientific American*, **268**, 94.

Kessler, R. C., K. A. McGonagle, S. Zhao, C. B. Nelson, M. Hughes, S. Eshleman, et al. (1994). Lifetime and 12-month prevalence of DSM-III-R psychiatric disorders in the United States. Results from the National Comorbidity Survey. *Archives of General Psychiatry*, **51**(1), 8–19.

Kessler, R. C., R. M. Crum, L. A. Warner, C. B. Nelson, J. Schulenberg and J. C. Anthony (1997). Lifetime co-occurrence of DSM-III-R alcohol abuse and dependence with other psychiatric disorders in the National Comorbidity Survey. *Archives of General Psychiatry*, **54**(4), 313–21.

Lacy, T. J. and K. G. Khatain (1993). Obsessive compulsive disorder manifesting as demonic attack. *Journal of Clinical Psychiatry*, **54**(10), 398.

Lawton-Craddock, A., S. J. Nixon and R. Tivis (2003). Cognitive efficiency in stimulant abusers with and without alcohol dependence. *Alcoholism – Clinical and Experimental Research*, **27**(3), 457–64.

Lifford, K. J., K. H. S., Frances Rice, T. Fowler, A. Thapar and M. B. M. van den Bree (2005). A twin study of alcohol use and school-related factors. *Alcohol and Alcoholism*, **40**(Supplement 1), S09–04.

March, J. C., E. Oviedo-Joekes and M. Romero (2006). Drugs and social exclusion in ten European cities. *European Journal of Addict Research*, **12**(1), 33–41.

Meise, U., H. Sulzenbacher and H. Hinterhuber (2001). Attempts to overcome the stigma of schizophrenia. *Fortschr Neurol Psychiatr*, **69**(Supplement 2), S75–80.

Menezes, P. R., S. Johnson, G. Thornicroft, J. Marshall, D. Prosser, P. Bebbington, *et al.* (1996). Drug and alcohol problems among individuals with severe mental illness in south London. *British Journal of Psychiatry*, **168**(5), 612–19.

Miller, L. (1985). Neuropsychological assessment of substance abusers: review and recommendations. *Journal of Substance Abuse Treatment*, **2**(1), 5–17.

Myers, M. G., S. A. Brown and M. A. Mott (1993). Coping as a predictor of adolescent substance abuse treatment outcome. *Journal of Substance Abuse*, **5**(1), 15–29.

Neale, J. and C. Kennedy (2002). Good practice towards homeless drug users: research evidence from Scotland. *Health and Social Care in the Community*, **10**(3), 196–205.

Otter, C., J. Huber and A. B. Bonner (1995). Cloninger's tri-dimensional personality questionnaire: reliability in an English sample. *Personality and Individual Differences*, **18**, 471–80.

Parsons, O. A. (1998). Neurocognitive deficits in alcoholics and social drinkers: a continuum? *Alcoholism – Clinical and Experimental Research*, **22**(4), 954–61.

Peters, T. J. and R. J. Ward (1988). Role of acetaldehyde in the pathogenesis of alcoholic liver disease. *Molecular Aspects of Medicine*, **10**(2), 179–90.

Pirkola, S. P., K. Suominen and E. T. Isometsa (2004). Suicide in alcohol-dependent individuals: epidemiology and management. *CNS Drugs*, **18**(7), 423–36.

Preuss, U. W., M. A. Schuckit, T. L. Smith, G. P. Danko, K. K. Bucholz, M. N. Hesselbrock, *et al.* (2003). Predictors and correlates of suicide attempts over 5 years in 1237 alcohol-dependent men and women. *American Journal of Psychiatry*, **160**(1), 56–63.

Regier, D. A., W. E. Narrow and D. S. Rae (1990). The epidemiology of anxiety disorders: the Epidemiologic Catchment Area (ECA) experience. *Journal of Psychiatric Research*, **24**(Supplement 2), 3–14.

Ribeiro, M., J. Dunn, R. Laranjeira and R. Sesso (2004). High mortality among young crack cocaine users in Brazil: a 5-year follow-up study. *Addiction*, **99**(9), 1133–35.

Rodriguez Holguin, S., M. Corral and F. Cadaveira (1999). Event-related potentials elicited by a visual continuous performance task in children of alcoholics. *Alcohol*, **19**(1), 23–30.

Rossow, I., A. Romelsjo and H. Leifman (1999). Alcohol abuse and suicidal behaviour in young and middle aged men: differentiating between attempted and completed suicide. *Addiction*, **94**(8), 1199–207.

Saunders, S. A., J. Democratis, J. Martin and I. A. Macfarlane (2004). Intravenous drug abuse and Type 1 diabetes: financial and healthcare implications. *Diabetic Medicine*, **21**(12), 1269–73.

Seidman, L. J., J. M. Goldstein, J. M. Goodman, D. Koren, W. M. Turner, S. V. Faraone, *et al.* (1997). Sex differences in olfactory identification and Wisconsin Card Sorting performance in schizophrenia: relationship to attention and verbal ability. *Biological Psychiatry*, **42**(2), 104–15.

SEU (2001). *Preventing Social Exclusion*. London, Social Exclusion Unit.

Smith, E. M., C. S. North and E. L. Spitznagel (1993). Alcohol, drugs, and psychiatric comorbidity among homeless women: an epidemiologic study. *Journal of Clinical Psychiatry*, **54**(3), 82–7.

Sokol, R. J. (1980). Alcohol and spontaneous abortion. *Lancet*, **2**(8203), 1079.

Sowell, E. R., S. N. Mattson, P. M. Thompson, T. L. Jernigan, E. P. Riley and A. W. Toga (2001). Mapping callosal morphology and cognitive correlates: effects of heavy prenatal alcohol exposure. *Neurology*, **57**(2), 235–44.

Tabernero M., M. Sancho-Tello and J. Renau Piqueras (2005). Ethanol delays proliferation of neural precursor cells in vitro. *Alcohol and Alcoholism*, **40**(Supplement 1), P035.

Taylor, A. N., H. E. Romeo, A. V. Beylin, D. L. Tio, S. U. Rahman and D. A. Hovda (2002). Alcohol consumption in traumatic brain injury: attenuation of TBI-induced hyperthermia and neurocognitive deficits. *Journal of Neurotrauma*, **19**(12), 1597–608.

Teicher, M. H. (2002). Scars that won't heal: the neurobiology of child abuse. *Scientific American*, **286**, 68.

Tuck, R. R. and M. Jackson (1991). Social, neurological and cognitive disorders in alcoholics. *Medical Journal of Australia*, **155**(4), 225–9.

van den Bree, M. B. M. (2005). Combining research approaches to advance our understanding of drug addiction. *Current Psychiatry Reports*, **7**, 125–32.

Wang, G. J., N. D. Volkow, R. Hitzemann, Z. H. Oster, C. Roque and V. Cestaro (1992). Brain imaging of an alcoholic with MRI, SPECT, and PET. *American Journal of Physiology*, **7**(3–4), 194–8.

Windle, M. and D. M. Scheidt (2004). Alcoholic subtypes: are two sufficient? *Addiction*, **99**(12), 1508–19.

Zuckerman, M. (1985). Sensation seeking, mania, and monoamines. *Neuropsychobiology*, **13**(3), 121–8.

CHAPTER 9

NUTRITION IN VULNERABLE GROUPS

NUTRITION AND SOCIAL DEPRIVATION

Social deprivation is associated with under-nutrition and obesity, both of which have adverse short- and long-term health effects. Public health strategies frequently address both under-nutrition and obesity in children and adolescents in response to the increases in eating disorders (anorexia and bulimia nervosa), which are appearing at increasingly younger ages. These problems affect predominantly adolescent females 12 to 25 years of age (Martin *et al.* 1999). Much less attention has been paid to related problems in adults, which are important in the expression of mental health disorders and are linked to cognitive functioning (Barnes 1976, Armstrong 2003). The problems of malnutrition are not restricted to developing countries, these problems have been reported in the UK and other countries in the western world (Stitt *et al.* 1994; Che 2001; Fletcher 2004).

Vulnerable groups, particularly affected by poor nutrition, include the homeless, young mothers (Botting *et al.* 1998), the elderly (Pirlich 2001), those at risk of mental health problems (Garmezy and Streitman 1974), those with cardiovascular problems (Lee and Cubbin 2002; Kelleher 2004), those with chronic physical illness (Gordon 2002) and those in the criminal justice system (Olubodun *et al.* 1996). There is increasing concern about alcohol and drug misuse, exacerbated by poor nutrition and associated with social deprivation.

Malnutrition has been defined as a disturbance of form or function due to lack of (or excess of) calories or of one or more nutrients (DHSS 1972). Malnutrition is an inappropriate reduction in lean body mass, which is lower than expected for the person's age, height, generic base and level of activity. It is an imbalance of energy and/or deficiency in one or more nutrients (proteins, vitamins, or trace elements), resulting in a reduction of organ mass and organ function. Interestingly, the brain is spared from this reduction due to a range of neuroprotective mechanisms, which ensure that this important neural control centre is protected in adverse nutritional and other environmental conditions. Chronic malnutrition leading to low protein intake, poor food choice and protein depletion may be due to unavailability of food but also may result from disease or medical conditions. Reduced food intake can result from disease, mental health problems (e.g. depression) and drugs, either used therapeutically or as a lifestyle choice, and alcohol abuse. In the case of disease, malnourished patients have high infection rates, poor wound healing and other complications which increase their stay in hospital. Increased energy is expended in hypermetabolic states such as trauma or surgery (Shizgal 1983).

Socially excluded populations are highly heterogeneous and difficult to study. However, the problems of inadequate family and social support mechanisms and the maladaptive life styles would be expected to result in increased incidences in type II diabetes mellitus, cardiovascular disease, diseases of the alimentary tract, dental cavities, cancer of mouth and pharynx, stomach/gastritis, gastric carcinoma, malabsorption syndrome, disorders of the liver and gall bladder and alcoholic liver disease. Additionally, a wide range of developmental problems is linked to nutritionally related disorders of the nervous system. Nutritional deficits impact on the growth and development of the brain, which increase the person's vulnerability to mental health problems including depression, senile dementia, Alzheimer disease and psychotic disorders such as schizophrenia. These clinical aspects of nutrition have been reviewed by Dickerson and Lee (1988).

NUTRITION AND THE HOMELESS

There is a limited number of studies which have considered the nutritional status of socially excluded people, these have mainly focused on the street homeless with less attention paid to other groups of homeless and the socially marginalised. A UK government report in 2004 (ODPM 2004) indicated that 95 060 households were homeless and living in temporary accommodation such as hostels, women's refuges, bed and breakfast hotels and other forms of temporary housing. However, it has been estimated that there are as many as two million 'unofficial homeless' in the UK.

The lack of nutritional studies of this significant group of people in the UK is partly due to the transient and heterogeneous nature of socially marginalised people and also the lack of funding to support this work. The observable tip of this demographic iceberg can be seen on the streets, in attendance at day centres and soup runs (Carillo et al. 1990). However, engaging with such people is difficult and obtaining valid information about their nutritional status virtually impossible. This heterogeneous group will consist of those who have been recently made homeless and the long-term homeless presenting with a range of mental health and substance abuse problems. An example from the literature where 'the homeless' was regarded, inappropriately, as a homogeneous group is that of Luder et al.

(1989), in the US, who collected nutritional data from users of two drop-in centres, bed and breakfast accommodation and two long-term accommodation units for previously homeless and psychiatrically ill people. The data was aggregated and the whole data set was analysed as one homogeneous group, preventing any investigation of the many confounding factors likely to affect the link between nutrition and successful rehabilitation.

Clearly it is important to understand the specific needs of those who are briefly homeless, due to some personal or family crisis, compared to the chronically homeless, some of whom might have periods of stable housing but are unable to sustain their tenancy. In both cases the individual's ability to function and be rehabilitated into the community will depend upon a range of physical and mental health factors, as outlined in Chapters 4 and 5. In these discussions the role of the brain in maintaining physical and mental homeostasis is paramount. In the case of physiological functioning, the activity of the endocrine, circulatory, immune and other systems is dependent on the interaction of specific brain regions such as the hypothalamus, which has the capacity to monitor and produce a range of regulatory factors. By means of a complex set of biochemical feedback reactions physiological homeostasis is maintained. Mental health functions are reliant on this physiological substrate for the supply of energy to maintain brain function and the availability of neurotransmitter precursors and cofactors needed for the functioning of neurons, essential for the management of information and production of behaviour (see Chapter 7).

Evidence of nutritional risk in a population of homeless adults has been reported by Silliman (1998) and in a study of 97 men (aged 18–72 years) visiting an emergency night shelter in Paris, Darmon *et al.* (2001) found that 54% had been homeless for more than 18 months. In this group 82% were smokers and 53% were regular and/or excessive drinkers. Nutritional status was measured using the BMI, which was shifted towards low values. The authors of this study found that the percentage of malnourished persons was four times higher than in the wider community. Intakes of potassium, calcium, zinc, vitamins B1, B2 and niacin were lower than European Population Reference Intakes but only the mean intake of vitamin B1 was significantly lower. The mean total energy intake was 2376 kcal and included a high and highly variable percentage of energy derived from alcohol found in 12% of the population. In this high drinking subgroup, the mean daily ethanol intake was 90 g and there was a significant negative correlation between ethanol and non-alcoholic energy intakes.

Homeless persons eat foods from community and voluntary-funded shelters, fast-food restaurants, delicatessens and refuse bins. In a survey of the adequacy of the dietary intake, the quality of shelter meals, Luder *et al.* (1990) measured a range of objective clinical parameters indicative of nutritional status in a heterogeneous group of urban homeless persons.

The group comprised mentally ill persons, alcohol and illicit drug users and temporarily unemployed persons. Although 90 % in this study reported that they obtained enough to eat, a low dietary adequacy score, based on the basic four food groups, indicated that the quality of their diets was inadequate. Shelter meals and diet records showed a high level of saturated fat and cholesterol. Serum cholesterol levels above the desirable limit of 5.17 mmol/l (200 mg) were observed in 79 subjects (82 %). In addition to a prevalence of hypertension and obesity (observed in 37 subjects (39 %)), these homeless persons were at high risk for development or worsening of cardiovascular disease. The conclusion from this study was that homeless persons who obtain meals at shelters are getting enough to eat. However, the shelter meals should be modified to meet the nutritional needs and dietary prescriptions of the large number of clients who suffer from various health disorders.

In the UK it has been reported that 30 % of all families with children spend less on food than is required to provide a diet which complies with the Department of Health's dietary recommended values (DRVs) (Stitt *et al.* 1994). The authors of this report point out that very little, if any, research has investigated the nutritional implications of a particularly extreme form of nutritional deficiency linked to material deprivation and homelessness. Their study reviewed the dietary intake of a number of homeless families in Liverpool, homelessness being defined as living in bed and breakfast accommodation. The study found that the families have inadequate cooking facilities and depend upon welfare benefits when purchasing their food. The results indicate that, in every single case, the dietary intake of these homeless families fell substantially short of the government's nutritional guidelines and is, without doubt, unhealthy in the extreme (Stitt *et al.* 1994). Homeless people with mental health problems are particularly at risk from nutritional deficiencies, see Chapters 6 and 7.

HOMELESS WOMEN

The role of women in childbirth, child rearing and their central role in the family presents important nutritional issues which become even more critical in the case of those who are homeless and socially deprived. The reproductive cycle of a woman includes nine months of pregnancy, and becomes extended beyond this time when the breast takes over from the placenta in providing nutrition for the newborn. A woman's ability to lactate is nutritionally significantly more demanding than that of bearing a foetus *in utero*. Nevertheless, pregnancy involves high physiological stress to the mother due to the increases in metabolism required for the production of new tissue in the placenta, foetal membranes, the foetus and mammary glands. A mother's ability to support these physiological demands depends not only on her nutritional status during pregnancy but also on her diet prior to conception (Thomson and Hytten 1973). Specific disorders such as obesity and hypertension provide complications in pregnancy, however, attention is also needed for the disadvantaged on low incomes or in extreme poverty or deprived conditions such as being without a home.

Pregnant homeless women present a number of challenges to health and social care providers. They are at risk for a variety of illnesses that could affect their pregnancies, including sexually transmitted diseases and substance abuse. Poor access to health care, inadequate prenatal care, poor nutrition and poor housing cause these women to suffer poor birth outcomes. They are more likely to deliver low birth weight infants and have higher rates of infant mortality. This heterogeneous group often contains pregnant adolescents and women in homeless families (Beal and Redlener 1995). Birth weight has an important influence on health and survival of the infant. Women who live in environmentally and economically deprived conditions give birth to a high incidence of low birth weight infants. Low birth weight is associated with inadequate maternal food intake which results in impaired foetal growth and shortened length of gestation, exacerbated by multiple pregnancies, poor hygiene and low socio-economic status.

Drake (1992) collected data on the nutrient intake and nutritional status of 96 single mothers and their 192 dependent children who had been displaced from their homes. This information on the dietary adequacy of a newly identified subgroup of homeless persons, single women and their dependent children, indicated that once situated in temporary housing, the women believed that they were receiving sufficient food. However, a nutrient analysis found that women in all age groups were consuming less than 50% of the 1989 recommended dietary allowances (RDA) for iron, magnesium, zinc and folic acid. Adults were consuming less than 50% of the RDA for calcium. The type and amounts of fats consumed were in higher than desirable quantities for a significant number of subjects of all ages. The health risk factors of iron deficiency anaemia, obesity and hypercholesterolemia were prevalent. These findings indicate a need to examine and remedy nutrient intake deficiencies among single women who are heads of household and their dependent children in temporary housing situations. Diet-related conditions found included low nutrient intakes that may affect child growth and development, risk factors associated with chronic disease and lack of appropriate foods and knowledge of food preparation methods in shelter situations.

For some women with children, alcohol and other drug use may be an important risk factor for homelessness because it may interfere with a woman's capacity to compete for scarce resources such as housing, employment or services (Robertson 1991). Women and children are the fastest growing segment of the homeless population, unfortunately there is a lack of research examining their nutrition status. Oliveira and Goldberg (2002) have reviewed the limited literature in order to increase an understanding of this important biological dimension and inform the development of effective strategies. For more information on nutrition in children, breast-feeding and the problems of children with a predisposition to obesity and anorexia, see Chapters 2, 6 and 7 in Dickerson and Lee (1988).

NUTRITION IN THE ELDERLY

Malnutrition in the elderly is brought about by changes in social, physical and economic circumstances. Alterations in life style, social networking and the increasing incidence of disease and disabilities lead to a modification of dietary intake, absorption and metabolism of nutrients occurring particularly in the eighth decade. Although restriction of food intake has been shown to extend the life span in laboratory rats (Berg and Simms 1965; McCay *et al.* 1989), increased life span is accompanied by increases in the incidence of age-related diseases (Ross *et al.* 1983). This observation is also found in humans (Williamson *et al.* 1964). Nutritional factors influence not only growth and development (see Chapter 3) but also the process of ageing of the mature individual. In contrast to studies in animals it is difficult, in elderly humans, to distinguish between the effects of nutritional factors that are significant in old age and those that have influenced nutritional status in the early years of development.

Age-related changes in nutritional demand are associated with physiological changes such as a reduction in cardiac output and efficiency of oxygen transport around the body. Low levels of circulating nutrients, in this age group, might represent subclinical malnutrition, however, what is clear is that homeostatic control mechanisms become increasingly impaired. This disturbance of physiological balance leads to vulnerabilities in the elderly, resulting from medical and environmental hazards and a resulting inability to respond appropriately to the changing inner and external world. The appearance of malnutrition in the elderly may result from the stress of pathological processes in those individuals whose nutrition is marginally adequate. Disease and disability are increasingly prevalent after 75 years and the resulting reduced capacity for exercise. To overcome the effects of disability an individual must expend more energy than normally required to perform specific tasks. With a balanced diet, dietary intake required to meet energy expenditure in old people who maintain their activities will normally have an adequate nutritional intake. However, a reduction in physical activity, particularly in the housebound, may result in an insufficient intake of nutrients (Exton-Smith 1972).

Prevalence of nutritional deficiencies

The DHSS (1972) definition of malnutrition includes both obesity and under-nutrition. The former is a problem in old age, and is more common in women than men after 75 years, usually the result of long-standing faulty eating habits. Under-nutrition, on the other hand, results from environmental and physical factors which become important in later life. During the last 30 years there appears to be very little change from the DHSS nutrition surveys of the elderly in the UK, in 1972, which indicated malnutrition in 3% of the population over 65 years. Finch (1998) found that in independent older people 3% of men and 6% of women are underweight, and in residential and nursing homes, these figures rise to 16% and 15%, respectively. These nutrition problems include protein calorie malnutrition (PCM), iron deficiency and vitamin deficiencies. In a five-year follow up of this study the proportion malnourished had increased to 7%, and prevalence was twice as high in those over the age of 80 compared to those aged 70–79 years. These problems become exacerbated when acute medical care is considered, in that 30–50% of patients, when admitted to hospital, have been recorded with PCM. Of these patients, 25–30% will develop malnutrition during their hospital stay, and as many as 69% will undergo declining nutritional status during their hospital stay (Reilly *et al.* 1988). Exton-Smith (1971) has summarised the main causes of nutritional deficiencies in the elderly, see Table 9.1.

Social isolation is common in many old people living alone. These people frequently have lost interest in life and neglect food preparation, and what food is taken is usually in the form of snacks. The Stockport survey of social needs of the over 60s indicated that dietary intake was related to the number of outside interests. Those who eat at clubs, in the company of others, had higher dietary intakes (Brockington and Lampert 1967).

Table 9.1   The main causes of nutritional deficiencies in the elderly.

Primary	Secondary
Ignorance	Impaired appetite
Social isolation	Masticatory inefficiency
Physical disability	Malabsorption
Mental disturbance	Alcoholism
Iatrogenic	Drugs
Poverty	Increased requirements

Source: Reproduced with permission from Exton-Smith, A. N. (1971). Maintenance of health in old age. *Transactions of the Medical Society of London*, **87**, 175–84.

Malnutrition is greatest in older people with psychiatric disorders (Stokoe 1965). Those suffering from chronic brain syndrome and confusional states are frequently malnourished, but the most conspicuous association is found in those with depressive illness, which leads to a lack of motivation to obtain, to cook, even in some cases, to eat food. Lack of money can lead to a diet which is dull, monotonous and tasteless. In the winter months many old people must choose between spending money on food or fuel. Old people, who can supplement their income from savings or from part-time earnings, have better diets than those whose only income is the state pension.

Excessive alcohol intake can result in reduced nutritional status, when the calorie needs are derived mainly from this source (see Chapter 8). This can result in impaired folic acid metabolism and the consequential mega-loblastic anaemia. Other drugs such as barbiturates, including anticonvul-sant and antipsychotic medications, cause malnutrition. A range of primary and secondary factors combine in a complex way to provide a wide range of individual vulnerabilities. Frequently these factors are interrelated, for example limited mobility, loneliness, social isolation and depression are all found in the elderly who are housebound. Such individuals are particularly liable to malnutrition.

Many countries have funded nutritional community programmes (Dodds and Melnik 1993) but these programmes give inadequate support for certain groups of elders, including those who are socially impaired and homeless and members of ethnic and other minority groups. Balsam and Rogers (1991) have reviewed the issues involved in supporting elders in greatest social and economic need. They suggest that reaching all of these elders with community services is not only praiseworthy but also, using innovative models, is clearly achievable. Although specific health professions such as community/district nurses have an important role to play (Strasser *et al.* 1991) there is a need for those working in the wide range of statutory and non-statutory services to be vigilant for vulnerable people who might be in need of dietary support. Nutritional supplementation in pregnant women, as suggested by Dickerson and Lee (1988), and other accessible groups is common practice but the evidence provided in the foregoing sections of this chapter suggests an important need for screening and assessment for other vulnerable groups, especially those who are socially isolated and/or homeless.

ASSESSING AND MONITORING NUTRITIONAL STATUS IN THE COMMUNITY

Poor nutrition is a significant clinical and public health problem in the community with the wider associations with health including poverty, social isolation and deprivation all exacerbating its incidence. It is frequently unde-tected and untreated. Effective nutritional screening is needed to reduce the prevalence of poor nutrition but barriers to implementation do exist. Working with health and social care staff to identify barriers that prevent the effective adoption of nutritional screening is key to ensuring that appropriate nutritional action always occurs in a timely manner. Profiling the local community helps to give a clearer overview of the high-risk population groups and provides robust evidence, which helps the process of identifying priorities for action (Todorovic 2004).

Although the home environment is the most appropriate place for the nutritional support of children and young adults, this is often poorly managed, can be of a transitory and changing nature and frequently is highly stressful, if not abusive (Perry and McLaren 2004). This provides a rationale for the development of community feeding programmes. In addressing nutritional needs in the community it is important to follow up the interventions with repeat surveys and modify the intervention in relation to the observed trends (Wrieden 2004). The main aims of nutritional assessment should be to:

- Define nutritional status at a particular time and evaluate the adequacy of recent nutrient intake.

- Detect overt and subclinical malnutrition and identify individuals requiring support.

- Provide guidelines on the relative amounts of nutrients required.

- Monitor, by repeated assessment, the effectiveness of nutritional support.

In addition to physical examinations and dietary history taking, there is a wide range of biochemical, anthropometric and immunological approaches that could be employed. Traditionally dieticians use dietary diaries and anthropometric measures to determine nutritional status. There are a number of methodological problems with these approaches, which are confounded when working with people with complex needs. The main problems relate to the validity of these tools in transient, often chaotic populations who have poor memory recall, and the community location of such observations mitigates against a controlled standardised environment for collection of the data. Additionally, intentional misreporting of food consumption has been reported in women (Lara *et al.* 2004).

Clinical examinations should be undertaken by trained personnel who may detect physical signs of nutritional deficiency which may or may not be linked to some underlying disease process. The person's general and physical appearance, e.g. excessive under- or overweight, may indicate obesity or starvation, while muscle wasting or tenderness suggests thiamine deficiency or lack of protein. Skeletal deformities point to vitamin D deficiency, whereas depletion of vitamin C, K or A could be underlying bruised or dry, rough, inflamed skin. Thiamine deficiency or other vitamin B complexes might also be expressed as sensory losses, detected by an examination of the central nervous system.

Protein energy malnutrition (PEM) can be detected by anthropometry, measurements of body fat, functional tests of skeletal muscle and by biochemical indices. Body weight is the sum of fat, protein, water and bone mineral mass; and total body energy (kcals) is the sum of the energy contained in fat stores, protein and glycogen reserves. In contrast to fat reserves, protein reserves have the *potential* for use as metabolic fuel, but its primary use is in the maintenance of a complex range of cellular functions. Depletion of the protein reserves can lead to serious functional impairment. Actual body weight can be compared with ideal body weight for height, sex and frame size, based on the Metropolitan Life Insurance tables (Weisberg 1983) as follows:

$$\text{Body mass index (BMI)} = \frac{\text{Weight (kg)}}{\text{Height x Height (m)}}$$

In a broad community-based sample of 457 homeless adults (344 men and 113 women) Gelberg *et al.* (1995) interviewed and examined in a variety of settings during the summer of 1985. Under-nutrition was examined using three anthropometric measures (weight, triceps skinfold and upper arm muscle area in the lowest 15th percentile) and one observational measure. Of the sample, 33% were undernourished as defined by at least one of the anthropometric measures. Malnutrition was significantly associated with more drug use, fewer free food sources, less income and male sex.

The accuracy and limitations of these approaches in a clinical setting have been reviewed (Anderson 1979; Kelly and Kroemer 1990; Watts *et al.* 2006) and relate to time of day of the measurements, clothing and training of the observers. The unreliability of this approach becomes more severe in cases of dehydration, oedema and ascites and the interaction between drugs and nutrition. In the case of the elderly, changes in height, weight and body composition occur with advancing years and current reference standards are not suitable for use with the elderly. Waist circumference has been used for abdominal obesity, but this measure varies across ethnic groups (Misra *et al.* 2005). Measurement of body fat can be estimated by *skinfold thickness* using Harpenden or Lange callipers, at six sites on the body. Skinfold thickness of the triceps muscles (TSF) is most commonly used, but a high degree of training of the observers is required to provide validity of this measure. *Mid arm muscle circumference* provides an indirect assessment of skeletal muscle protein reserves.

These anthropometric approaches are generally inappropriate for socially excluded groups due to a number of limitations:

- Distribution of body fat varies with sex, ethnic group and age.

- Changes in muscle mass can occur independently of changes in muscle composition.

- Skinfold compressibility varies with age, sex, anatomical site and hydration status.

- Assumptions are made in the calculations, noted above, that the arm cross-section is circular, when it is elliptical, and bone area is neglected.

- Limbic oedema and surgical emphysema render the measurements invalid.

In contrast to anthropometric measurements biochemical assessments are more objective and can provide an important insight into PEM and also specific nutritional deficiencies. Clinical laboratory procedures are available for measuring amino acids, vitamins, trace elements, acute phase proteins and many other standard medical indicators. The new disciplines of genomics and proteomics are beginning to provide a great insight into metabolic functions and disease processes, but are presently expensive and largely used in an experimental context. Measurement of plasma proteins is perhaps the most useful biochemical assessment tool in assessing the protein energy status of the population groups discussed in this book. Unlike carbohydrates and fats, the body does not store protein in a nonfunctional form. Therefore gain or loss of protein is reflected in functional loss. When measured serially, circulating protein provides an index of the rate of protein synthesis or degeneration. These changes are good indicators of physiological stress relating to organ dysfunction, immune responses to infections and healing.

SPECIFIC NUTRIENT DEFICIENCIES

A number of vitamin deficiencies have been found in the vulnerable groups that are the subject of this chapter. These include B complex (vitamins B1, B6, B12), folate, ascorbic acid (vitamin C) and vitamin D deficiencies. A high risk of deficiencies exists in elderly people who are isolated, due to physical disability, sensory degeneration, recent bereavement, very old men living alone and those with mental health problems, particularly depression.

In the case of B complex deficiencies, Brin *et al.* (1964) proposed five stages in the development of deficiency, based on observations of B1 (thiamine) status. Loss of appetite, general malaise and increased irritability occurred in the *physiological* stage three. These symptoms are in common with a number of other origins in the elderly. Stages four and five are typified by cardiac, neurological, mental confusion and ophthalmoplegia problems. There is very clear evidence that Wernicke's encephalopathy is due to thiamine deficiency; the clinical features include diplopia and nystagmus progressing to ophthalmoplegia and cognitive changes of Korsakoff's psychosis, which include loss of memory, disorientation, confabulation and hallucinations. In the UK, US, Australia and other countries in the western world this progressive condition is associated with alcohol abuse (see Chapter 8), however,

Wernicke's encephalopathy has also been described in the elderly with accidental hypothermia (Philip and Smith 1973). Thiamine deficiency associated with confusional states in elderly orthopaedic patients has been reported (Older and Dickerson 1982).

In a study of 107 homeless men in Sydney, Darnton-Hill and Truswell (1990) have concluded that the incidence and prevalence of Wernicke–Korsakoff syndrome in Australia may be the highest in the world. In their study a high prevalence of signs consistent with thiamine deficiency were found. Of the subjects, 24% showed three or more signs of Wernicke–Korsakoff syndrome (ophthalmoplegia, nystagmus, ataxia, peripheral neuropathy and global confusion). These homeless men showed a high prevalence of dietary, biochemical and clinical features to indicate subclinical or early clinical thiamine deficiency. In this sample about half reported taking vitamin supplements (with varying duration and regularity), usually a regimen consisting of thiamine, vitamin C, folic acid and a multivitamin-B-complex capsule. In this cross-sectional study, little effect could be seen on clinical health between those reporting taking vitamin supplementation and those not doing so. However, biochemical measurements showed significant differences. The numbers of men classified as deficient were higher by about 20% for those reporting not taking vitamins. On the basis of the biochemically assayed vitamin status, the supplemented group had better health outcomes.

ALCOHOL AND NUTRITION

Chronic alcohol problems are one of the main causes of malnutrition in countries in the northern hemisphere. Nutritional status of chronic problematic alcohol users is not as severe as previously thought, however, it should be anticipated that at-risk groups including the socially excluded and the elderly might not receive adequate nutrition to maintain physiological homeostasis. Early studies reported grossly deficient nutrition in individuals with poor dietary intake and with alcohol-related diseases, in particular liver dysfunction. More recent studies of alcohol problem users without major complicating disease have reported mean daily intake of carbohydrates, proteins and fats similar to control populations. However, people from lower socio-economic classes and those with alcohol-related disease do have significantly low calorie intake, and in these cases alcohol may be a secondary cause of malnutrition. Mendenhall *et al.* (1986) concluded that 100% of the patients with alcoholic hepatitis and 60% of chronic alcoholics with cirrhosis were malnourished. Treating malnutrition in people with alcohol dependency problems is essential prior to the commencement of a programme of recovery and rehabilitation. However, this is complicated by linked problems of liver disease and neurological disorders.

Differences in levels of malnutrition between the low- and middle-income classes were found to be 32 % and 8 %, respectively (Goldsmith *et al.* 1983). However, when patients with alcohol-related diseases are ruled out no significant differences in nutritional status between chronic alcoholics without complications and controls were found by Estruch (1993). This was not the case for those with complications suggesting that adequate nutrition protects the individuals from tissue and organ damage. Total lifetime doses of alcohol and daily calorie intake are primary risk factors when liver cirrhosis has occurred.

Chronic alcoholics are most likely to be deficient in vitamins and minerals, and frequently have damaged livers. In such cases correction or prevention of nutritional deficiencies will not prevent liver damage (Lieber 1975). In the work by Cook and colleagues (Cook *et al.* 1991), who analysed 20 heavy drinkers admitted to hospital for detoxification, only serum levels of vitamin E were found to be significantly reduced compared with controls. Sgourus *et al.* (2004) found that 53.4 % of patients admitted to a community substance misuse department for detoxification in Stoke-on-Trent (UK), were deficient in vitamin B1 before treatment in contrast to only 13.8 % of the patients classified as 'underweight' on the basis of having a BMI less than 20. The normal range for the BMI is 20–24.

Vitamin B1 concentration has been found to be lower in female alcoholics in comparison with male alcoholics (Mancinelli 2005). This observation was reflected in liver function tests; these showed strikingly significant severe problems which were considerably greater in the females than males. In this study, women started drinking heavily later, but for a shorter time than men. However, more severe alcohol damage occurred in women than in men, confirming the so-called 'telescoping effect'. This work highlights the need of prevention programmes especially aimed at women with particular attention paid to nutritional status, as alcohol abuse and nutritional deficits appear to have a detrimental effect on the health of women and their children. Special consideration should be paid to alcohol and diet in pregnancy in view of the leads to the well-known foetal alcohol spectrum disorder (FASD) and perhaps less pronounced developmental effects (see Chapter 3).

REFERENCES

Anderson, M. A. (1979). Comparison of anthropometric measures of nutritional status in preschool children in five developing countries. *American Journal of Clinical Nutrition*, **32**(11), 2339–45.

Armstrong, J. (2003). Coexistence of social inequalities in undernutrition and obesity in preschool children: population-based cross-sectional study. *Archives of Disease in Childhood*, **88**(8), 671–5.

Balsam, A. L. and B. L. Rogers (1991). Serving elders in greatest social and economic need: the challenge to the Elderly Nutrition Program. *Journal of Aging and Social Policy*, **3**(1–2), 41–55.

Barnes, R. H. (1976). Dual role of environmental deprivation and malnutrition in retarding intellectual development. A. G. Hogan Memorial Lecture. *American Journal of Clinical Nutrition*, **29**(8), 912–17.

Beal, A. C. and I. Redlener (1995). Enhancing perinatal outcome in homeless women: the challenge of providing comprehensive health care. *Seminars in Perinatology*, **19**(4), 307–13.

Berg, B. N. and H. S. Simms (1965). Nutrition, onset of disease, and longevity in the rat. *Canadian Medical Association Journal*, **93**(17), 911–13.

Botting, B., M. Rosato and R. Wood (1998). Teenage mothers and the health of their children. *Population Trends*, **93**, 19–28.

Brin, M., H. Schwartzberg and D. Arthur-Davies (1964). A vitamin evaluation program as applied to 10 elderly residents in a community home for the aged. *Journal of the American Geriatric Society*, **12**, 493–9.

Brockington, F. and S. M. Lampert (1967). *The Stockport Survey. The Social Needs of the Over 60s*. Manchester: University Press, Manchester.

Carillo, T. E., J. A. Gilbride and M. M. Chan (1990). Soup kitchen meals: an observation and nutrient analysis. *Journal of the American Diet Association*, **90**(7), 989–91.

Che, J. (2001). Food insecurity in Canadian households. *Health Reports*, **12**(4), 11–22.

Cook, C. C., R. J. Walden, B. R. Graham, C. Gillham, S. Davies and B. N. Prichard (1991). Trace element and vitamin deficiency in alcoholic and control subjects. *Alcohol and Alcoholism*, **26**(5–6), 541–8.

Darmon, N., J. Coupel, M. Deheeger and A. Briend (2001). Dietary inadequacies observed in homeless men visiting an emergency night shelter in Paris. *Public Health Nutrition*, **4**(2), 155–61.

Darnton-Hill, I. and A. S. Truswell (1990). Thiamine status of a sample of homeless clinic attenders in Sydney. *Medical Journal of Australia*, **152**(1), 5–9.

DHSS (1972). *A Nutritional Survey of the Elderly*. London: HMSO.

Dickerson, J. W. T. and H. A. Lee (1988). *Nutrition in the Clinical Management of Disease*. London: Edward Arnold.

Dodds, J. M. and T. A. Melnik (1993). Development of the New York State Nutrition Surveillance Program. *Public Health Reports*, **108**(2), 230–40.

Drake, M. A. (1992). The nutritional status and dietary adequacy of single homeless women and their children in shelters. *Public Health Reports*, **107**(3), 312–19.

Estruch, R., J. M. Nicolas, E. Villegas, A. Junque and A. Urbano-Marquez (1993). Relationship between ethanol-related diseases and nutritional status in chronically alcoholic men. *Alcohol and Alcoholism*, **28**(5), 543–50.

Exton-Smith, A. N. (1971). Maintenance of health in old age. *Transactions of the Medical Society of London*, **87**, 175–84.

Exton-Smith, A. N. (1972). Physiological aspects of aging: relationship to nutrition. *American Journal of Clinical Nutrition*, **25**(8), 853–9.

Finch, S. (1998). *National Diet and Nutrition Survey: People aged 65 years and over*. London: The Stationery Office.

Fletcher, E. S. (2004). Changes over 20 years in macronutrient intake and body mass index in 11- to 12-year-old adolescents living in Northumberland. *British Journal of Nutrition*, **92**(2), 321–33.

Garmezy, N. and S. Streitman (1974). Children at risk: the search for the antecedents of schizophrenia. Part I. Conceptual models and research methods. *Schizophrenia Bulletin*, **8**, 14–90.

Gelberg, L., J. A. Stein and C. G. Neumann (1995). Determinants of undernutrition among homeless adults. *Public Health Reports*, **110**(4), 448–54.

Goldsmith, R. H., F. L. Iber and P. A. Miller (1983). Nutritional status of alcoholics of different socioeconomic class. *Journal of the American College of Nutrition*, **2**(3), 215–20.

Gordon, M. M. (2002). Can intervention modify adverse lifestyle variables in a rheumatoid population? Results of a pilot study. *Annals of the Rheumatic Diseases*, **61**(1), 66–9.

Kelleher, C. C. (2004). Hurling alone? How social capital failed to save the Irish from cardiovascular disease in the United States. *American Journal of Public Health*, **94**(12), 2162–9.

Kelly, P. L. and K. H. Kroemer (1990). Anthropometry of the elderly: status and recommendations. *Human Factors*, **32**(5), 571–95.

Lara, J. J., J. A. Scott and M. E. Lean (2004). Intentional mis-reporting of food consumption and its relationship with body mass index and psychological scores in women. *Journal of Human Nutrition and Dietetics*, **17**(3), 209–18.

Lee, R. E. and C. Cubbin (2002). Neighborhood context and youth cardiovascular health behaviors. *American Journal of Public Health*, **92**(3), 428–36.

Lieber, C. (1975). Alcohol and malnutrition in the pathogenesis of liver disease. *Journal of the American Medical Association*, **233**(10), 1077–80.

Luder, E., E. Boey, B. Buchalter and C. Martinez-Weber (1989). Assessment of the nutritional status of urban homeless adults. *Public Health Report*, **104**(5), 451–7.

Luder, E., E. Ceysens-Okada, A. Koren-Roth and C. Martinez-Weber (1990). Health and nutrition survey in a group of urban homeless adults. *Journal of the American Diet Association*, **90**(10), 1387–92.

Mancinelli, R. (2005). Female alcoholism and biomarkers: gender differences in vitamin B1 (thiamine) levels. *Alcohol and Alcoholism*, **40**(Supplement 1), Po 02.

Martin, A. R., J. M. Nieto, M. A. Jimenez, J. P. Ruiz, M. C. Vazquez, Y. C. Fernandez, *et al.* (1999). Unhealthy eating behaviour in adolescents. *European Journal of Epidemiology*, **15**(7), 643–8.

McCay, C. M., M. F. Crowell and L. A. Maynard (1989). The effect of retarded growth upon the length of life span and upon the ultimate body size. *Nutrition*, **5**(3), 155–71; discussion 172.

Mendenhall, C. L., T. Tosch, R. E. Weesner, P. Garcia-Pont, S. J. Goldberg, T. Kiernan, *et al.* (1986). A cooperative study on alcoholic hepatitis. II: Prognostic significance of protein-calorie malnutrition. *American Journal of Clinical Nutrition*, **43**(2), 213–18.

Misra, A., J. S. Wasir and N. K. Vikram (2005). Waist circumference criteria for the diagnosis of abdominal obesity are not applicable uniformly to all populations and ethnic groups. *Nutrition*, **21**(9), 969–76.

ODPM (2004). *Monitoring and Review of Supporting People Services: Quality Assessment Framework – Core Service Objectives*. London: Office of the Deputy Prime Minister.

Older, M. W. and J. W. Dickerson (1982). Thiamine and the elderly orthopaedic patient. *Age and Ageing*, **11**(2), 101–7.

Oliveira, N. L. G., and J. P. Goldberg (2002). The nutrition status of women and children who are homeless. *Nutrition Today*, **37**(2), 70–7.

Olubodun, J. O., H. A. Akinsola and O. A. Adeleye (1996). Prison deprivation and protein nutritional status of inmates of a developing community prison. *European Journal of Clinical Nutrition*, **50**(1), 58–60.

Perry, L. and S. McLaren (2004). An exploration of nutrition and eating disabilities in relation to quality of life at 6 months post-stroke. *Health and Social Care in the Community*, **12**(4), 288–97.

Philip, G. and J. F. Smith (1973). Hypothermia and Wernicke's encephalopathy. *Lancet*, **2**(7821), 122–4.

Pirlich, M. (2001). Nutrition in the elderly. *Best Practice and Research in Clinical Gastroenterology*, **15**(6), 15.

Reilly, J. J., Jr., S. F. Hull, N. Albert, A. Waller and S. Bringardener (1988). Economic impact of malnutrition: a model system for hospitalized patients. *Journal of Parenteral and Enteral Nutrition*, **12**(4), 371–6.

Robertson, M. J. (1991). Homeless women with children. The role of alcohol and other drug abuse. *American Journal of Psychology*, **46**(11), 1198–204.

Ross, M. H., E. D. Lustbader and G. Bras (1983). Dietary practices of early life and age at death of rats with tumors. *Journal of the National Cancer Institute*, **71**(5), 947–54.

Sgouros, X., M. Baines, R. N. Bloor, R. McAuley, L. O. Ogundipe and S. Willmott (2004). Evaluation of a clinical screening instrument to identify states of thiamine deficiency in inpatients with severe alcohol dependence syndrome. *Alcohol and Alcoholism*, **39**(3), 227–32.

Shizgal, H. M. (1983). Nutritional assessment. In: R.W. Winters and H. L. Greene (eds), *Nutritional Support of the seriously ill patient*. New York: Academic Press.

Silliman, K., M. M. Yamanoha and A. E. Morrissey (1998). Evidence of nutritional risk in a population of homeless adults in rural northern California. *Journal of the American Diet Association*, **98**(8), 908–10.

Stitt, S., G. Griffiths and D. Grant (1994). Homeless and hungry: the evidence from Liverpool. *Nutrition Health*, **9**(4), 275–87.

Stokoe, I. H. (1965). *The Physical and Mental Care of the Elderly at Home. Psychiatric Disorders of the Aged*. London. World Psychiatric Association.

Strasser, J. A., S. Damrosch and J. Gaines (1991). Nutrition and the homeless person. *Journal of Community Health Nursing*, **8**(2), 65–73.

Thomson, A. M. and F. E. Hytten (1973). Nutrition during pregnancy. *World Review of Nutrition and Dietetics*, **16**, 23–45.

Todorovic, V. (2004). Nutritional screening in the community: developing strategies. *British Journal of Community Nursing*, **9**(11), 464–70.

Watts, K., L. H. Naylor, E. A. Davis, T. W. Jones, B. Beeson, F. Bettenay, *et al.* (2006). Do skinfolds accurately assess changes in body fat in obese children and adolescents? *Medicine and Science in Sports and Exercise*, **38**(3), 439–44.

Weisberg, H. F. (1983). Evaluation of nutritional status. *Annals of Clinical and Laboratory Science*, **13**(2), 95–106.

Williamson, J., I. H. Stokoe, S. Gray, M. Fisher, A. Smith, A. McGhee, *et al.* (1964). Old people at home. Their unreported needs. *Lancet*, **13**, 1117–20.

Wrieden, W. L. (2004). Secular and socio-economic trends in compliance with dietary targets in the north Glasgow MONICA population surveys 1986–1995: did social gradients widen? *Public Health Nutrition*, **7**(7), 835–42.

Part III

Addressing Social Exclusion: The Way
Out?

CHAPTER 10

NEEDS ASSESSMENT OF SOCIALLY EXCLUDED POPULATIONS

In addressing the complex needs of the socially excluded, the first contact is a critical stage in providing support and appropriate interventions. The complex needs of particularly 'hard-to reach' people require a range of specialist interventions and the activities of professionally trained personnel working together with non-clinical staff, some of whom might be volunteers, to provide an integrated set of interventions. This interagency working as proposed in Models of Care (NTA 2005), is a good way forward but there are a number of obstacles to effective working. These include different methods of working practice and the specific language (jargon) of the disciplines in which the staff have been trained. At first contact, the identification of primary needs is pivotal to the organisation of future support when less overt needs can be addressed. In deciding which screening and assessment questionnaires to use it is important to decide which of the many tools are appropriate and at what stage of engagement with the client they should be employed. The organisation of the assessment process should be considered in relation to the location of the assessment, i.e. on the street, in the client's home, in the reception area of a hostel or in a clinical setting within the centre or hospital. The choice of tools will also depend on the competency of the staff and the main objectives of the project.

ENGAGEMENT AND INITIAL SCREENING

The forgoing chapters have covered the many biological, psychological and social factors that impact on socially excluded people. Exclusion from society occurs in a variety of ways and involves highly complex issues such as neuropsychological deficits, developmental problems and negative health behaviours. The complex interaction of mental health problems, problematic alcohol and drug use, criminal behaviour and the social isolation caused by the ageing process, contribute to the difficulties in understanding and developing a suitable response for each client. Social exclusion might occur due to the lack of an immediate family, family break up or from immigration and coercion due to the international trafficking of women for work in the sex industry, a contemporary form of slavery (Munro 2006).

Each of these routes into exclusion results in a large range of client groups with overlapping complex needs including: physical disability, degenerative illness, mental health problems, alcohol and drug problems, refugee status, women with children, frail elderly, AIDS/HIV, learning difficulties, leaving prison, young leaving care, domestic violence and single homelessness. Not surprisingly the services required to address these diverse complex groups are also diverse. These include residential accommodation for the homeless, specialist services for substance misusers, elderly care and nursing homes and secure places for women and children. Non-residential care services are available to cater for rough sleepers and street women, and community care is provided by a range of agencies including church groups, drop-in counselling services, missing persons agencies and street-based health centres.

Being homeless clearly indicates that accommodation is a major issue, but the underlying contributing issues are not so obvious. Simply providing accommodation will not necessarily solve the person's problems. However, a person seeking accommodation may well become engaged with a support agency, which provides an opportunity to help the person identify the range of issues that has resulted in the acute accommodation problem.

In working with socially excluded people the primary presenting need is often not the most significant issue causing distress and loss of social functioning of the individual. In the case of those who seek help from a homeless service the initial information provided by the potential client might not give an indication of, for example, the underlying alcohol, drug or mental health problem. This deliberate non-disclosure frequently occurs in order to obtain accommodation.

The voluntary sector in the UK provides the most accessible interface with the street-level mainline services for alcohol, drugs, health and accommodation support. The initial period of contact is an opportunity for a relationship with the client to begin. It is a period of uncertainty for the potential client and for the agency staff. The first contact meeting with a statutory or non-statutory agency, the initial contact phase, should be regarded as *screening*, akin to triage in a healthcare setting and is not necessarily the best time to gain valid information about the client. Luscombe and Brook (2005), in analysing the initial screening data from the Salvation Army social service centres in the UK, found that 10 % of those seeking accommodation reported substance misuse as a reason for being homeless. This is a gross under-estimation of the 60–80 % of the Salvation Army hostel population with substance misuse problems.

This first contact may be considered as a pretreatment phase or a low threshold stage into treatment. Here the immediate presenting needs should be identified in order to determine whether the needs are life threatening, require emergency accommodation or present a threat to the staff of the agency. Risk assessment is essential to protect the health and safety of the staff and also to determine whether emergency medical or mental health help is required. An important aim at this stage is to engage with the client to provide immediate assistance in a way that the client perceives that they are receiving personal attention and genuine concern. People at this stage are quite vulnerable emotionally and physically, in particular they may be intoxicated or hungry. However, those providing support should be very careful to *do no harm* (Logan 2005). Contact with a homeless service is not the only way that socially excluded people come into contact with support agencies. Referrals may be made via medical and social services and also from the criminal justice system and the armed forces.

ASSESSMENT AND MONITORING

As indicated above the initial screening phase will not usually provide a valid representation of the client's true needs. This is not the case with the admission of an elderly person into a care or nursing home. Here a detailed medical and behavioural assessment is often undertaken in a hospital or by a community health/social service care manager prior to a move into the next level of care. This pre-admission assessment of the elderly is used to develop a care plan, however, the disorientation and confusion associated by the move into new accommodation can invalidate the pre-admission assessment which should be repeated 3–4 weeks after admission.

The main aim of the assessment process should be to identify the characteristics of the client, including their life history, and by means of standardised questionnaires, health and behavioural measures should be obtained. Assessment should be seen as an ongoing process forming the basis of treatment/programme monitoring. This *outcome monitoring* enables the care provider to gain an insight into the progress of the client by the observation of changes within the client; changes relating to physical and psychological health, behaviour (including misuse of substances) and social circumstances.

Outcome monitoring involves the measurement of change between two or more points in time and might involve a combination of both subjective and objective measures. Subjective indicators include self-assessment and responses to questions such as 'How do you feel today?'. The use of standardised questionnaires, such as *General Health Questionnaire* (GHQ), the *Christo Inventory for Substance Misuse Services* and quality of life indicators are also useful at this stage. These might include the *Hospital Anxiety and Depression Scale* (HADS), *EurolQoL* and the *Social Problems Questionnaire* (SPQ31). These validated questionnaires can be helpful in structuring informal and more formal assessment sessions. However, there are problems with client recall in those with neuropsychological problems, in particular memory loss or confabulation (see Chapter 11, 'Capacity for change'). Objective measures are usually more robust, quantitative measures of, for example, height, weight or biomedical parameters give absolute data which can be used to monitor a client's physiological progress.

ASSESSING WELL-BEING

The interaction of biological, psychological, social and spiritual factors determine a person's sense of well-being. Indicators of well-being include *quality of life* measures which give an insight into functional ability and contribute to an assessment of impairment, disability and handicap from the client's perspective. Quality of life measures tend to focus on positive health and a holistic view of the functioning of mind, body and social adjustment. Quality of life is dependent on the experiences of the client and reflects interpersonal interactions and social participation.

Foster (2005) has compared the use of a number of health-related quality of life (HrQoL) indicators of alcohol-dependent subjects. These included *Severity of Alcohol Dependence* (SADQ), *Alcohol Problems Questionnaire* (APQ), *Rotterdam Symptoms Checklist* (RSCL), *Life Situation Survey* (LSS), *General Health Questionnaire* (GHQ-28), *Nottingham Health Profile* (NHP) and *Short-Form-36* (SF-36). He recruited 240 subjects from six sociodemographically diverse centres, subjects were then followed up at 3-, 6- and 12-month intervals when the RSCL, LSS, GHQ-28, NHP, SF-36 and alcohol consumption data were gathered.

At the first assessment stage, sociodemographic, tobacco/alcohol use history, family history, previous alcohol-related treatment and data concerning the use of prescription and illicit drugs were collected. In this study, at three months the baseline predictors of outcome were Jarman scores (an indicator of geographical area based social deprivation), SF-36 bodily pain scores and prescription of vitamins. At six months Jarman and SF-36 bodily pain scores both remained significant and there was one other predictor, living alone. The 12-months predictors were Jarman scores, number of residential treatments and units of alcohol consumed. In reviewing these results the sociodemographic factors had the greatest impact on quality of life.

A potentially useful quality of life indicator for socially excluded clients with alcohol problems is the *Hospital Anxiety and Depression Scale* (HADS; Zigmond and Snaith 1983). This is a widely used self-report case detector for anxiety and depression, however, there is increasing evidence that the measure may be unsuitable for use in certain clinical groups because pathology adversely impacts on the underlying factor structure of the instrument. However, Martin *et al.* (2006) have demonstrated that the HADS is likely to be useful as a screening tool in alcohol dependency.

Quality of life indicators are becoming available for an increasing range of clinical problems. Diabetes is frequently found in homeless, disadvantaged groups and the elderly. Garratt *et al.* (2002) have reviewed five of the diabetes-specific instruments; ADDQoL, DHP-1/18, DSQOLS, D-39 and QSD-R. Each of these measures were found to have good reliability and internal and external construct validity. Stroke is a major cause of long-term disablement and can lead to social exclusion. Nutritional issues in those recovering from stroke have been poorly researched despite the deleterious effects of malnutrition and other culturally related issues. Perry and McLaren (2004) used quality of life measures to investigate the contribution of dietary and nutritional factors after stroke. In a study of 206 survivors of a cohort of acute stroke patients consecutively admitted, within a 12-month period to an NHS trust hospital in south London. The results demonstrated relatively minor degrees of physical disablement. Poor nutritional status and substantial dietary inadequacy were revealed, linked with reduced appetite and depression reflected in *mood state* as indicated in quality of life scores. Such scores were also significantly influenced by social support, eating-related disabilities and age.

After alcohol and drug problems in socially excluded homeless populations, mental health problems are the second most apparent issues to be addressed. An awareness of the comorbidity of mental health problems and substance misuse has developed during the last two decades. The most conspicuous changes in the community which have contributed to the increase in dual diagnosis are the closure of large psychiatric hospitals and the increasing prevalence of drug use in the community. Individuals who are comorbid for mental health problems and substance misuse have a requirement for both medical and social care needs and are particularly at risk of social exclusion. Todd *et al.* (2004) have reviewed recent government policy, which advocates treating comorbid clients within mainstream mental health services, and highlight the need for health and social care workers to recognise the likelihood of high levels of social exclusion among clients with comorbid problems. This has implications for the assessment of clients, and points to the need for a *single shared assessment.*

COMPREHENSIVE ASSESSMENTS

In the first part of this chapter the main focus was on the need for appropriate screening and assessments in order to determine the immediate needs of the client and then facilitate the construction of a *personal development plan.* A further need for appropriate assessment protocols should be considered in order to reduce relapse. The role of health and social support agencies should be to support the clients to the point where their chances of relapse are significantly reduced. Relapse can be minimised by limiting the harm associated with relapse, which frequently occurs in clients who are comorbid with mental health and substance misuse problems. During the last two decades the emergence of the *biopsychosocial* models of health and social issues has provided an insight into the complex needs of clients who are socially excluded. This is particularly relevant in the advances in our understanding of smoking behaviour, alcohol and drug dependence, gambling, sexual addiction and eating disorders, as reflected by Moos and Holahan (2003).

An integrated biopsychosocial orientation and a theoretical paradigm of evaluation research have supplanted earlier adherence to an oversimplified biomedical model and reliance on a restrictive methodological approach to treatment evaluation. And yet in an ironic way, more remains to be done than before, in part because of our increased knowledge and in part because of new clinical perspectives and treatment procedures and the evolving social context.

The integration of biopsychosocial approaches to addictive behaviours provides a useful strategy for working more generally with socially excluded people, as discussed in Chapter 11 (see under section, 'Interventions for addictive behaviours'). This approach to preventing relapse suggests the importance of helping the individuals to identify personal warning signs, negative mood states and compulsive and impulsive behaviours (Donovan and Marlatt 2005). These interventions should be followed by support in the development of coping skills, basic skills and work-related skills, as part of the process of rehabilitation. The implications for the assessment process, in the context of a biopsychosocial perspective to treatment, are that the appropriate assessment tools should be used in order to identify the potential factors which might elicit a relapse, identify high-risk situations and to determine deficits and strengths in coping skills.

Socially excluded people often present with a complex set of needs, which in many cases, consists of a number of chronic relapsing disorders or social problems. This may be considered from a *survival analysis* perspective (Curry and Marlatt 1988), which is based on a dichotomous outcome, that is *relapsed* or *not*. However, *multiple event analysis* provides a more relevant approach to relapse (Wang *et al.* 2002). Nevertheless, whichever statistical analytical strategy is used, the important issue is that relapse is not a discrete event, it is likely to recur and should be considered within a time-based framework. Assessments should be made periodically in order to capture the recovery and rehabilitation processes as they proceed (Shiffman *et al.* 2000).

Shiffman (1989) suggests that it is inappropriate to focus on a single level of assessment, as multiple layers of assessments may be required to predict relapse. If this approach is adopted then a multidimensional, multivariate assessment strategy, taking account of the various recovery stages and biopsychological parameters monitored at each stage, should be used. The comprehensive continuous assessment model suggested would involve important decisions regarding the type of assessments to be used and the appropriate timing. In the case of clients whose relapse is *mood-dependent*, the average length of time between assessments was found to be 2.4 days (Hodgins *et al.* 1995). This time between assessments might be too long to capture the rapidly fluctuating moods associated with relapse. This and other confounding factors indicate that a single baseline assessment (e.g. at the beginning of the programme) is inadequate to predict subsequent relapse.

The multiple confounding factors in individuals with complex needs may have co-occurring psychiatric conditions associated with specific and unique cues that promote relapse. This suggests that assessment of both general and substance-specific parameters should be assessed in order to facilitate the development of coping skills (Moggi *et al.* 1999). Donovan (1996) has proposed a heuristic model, consisting of a funnel, to reflect the transition from stability to relapse. In this progression towards relapse the variables become more focused and intense and are funnelled within an emergent relapsing situation.

In view of the complexity of the processes of social exclusion and social inclusion, the multidimensional models developed for relapse prevention, with regard to addictive behaviours, seem to be an appropriate starting point for the development of comprehensive assessments in the groups with complex needs, many of which are associated with comorbidity of substance misuse and mental ill health. In the development of this multivariate approach, an assessment of tools that might be used will now be considered.

GENERAL AND SPECIFIC ASSESSMENTS

In developing a multivariate assessment model, it is important to define the various stages of the linked processes of initial engagement, provision of accommodation (or links into community day programmes), entry into a treatment programme (e.g. detoxification, substance misuse rehabilitation, behavioural modification/cognitive behaviour treatment), basic and life skills training, and community resettlement support. Each of these phases will require appropriate assessments, which should inform both client and project worker of progress, and also indicate when the client has achieved the various agreed outcomes for that phase of support, prior to moving to the next phase. An integration of support through this period of change should be underpinned and informed by a number of general indicators. These should include socio-demographic, legal and health status, together with measures of behavioural functioning, biomedical status (e.g. nutrition, liver damage), mental health state and severity of addiction to substances and other nonsubstance behaviours. In view of the socio-economic disadvantage of a significant number of clients, the need to screen for deficits in basic skills (e.g. reading, writing and numerical ability) should be considered with a view to providing relevant support.

Socio-demographic, legal and financial information is normally required initially in order to make accommodation available via *Supporting People* (SP) funding (see Chapter 12, section 'Income support and homelessness'). This core data is required by the SP commissioning bodies and housing associations, which are supported by the government's Housing Corporation. First engagement might occur at the time when accommodation is requested (it can also take place in the community without accommodation needs, see Chapter 12). However, as noted above, this can be a time of personal disruption and confusion and is not a particularly good time to elicit key information about the true needs of the client. Within 2–3 days this information can be obtained by means of a number of screening tools such as the *Christo Inventory for Substance Misuse Services* (CISS) (Christo *et al.* 2003; NTA 2005). This 10-item questionnaire can be used to produce a single score of 0–20, which is a general index of client problems. The CISS can be used to give a quick standardised and reliable view of outcome areas, which can be used repeatedly to monitor client's problems at intake and at standardised follow-up time. A review of assessments for use with clients with alcohol problems is included in Appendix B.

ASSESSMENT OF MENTAL HEALTH STATUS

People with mental health problems are quite commonly found in services providing help and shelter for the homeless. Timms and Fry (1989) interviewed a sample of men, newly arriving at a Salvation Army hostel, and compared the new arrivals with the total resident group of men who had spent one year or more in the hostel. Results from this study showed that 31% fulfilled the diagnostic and statistical manual (DSM: 111R) criteria for a diagnosis of schizophrenia and more than half were not in contact with psychiatric services. This suggests that a significant number of male schizophrenics are lost to follow up and become homeless. Implications for service provision are discussed (Timms and Fry 1989) in the light of these findings.

CRISIS has reported witnessing an increase of people with mental health problems within its services in recent years. Research carried out by CRISIS suggests that this increase may be due to a rise in younger people who are homeless and have associated drug addictions (Dean and Craig 1999). The relationship between mental health problems and homelessness is complex, however. Mental health problems can lead to an initial loss of accommodation and may also contribute to people remaining homeless due to lack of support upon rehousing but there is a lack of explicit research into this relationship. Assessment of the mental health status and its monitoring during the progress of rehabilitation and resettlement should be an important aspect of statutory and non-statutory service provision.

In a busy health or social service setting there will be a considerable limitation on the amount of time and staff commitment to the assessment process. The *Mini Mental State Examination* (MMSE) can be performed within 5 minutes to reveal signs of dysfunction. Other assessments which might be considered\ include: the *Symptom Checklist-90-Revised* (SCL-90-R), which requires specific training and takes 15–30 minutes to administer; or the *Brief Symptom Inventory* (BSI), which also requires specific training and takes 8–10 minutes to administer. Mood state can be assessed by means of the *Beck Depression and Anxiety Scale,* which is well respected, but has limitations and is not as easy to use as the *HADS.* Levels of stress can be monitored by the *DASS-42.*

A useful comparison of the various tools, which might be considered within an assessment framework, can be found at http://www.priory.com/psych/ratings.htm. In addition to time limitations in administering mental assessments, the level of training and experience of the assessors is critical. In the case of the *Present State Examination* (PSE), and the *Clinical Interview Schedule* (CISr) there is evidence that lay interviewers can assess nonpsychotic symptoms in clients. However, Wing *et al.* (1990) has advised against the use of clinically inexperienced interviewers to assess psychotic symptoms. The *Schedules for Clinical Assessment in Neuropsychiatry* (SCAN) provides a very reliable measure of psychosis in adults. However, this semi-structured interview technique requires a high level of training of clinically experienced staff. Brugha *et al.* (1999) has carried out a pilot study into the possibility of using experienced lay staff to reliably carry out a semi-structured survey form of SCAN in psychotic and nonpsychotic disorders. This study indicates the potential and training needs for lay staff to become reliable in carrying out mental health assessments.

COGNITIVE DYSFUNCTION

In view of the potential treatment implications of impaired cognitive status among socially excluded people, in particular alcohol and drug misusers, several authors (Goldman and Darkes 2004; Miller 1985; Tuck and Jackson 1991) have argued for more widespread use of neuropsychological testing in treatment programmes. However, evaluation with comprehensive neuropsychological test batteries, such as the Halstead–Reitan Neuropsychological Test Battery (Reitan and Wolfson 1994), is costly in terms of administration and scoring time (approximately 3–10 hours), making their routine use impractical in most settings. Short-version neuropsychological instruments emphasising the assessment of known deficit areas of alcoholics have been introduced but none show high correlation with deficits found in more robust and comprehensive instruments. In light of recent technological advancements in the computer industry, a new alternative has become available. Computer-based assessment has become an attractive alternative to traditional assessment procedures in psychological testing. Computer-assisted assessment packages have gradually progressed from software that merely scores item responses to comprehensive programs that administer the test, then immediately compute the scores and generate the interpretative reports that summarise the test results.

A relatively new brief neuropsychological assessment device that addresses the related alcohol deficit areas of verbal problem solving, conceptual shifting, perceptual-spatial and abstracting abilities, motor speed, information-processing speed and memory has recently been developed as a computer-based instrument. It is called the Bexley–Maudsley Automated Psychological Screening Test (BMAPS), derived from the well-known paper and pencil instrument used by Acker and Shaw. This is a collection of psychological screening tests based on original research and designed for automated presentation by computer. It was originally developed for the Commodore Pet computer by William and Clare Acker (Acker *et al.* 1984; Waugh *et al.* 1989; Zur and Yule 1990). The current version has been updated to run on an IBM-compatible computer using Microsoft Windows XP or Windows NT. The theoretical emphasis of the BMAPS test is towards 'nonverbal skills' because these abilities can be identified only by testing and are found in spite of intact verbal intelligence. Therefore, nonverbal deficits are easy to overlook unless specific means of assessment are available. The tests included are ones that have been used for distinguishing between alcoholic and other psychological problems. Presently, normative and clinical values of the PC version of BMAPS are being determined for a range of clinical applications (Martin *et al.* 2002). By providing an insight into the severity of cognitive dysfunction the effectiveness of interventions may be measured with the ultimate objective of improving cognitive performance.

BIOMEDICAL ASSESSMENTS

The questionnaire-based assessment tools reviewed above give an important insight into the support needs of clients. However, this approach, to a large extent, depends on client recall, honesty and the interviewing skills of the project worker. In some situations biomedical tests can provide a more quantitative, objective measure of the client's status. This approach requires a reasonably high level of service organisation and some basic staff training to permit the collection of urine, saliva or blood.

Tests for amphetamines, barbiturates, benzodiazepines, cannabis, cocaine, methadone and opiates are commonly undertaken in substance misuse services, prisons and in some homeless rehabilitation services. The use of

Drug Testing and Treatment Orders (DTTOs) requires clients who would otherwise be subjected to a custodial sentence, to attend a day centre in order that they can supply a specimen for drug testing. Drug testing is possible using both urinary and salivary samples. Urinary testing is a well-established technique and problems, such as adulteration by the clients to falsify the results, are well understood and can be controlled. Urine is easy to produce in large volumes whereas some addicts may find it difficult to produce enough saliva.

Saliva testing has some benefits as a *Point Of Care Test* (POCT), however, these tests are more likely to generate false positives and negatives, and at best only give an indication as to the presence or absence of the drugs. There are a number of different companies that produce POCT products for drugs of abuse in urine. In an MHRA evaluation (Burtonwood *et al.* 2003) of 16 different products (from eight different companies), a large variation in quality between different products (or their batches) was found. The various products use different technologies so it is important to know which assessment method is used by a particular device in order to be aware of its potential for cross-reaction with other compounds, which might confound the test results.

The use of POCT dipsticks is convenient and provides a rapid result. However, the results are sometimes confusing, may be hard to read or even depend on the room lighting. The results can be equivocal (for example it is sometimes hard to be sure if a test line was even there or not) and some have unclear labels and instructions. Information on cross-reactivity is not always available. Because of the convenience of *POC* testing, it is easy for an untrained worker to undertake management of testing and either not carry out the test according to the set protocols or misinterpret the results (George and Braithwaite 2002).

The concentration of the drugs is at a much lower concentration in saliva than in urine, and saliva concentrations are likely to vary in relation to diurnal variation in the client's metabolism. Urine on the other hand accumulates in the bladder over several hours and is likely to give a more 'aggregated' test result, as opposed to episodic sampling of saliva.

Laboratory-based tests are significantly more reliable than dipsticks (Wilson and Smith 1999). These usually involve mass screening procedures using an EMIT system, a well-established detection using immunofluorescence as a detection method. A laboratory undertaking such testing should regularly undergo quality assurance checks by a national agency such UKNEQUAS. Here the quality assurance agency provides support and sends three 'blind' samples four times a year in order that the laboratory procedures and instrumentation comply with national standards of testing. In view of these quality assurance procedures this approach is considered a legally valid screening technique in the UK, Europe and the US. In the US, the Substance Abuse and Mental Health Services Administration (SAMHSA) (Anon 2001) has recently permitted the use of alternative matrices such as hair, sweat and saliva albeit with some degree of caution. Saliva can be used but a urine sample is required as well (Guidelines subpart B, Section 2.3). The benefit of EMIT-based urinary testing is that the results are quantifiable. This means that reducing concentrations of the drugs can be monitored during repeated sampling of the client during the course of the treatment programme.

Nutritional monitoring

The chronic effects of alcohol consumption in socially excluded people have been highlighted in Chapter 9. The critical link between vitamin deficits and alcohol brain damage suggests that the detection of and correction of vitamin B1 deficiencies in these clients is essential in order to prevent further cognitive damage and, if possible, prevent the people developing WKS (Thomson and Marshall 2006).

There is a considerable individual variation in the metabolic functioning of elderly people. Additionally, there is an increasing concern regarding the nutritional deficiencies in the elderly population, especially those in hospitals, care and nursing homes (see Chapter 9) (Russell 2000). In view of the link between nutrition and cognitive functioning and general health in the frail elderly, it is important to assess the nutritional status of elderly people generally and especially those in care. Although large-scale screening of all elderly people in care would be difficult to undertake, nutritional assessment should be targeted at those who are at particular risk. This targeted approach should include those who have not had a meal during the last 24 hours and those with a metabolic complication due to diabetes, excessive alcohol or drug use. In general macronutrients seem to absorbed quite well by the gut, however, decreases in efficiency of absorbing micronutrients (e.g. calcium, vitamins D and B12) in the elderly indicates that older people require higher recommended daily allowances (RDAs).

A good indicator of general health and metabolic status can be obtained from liver function tests (LFTs). LFTs include measurement of albumin, however, a more valid indicator of poor nutrition is prealbumin. Traditionally *protein albumin* has been measured as part of an LFT. However, because albumin has a long half-life it is a poor indicator of acute malnutrition (serum levels above 3.5 g/dl are considered normal; values in the range 2.8–3.5 g/dl indicate mild malnutrition; severe malnutrition is present below 2.5 g/dl). Alternatively, *prealbumin* (also referred to as thyroxin-binding prealbumin or transthyretin) is now considered to be a more useful measure of malnutrition. *Prealbumin* occurs in smaller concentrations than albumin, has a short half-life and responds rapidly to low energy intake. It is a sensitive indicator of protein deficiency and it responds to the availability of tryptophan and a high essential to non-essential amino acid ratio (Spickerman 1993). In addition to albumin, and prealbumin other biochemical markers of malnutrition include retinol-binding protein (RBP), transferrin and C-reactive protein (CRP).

In at-risk socially excluded client groups, LFTs and vitamin B1 (thiamine) levels assays should be considered. These tests require blood sampling, which can be undertaken by a visiting nurse or general practitioner. Other nutritional markers that are currently being developed in our laboratories at the University of Kent include tryptophan metabolites (linked to cognitive assessments), and other vitamins and indicators of oxidative stress.

THE MANAGEMENT OF SCREENING AND ASSESSMENT

Screening, assessments and outcome monitoring are essential to provide the most appropriate support for the needs of the client. This ongoing process is required for *care planning* and *personal development plans* leading from initial engagement through various treatment programmes to rehabilitation in the community. In addition to identifying and monitoring the ongoing needs of the clients, information is also needed for a range of management purposes including monitoring the quality of the service provided by the agency and reporting to the funding agencies.

The views of users and reporting to purchasers of the service require a different presentational style compared to the client-centred data. However, some general principles are common to both client and management reporting. These include: clarity of descriptions; reporting selectively to different purchasers; explanations of why outcomes are relevant to purchasers; a good balance between text and figures; details of reliability and validity; definition of the time period and presentation of outcomes (e.g. changes occurring as result of the intervention); in addition to outputs, for example the percentage number of clients relapsing (Burns 1997).

For both client and management reports valid information is dependent on accurate collection of data. This involves good agreement between observers (inter-observer reliability), achieved by training and ongoing quality assurance processes. Analysis of data is normally done by means of a database and statistical software such as SPSS. Consideration of statistical validity, sample size and design are beyond the scope of this book. A very useful introduction to the analysis of qualitative and quantitative data is found in Martin and Thompson (2000).

The reader will now be aware that developing a workable set of screening and assessment tools and using the data appropriately for the benefit of the client and the management needs of the agency, involves a complex set of decisions which will be specific to a particular agency. The use of *logical framework analysis* (LFA) can help to identify the most relevant set of tools in relation to the mission, activities and outputs of the service provided. An LFA (USAID 1969) focuses on the key parameters that give rise to success or failure of the programme or service, and should consider the requirements for particular data in order to address the needs of the client and the reporting process essential to maintain the funding and stakeholder support for the project.

Having established the assessment tools, the data collection, data analysis and the reporting process, a management framework needs to be established. The service organisation might consider that this multilevel, repeated measures approach to client assessment would best be managed within a computer-based framework. An example of such an IT-based based system has been described by Clayden and Bonner (2003), see Figure 10.1.

This chapter has presented a review of the range of screening and assessment tools that might be used to identify the specific needs of clients. An objective view of the most appropriate and practical tools, and the context in which these should be used, can be developed by means of a *logical framework analysis*. The main purpose of the needs identification is to help the agency staff develop a client-centred approach to supporting the client

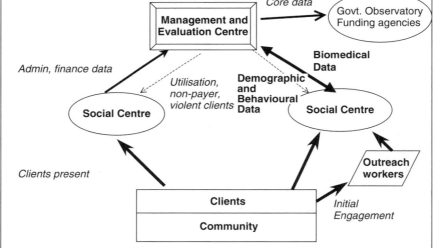

Client Information Management

Figure 10.1 Proposed data flow between community agencies and a central evaluation centre, linked to statutory observatories. A single shared assessment process should provide information to support client needs and also management information required for quality assurance and funding

Source: Reproduced from Clayden, D. and A. B. Bonner (2003). Establishing and monitoring outcomes in social care in quantitative approaches in health care management. In: *Proceedings of the 27th Meeting of the European Group on Operational Research Applied to Health Services (ORAHS)*. Frankfurt: Peter Lang

through the vulnerable period of behavioural change. This set of interventions is explored in more detail in the next chapter.

REFERENCES

Acker, C., W. Acker and G. K. Shaw (1984). Assessment of cognitive function in alcoholics by computer: a control study. *Alcohol and Alcoholism*, **19**(3), 223–33.

Anon (2001). *Drug Testing*. Vol. Federal Register 66. Substance Abuse and Mental Health Services Administration, pp. 43876–82.

Brugha, T. S., P. E. Bebbington, R. Jenkins, H. Meltzer, N. A. Taub, M. Janas, *et al.* (1999). Cross-validation of a general population survey diagnostic interview: a comparison of CIS-R with SCAN ICD-10 diagnostic categories. *Psychological Medicine*, **29**(5), 1029–42.

Burns, S. (1997). *A DIY Guide to Implementing Outcome Monitoring*. London: Alcohol Concern.

Burtonwood, C. A., A. Marsh, S. P. Halloran and B. L. Smith (2003). *Sixteen devices for the detection of drugs of abuse in urine*. London: Evaluation Unit.

Christo, G., S. L. Jones, S. Haylett, G. M. Stephenson, R. M. Lefever and R. Lefever (2003). The Shorter PROMIS Questionnaire: further validation of a tool for simultaneous assessment of multiple addictive behaviours. *Addictive Behaviors*, **28**(2), 225–48.

Clayden, D. and A. B. Bonner (2003). Establishing and monitoring outcomes in social care in quantitative approaches in health care management. In: *Proceedings of the 27th Meeting of the European Group on Operational Research Applied to Health Services (ORAHS)*. Frankfurt: Peter Lang.

Curry, S. and G. A. Marlatt (1988). Survival analysis and assessment of relapse. In: Donovan, D. M. and G. A. Marlatt (eds), *Assessment of Addictive Behaviours*. New York: Guilford Press, pp. 454–83.

Dean, R. and T. Craig (1999). *Pressure Points: Why People with Mental Health Problems become Homeless*. London: Crisis.

Donovan, D. M. (1996). Assessment issues and domains in the prediction of relapse. *Addiction*, **91**(Supplement 12), S29–36.

Donovan, T. and G. A. Marlatt (2005). *Assessment of Addictive Behaviours*. New York: Guilford Press.

Foster, J. (2005). Alcohol dependency and quality of life. *Alcohol and Alcoholism*, **40**(Supplement 1), S15-01.

Garratt, A. M., L. Schmidt and R. Fitzpatrick (2002). Patient-assessed health outcome measures for diabetes: a structured review. *Diabetic Medicine*, **19**(1), 1–11.

George, S. and R. A. Braithwaite (2002). Use of on-site testing for drugs of abuse. *Clinical Chemistry*, **48**(10), 1639–46.

Goldman, M. S. and J. Darkes (2004). Alcohol expectancy multiaxial assessment: a memory network-based approach. *Psychological Assessment*, **16**(1), 4–15.

Hodgins, D. C., J. Armstrong, D. C. Hodgins, N. El-Guebaly and J. Armstrong (1995). Prospective and retrospective reports of mood states before relapse to substance use. *Journal of Consulting and Clinical Psychology*, **63**(3), 400–7.

Logan, D. L. (2005). Now it's personal! Maximising the 'first contact' opportunities with homeless and vulnerable people: the 'Pre-treatment' role of the voluntary sector. *Alcohol and Alcoholism*, **40**(Supplement 1), S02-03.

Luscombe, C. and A. Brook (2005). Prevalence of alcohol abuse in homeless populations: the use of holistic assessments in the non-statutory sector. *Alcohol and Alcoholism*, **40**(Supplement 1), S02-04.

Martin, C. R., A. B. Bonner, A. Brook and C. Luscombe (2006). Factor structure and use of the Hospital Anxiety and Depression Scale in the homeless and socially marginalized. *Psychology, Health and Medicine*, **11**(2), 190–7.

Martin, C. R., A. B. Bonner and C. C. H. Cook (2002). Development of the PC version of the Bexley–Maudsley automated psychological screening test. *Proceedings of the British Psychological Society*, **10**(1).

Martin, C. R. and D. R. Thompson (2000). *Design and Analysis of Clinical Nursing Research Studies*. London: Routledge.

Miller, L. (1985). Neuropsychological assessment of substance abusers: review and recommendations. *Journal of Substance Abuse and Treatment*, **2**(1), 5–17.

Moggi, F., P. C. Ouimette, R. H. Moos and J. W. Finney (1999). Dual diagnosis patients in substance abuse treatment: relationship of general coping and substance-specific coping to 1-year outcomes. *Addiction*, **94**(12), 1805–16.

Moos, R. H. and C. J. Holahan (2003). Dispositional and contextual perspectives on coping: toward an integrative framework. *Journal of Clinical Psychology*, **59**(12), 1387–403.

Munro, G. (2006). *An Exploratory Research Study into the Substance Misuse and Health Related Needs of Migrant and Trafficked Women Engaged in Prostitution in Tower Hamlets and the City*. London: The Research Department, The Salvation Army.

NTA (2005). *Models of Care: Update 2005*. London: National Treatment Agency, NHS.

Perry, L. and S. McLaren (2004). An exploration of nutrition and eating disabilities in relation to quality of life at 6 months post-stroke. *Health and Social Care in the Community*, **12**(4), 288–97.

Reitan, R. M. and D. Wolfson (1994). A selective and critical review of neuropsychological deficits and the frontal lobes. *Neuropsychological Review*, **4**(3), 161–98.

Russell, R. M. (2000). The aging process as a modifier of metabolism. *American Journal of Clinical Nutrition*, **72**(Supplement 2), 529S–32S.

Shiffman, S. (1989). Trans-situational consistency in smoking relapse. *Journal of Health Psychology*, **8**(4), 471–81.

Shiffmann, S., M. H. Blabanis, J. Engberg, C. J. Gwaltney, K. S. Liu, M. Gnys, *et al.* (2000). Dynamic effects of self-efficacy on smoking lapse and relapse. *Journal of Health Psychology*, **19**(4), 315–23.

Spickerman, A. M. (1993). Proteins used in nutritional assessment. *Clinical and Laboratory Medicine*, **13**, 353–69.

Thomson, A. D. and E. J. Marshall (2006). The treatment of patients at risk of developing Wernicke's encephalopathy in the community. *Alcohol and Alcoholism*, **41**(2), 159–67.

Timms, P. W. and A. H. Fry (1989). Homelessness and mental illness. *Health Trends*, **21**(3), 70–1.

Todd, J., G. Green, M. Harrison, B. A. Ikuesan, C. Self, D. J. Pevalin, *et al.* (2004). Social exclusion in clients with comorbid mental health and substance misuse problems. *Social Psychiatry and Psychiatric Epidemiology*, **39**(7), 581–7.

Tuck, R. R. and M. Jackson (1991). Social, neurological and cognitive disorders in alcoholics. *Medical Journal of Australia*, **155**(4), 225–9.

USAID (1969). *The Logical Framework Approach*. US Agency for International Development.

Wang, S. J., C. J. Winchell, C. G. McCormick, S. E. Nevius and R. T. O'Neill (2002). Short of complete abstinence: analysis exploration of multiple drinking episodes in alcoholism treatment trials. *Alcohol: Clinical and Experimental Research*, **26**(6), 671–80.

Waugh, M., M. Jackson, G. A. Fox, S. H. Hawke and R. R. Tuck (1989). Effect of social drinking on neuropsychological performance. *British Journal of Addiction*, **84**(6), 659–67.

Wilson, J. F. and B. L. Smith (1999). Evaluation of detection techniques and laboratory proficiency in testing for drugs of abuse in urine: an external quality assessment scheme using clinically realistic urine samples. *Annals of Clinical Biochemistry*, **36**(5), 592–600.

Wing, J. K., T. Babor, T. Brugha, J. Burke, J. E. Cooper, R. Giel *et al.* (1990). SCAN. Schedules for Clinical Assessment in Neuropsychiatry. *Archives of General Psychiatry*, **47**(6), 589–93.

Zigmond, A. S. and R. P. Snaith (1983). The Hospital Anxiety and Depression Scale. *Acta Psychiatrica Scandinavica*, **67**, 361–7.

Zur, J. and W. Yule (1990). Chronic solvent abuse. 1. Cognitive sequelae. *Child: Care, Health and Development*, **16**(1), 1–20.

CHAPTER 11

INTERVENTIONS: CHANGING BEHAVIOUR

DELIVERING SERVICES

The previous chapter provided an introduction into the processes of screening, assessment and outcome monitoring. The identification of needs is clearly important prior to intervening and providing help for the vulnerable person. These previous discussions highlighted the problems of understanding the true needs of the person as opposed to those needs apparent when the client initially contacted the social or health service. Additionally, the changing nature of the client's needs suggests the requirement for ongoing assessments with a focus on the appearance of cues which forewarn of relapse from recovery, especially in programmes to support clients with mental health and/or substance misuse problems. Motivational issues should be monitored as the client progresses towards living independently. Cues that reflect possible tenancy failure need to be monitored and appropriate support provided. Interventions, which are provided in the absence of appropriate screening, assessment and outcome monitoring, are likely to be less effective than those developed with a relevant assessment framework. Furthermore important information relating to the effectiveness of the service will not be available, a consideration at this time of evidence-based practice, which is essential for service development, delivery and funding.

The type of intervention offered by a particular service will depend on a range of factors, including the physical and human resources available, all of which will be determined by the funding available. However, bearing in mind the very significant impact that the non-statutory services have in helping vulnerable people in the community, the role of volunteers should not be underrated. In working with people with complex needs, the skills and range of staff are important, and conducting a training needs analysis should be regularly undertaken by both non-statutory and statutory services. With regard to volunteers, minimal standards should be in place in order to protect vulnerable clients and also to avoid risk to the volunteer. Minimum training standards should not be restricted to volunteers and new members of staff, they should form the basis of an ongoing training and educational process, available for all members of staff, including senior managers. These human resource issues are part of the management of the service's quality assurance mechanism and should be seen as part of the strategic development of the service.

In the UK the *Commission for Social Care Inspection* (CSCI) ensures that registered care homes comply with *National Care Standards*. CSCI inspections involve collection of evidence and the awarding of scores (1–4), depending on the subjective evaluation of the service, by the local inspector. Projects and services funded by *Supporting People* (see Chapter 12) are monitored within a *Quality Assessment Framework* (QAF) according to their performance on 17 standards. This well-developed audit tool provides a standardised assessment approach leading to the scores of A (very good) to D (bad), depending on written evidence and evidence collected during an inspection visit.

Quality in Alcohol and Drug Services (QuADS) has been developed to encourage the development of substance misuse services. QuADs, like QAF, is a standardised quality assessment tool developed in response to *Task Force to Review Services for Drug Misusers* in 1996. The 37 standards of QuADS span a wide range of activities including: core management standards; core care standards; assessments; treatment; care planning; counselling and psychotherapy; prescribing; alcohol detoxification; needle exchange and services for young people.

Increasingly, care for the socially excluded is becoming regulated, a good development to protect vulnerable people who often are not represented due to their own communication difficulties, or lack of channels through which their views can be articulated. The views of service users are becoming an important aspect of statutory inspections and the development of services in the community. The downside of this increasingly regulated system of care and support is the impact on the morale of staff, who are faced with seemingly ever-increasing numbers of forms to complete, putting more pressure on hard-pressed project workers.

PHILOSOPHY OF CARE

An emerging element in statutory inspections is the *mission and objectives of the service*. Self-assessment of the service should now include a comparison of outputs of the service against the key strategic objectives for which the service is being funded. This is a very welcome development as the need for objectivity regarding the impact that a service is having on people's lives is long overdue. However, there is a difference between an aspirational aim, for instance 'to reduce chaos, develop life skills and reintegrate individuals into the community' and a deeper consideration of the underlying individual and community issues which are the focus of this book.

The main problem areas leading to exclusion from society include stigmatisation, lack of social networks (especially family structure), employment and accommodation opportunities. An absence of *meaning and belonging* and *purpose in life* have been cited in Chapter 2, as the expressions of these socially mediated problems, exacerbated in some by the confounding issues of learning difficulties, mental health and substance misuse.

In developing a *philosophy of care* for a service that aims to address the complex needs of this heterogeneous group of potential clients, a range of intervention strategies has to be considered. This raises a question as to whether a unitary *philosophy of care*, which encompasses such a wide range of diverse support services, could be agreed by the stakeholders. Common features of this range of interventions include the *process of change*, which involves a consideration of motivation, cognitive capacity for change, physiological functioning, inherited tendencies, developmental experiences and an appropriate social environment in which to operate as a functional individual. This *biopsychosocial* approach is a useful conceptual model, which draws on a number of ideas from treatment modalities that involve acute or chronic motivational issues including:

- Harmful environments in which an individual has difficulties in coping. These include social situations or life styles in which an individual is ill equipped to respond.

- Sensitisation to the effects of stimulant drugs, tolerance, withdrawal and other features of addictive behaviours.

- Motivational problems related to poor impulse control, chronic anxiety, depression, low self-esteem and other mental health related issues.

Another feature common to the various treatment modalities used to address the needs of the socially excluded is that of increasing personal organisation and orderliness. Physicists describe this process in terms of an increase in *entropy*. Left to itself the universe is regarded as continually moving towards a state of disorder (Maxwell *et al.* 1875, in Haynie 2001). Change in chaotic systems provides a good analogy of an individual's motivational state, with increasing orderliness the individual becomes more able to function as an individual in society. At a biological level increased orderliness results from integration and synchronicity of a wide range of physiological feedback mechanisms, which are involved in, for instance, the regulation of neurotransmitters and concentration of hormones in the body. This is discussed in Chapter 6 with respect to the *dysregulation hypothesis* of depression. At a behavioural level, reduction of chaos is reflected in improvements of the sleep–wake cycle, an important indicator of progress in substance misuse treatment programmes.

Reality orientation is a well-established approach used in elderly care support programmes. A modification of this approach has some relevance for younger people who suffer from a sense of disorientation due to their life style and problematic alcohol and drug misuse. These time-based changes underpin increasing functionality of the client and are important requisites for social inclusion. Holding down a job, maintaining a tenancy and generally participating in civil society requires a great deal of personal organisation including keeping appointments and generally managing time effectively.

These ideas suggest that an inclusive *philosophy of care* should include an overall service objective to facilitate the process of change, in order to increase personal organisation and effectiveness, and develop a purpose in life within a socially supportive context.

THE PROCESS OF CHANGE

Change is something that we experience on a daily basis, it allows us to respond to the changing environment and different physiological and psychological states. The ability to adapt appropriately to changing circumstances is an important attribute which has survival value. The process of change is central to rehabilitation and resettlement in socially excluded people, in order that they may improve their accommodation situation, become more financially independent by gaining employment and reduce their negative health behaviours.

Behavioural change strategies should be embedded in a framework for working with the 'whole' person and should include ways of structuring conversation in an unbounded environment with the clients feeling they have the freedom to talk and think about change from *their* perspective. In the case of clients with multiple needs, negotiation between the client and the helper is required so that a decision can be made as to which of the multiple needs should be addressed first. In increasing the confidence of the client to change the desired behaviour or present situation, an exploration and an assessment of the importance of the desired change is a good starting point. Exchanging information and reducing resistance should then be central elements in the consultative process. The time available for the consultation will determine what is possible. Clearly the time available in the initial contact stage will be limited and *brief motivational interviewing* might be appropriate at this stage of the client–helper relationship. In the later assessment phases, more time will be available, which might range from a few hours, to a day or more, depending on the structure of the programme and staff resources.

Listening skills are needed by anyone engaged in any contact with clients, although it is important to distinguish between the use of *counselling skills* and *counselling per se*. Appropriate training and professional recognition is required for the development of counselling as part of the therapeutic process, beyond the initial contact phase. However, counselling skills can be used effectively by project workers to support clients and help them into an appropriate therapeutic programme.

The promotion of behaviour change involves *readiness* to change and a recognition of the salience of a potential change within the person's world, together with the *confidence* to move forward. The *transtheoretical model of stages of change* (Prochaska and DiClementi 1986) provides a useful guide to describe how people move towards making decisions and changing their behaviour. This approach was developed in addiction services, and now is widely used among a number of different health and social care professionals. However, it has been estimated that no more than 20% of people in healthcare settings are ready to move forward and actively seek change.

Clearly *motivation* is a pivotal factor in the process of change. This will depend on whether the client considers the change to be important, their mood state and their perceived notion of a way out of their problematic situation (see Chapter 2). Overcoming *resistance* will be determined by the style of the interviewer. For instance a confrontational interviewing style will increase *resistance*. An additional obstacle is the window of opportunity – it might not be an appropriate time for change.

It is beyond the scope of this book to delve further into managing the process of change, the application of this approach is succinctly given by Rollnick *et al.* (2002). A useful overview is provided by Davis (1996) and an interesting view on the use of *motivational interviewing* in working with clients was produced by Kent (2004). The use of *brief motivational interviewing* has been reported in excessive drinkers (Rollnick *et al.* 1992), smokers (Rollnick *et al.* 2002) and diabetic patients (Stott *et al.* 1995). The more extensive and time-consuming *motivational interviewing* has its foundation in the work of Miller and Rollnick (1991).

In addition to the *transtheoretical model of stages of change*, a number of other approaches may be considered by the reader, as indicated in Table 11.1. The use of some of these methods will require extensive training and some require professional registration. However, it should be noted that in well-controlled comparative studies in the use of various therapeutic approaches, as in Project Match (1993) and the UKAT study Team (2001), no one technique appears to be significantly better than the others. What does impact on client outcome is the nature of the relationship between the client and the therapist and also the place of safety available to the client. The relationship between client and helper should therefore form the main support element in the processes of change in the rehabilitation and resettlement of socially excluded people. These clients become even more vulnerable when engaging with helpers and linking into the non-statutory and statutory services. An example of this is in the case of needle exchange schemes, aimed at reducing harm and making a contact with hard to reach injecting drug users. These services are

Table 11.1 Summary of theories for the promotion of behavioural change.

Individual level	Stages of change model	Individuals' motivation and readiness to change a problem or behaviour	• Precontemplation • Contemplation • Decision • Action • Maintenance
	Health belief model	Individuals' perceptions of the threat posed by a health problem, the benefits of avoiding the threat and factors influencing the decision to act	• Perceived susceptibility • Perceived severity • Perceived benefits • Perceived barriers • Cues to action • Self-efficacy
	Theory of planned behaviour	Individual's attitudes towards a behaviour, perceptions of norms and beliefs about the ease or difficulty of changing	• Behavioural intention • Attitude • Subjective norm • Perceived behavioural control
	Precaution adoption process model	Individuals' journey from lack of awareness to action and maintenance	• Unaware of issue • Unengaged by issue • Deciding about acting • Deciding not to act • Acting • Maintenance
Interpersonal level	Social cognitive theory	Personal factors, environmental factors and human behaviour exert influence on each other	• Reciprocal determinism • Behavioural capability • Expectations • Self-efficacy • Observational learning • Reinforcements
Community level	Community organisation	Community-driven approaches to assessing and solving health and social problems	• Empowerment • Community capacity • Participation • Relevance • Issue selection • Critical consciousness

Source: Reproduced from *Theory at a Glance: A Guide for Health Promotion Practice*. US Department of Health and Human Science, NIH, Washington.

normally operated in such a way as to protect the identity of the service users. Dealing with the vulnerability of clients is important in these front-line services and also in more mainstream services in which counselling skills and counselling are used. Rose Kent (2004) has drawn attention to the use and abuse of power in these psychosocial interventions. The use of low intensity counselling skills and more penetrating psychosocial interventions involve working with psychologically vulnerable people. The setting and maintaining of boundaries within an ethical framework and the recognition of 'accountability and transparency' should help to protect vulnerable clients, and reduce professional and legal risks for the helper.

MAINTAINING CHANGE

The approach to preventing relapse, as described in Chapter 10, suggests the importance of helping the individuals to identify personal warning signs, which might include 'euphoric recall', for example positive thoughts about previous maladaptive behaviours. Other warning signs include emotional warnings such as positive emotional states (e.g. excitement, celebration, arousal) and negative mood states (e.g. depression, loneliness, anger, boredom). A third set of issues relating to relapse includes compulsive and impulsive behaviours (see above), in particular related to drug use, drinking, re-establishing social contact with drinkers and other drug users (Donovan and Marlatt 2005). A key element of the intervention process is, after having identified the specific factors which when triggered may lead to relapse, to help the clients to develop behavioural and cognitive strategies. This involves developing coping skills, which might initially be concerned with addressing problematic alcohol or drug misuse, requiring ways of dealing with cravings and urges to engage in addictive behaviours.

The past decade has brought an exponential increase in our knowledge of the pharmacotherapeutic management of depression and other affective states. Much has been learned about the prevalence, risks and course of depression in the general population, the elderly and patients with comorbid medical illnesses and about the biological basis of depression. Nemeroff (1994) has reviewed the evolving trends in the diagnosis and management of depression and provides an evaluation of the main classes of antidepressants. The main conclusions from this review are that although depression carries a high risk of morbidity and mortality, it is very treatable, and early diagnosis and treatment are recommended. The role and effectiveness of medications in relapse prevention have been reviewed by Nunes (2004).

Frequently medication is continued after the patients' acute depressive symptoms diminish, sometimes for as long as one to five years to prevent relapse and recurrence of depression; maintenance therapy often involves the prescription of full doses, rather than lower doses of antidepressant. The choice of antidepressants has been extended over recent years. In addition to tricyclic and tetracyclic antidepressants and monoamine oxidase inhibitors, the serotonin reuptake inhibitors fluoxetine, sertraline and paroxetine have been developed. Additionally, antidepressants with atypical mechanisms of action that include bupropion, trazodone, venlafaxin, and nefazodone have been developed. These new medications are safer and better tolerated because they are believed to act selectively on specific neurotransmitter systems, and are comparable in efficacy to the tricyclic antidepressants. However, the use of pharmacological tools needs to be managed judiciously to avoid overdependency on chemicals (Goodchild and Laurance 2006).

INTERVENTIONS FOR ADDICTIVE BEHAVIOURS

A wide range of residential and non-residential services is available in the community. These services use a range of treatment strategies including twelve-step, cognitive behaviour therapy (CBT), solution focused therapy and family therapy.

Chapter 3 of this book provides a rationale for using a developmental approach in working with clients with complex needs. Bowlby (1977) laid the foundations of *attachment theory* by suggesting that members of some other animal species have an innate tendency to seek and maintain proximity to certain preferred others. The establishing of an 'affectional bond' is an important feature of mother–infant bonding, disruption of which can have consequences for personal attributes and sometimes results in later life psychopathologies. Reading (2002) has drawn attention to the role of the therapeutic alliance in using *attachment theory* in a therapeutic setting. It is proposed that the therapist acts as a temporary attachment figure, providing the client with a secure anchor as the client begins to explore the new world view which is revealed in the therapeutic relationship. The therapeutic alliance should promote confidence and reduce resistance to change. The attachment behavioural system is shown in Figure 11.1.

The entry point into this system is anxiety due to either perceived threat or separation concerns. The relevance of this model is that the relationship between the addict and his or her drug is that the *set* (Winnicott 1964) is laid down, after repeated experiences with the drug. An *internal working model* (IWM), formed in the mind, provides a secure base (see Figure 11.1). Attachment behaviour becomes activated when danger is perceived or the affectional bond is threatened. Cognitive behavioural therapy can be employed to help clients identify and modify their thoughts that increase the possibility of relapse, but CBT is thought to have a different influence on relapse than the use of attachment-based psychotherapy (Reading 2002). Deprivation of the secure base, the relationship between the client and

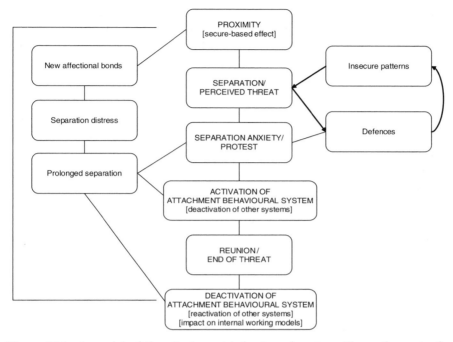

Figure 11.1 A model of the attachment behavioural system. The pathway to the left of the central column depicts the satisfactory movement back to a position of proximity/security base. To the right is depicted the possible route of entry into defensive/insecure patterns of attachment. Note that progress on both left and right routes forms the basis for a further impact on the organisation of internal working models. Note also the recursive interplay between attachment and other behavioural systems.

Source: Reprinted with permission from John Wiley and Sons, Ltd from Reading, B. (2002) The application of Bowlby's attachment theory to the psychotherapy of the addictions. In: Weegmann, M. and R. Cohen (eds), *The Psychodynamics of Addiction*. London: Whurr Publishers.

his or her drug, is a significant personal change which occurs in effective interventions. At this stage an ambiguous relationship develops with the therapist and the client may develop hostile feelings to the therapist. This is a result of a threat to the secure base, namely his or her relationship with the drug.

Cessation/reduction of the drug invites the potential to experience loss of both proximity to the drug use itself and of those relationships/social networks to which the drug use has facilitated membership in the past. Since the process of mourning losses seems to be crucial in freeing the bereaved individual to form new attachments (and to relinquish ties to old ones), the therapist needs to be able to acknowledge and facilitate the patient's need to grieve such losses where appropriate (Reading 2002).

In reviewing the overriding principles which should be considered in providing help for individuals who are addressing addictive behaviour problems, West (2006) concludes that the following guiding principles should be designed into the programme delivery:

- Interventions must reduce impulses or create inhibitions operating at the moments when opportunities for engaging in the addictive behaviour occur.

- Preventative interventions should increase vigilance for small signs that the motivational system is getting out of balance and add, remove, strengthen or weaken elements to restore motivational balance.

- Interventions to combat addiction should have a clear specification concerning how far they are seeking to reduce the strength or extent of excessive motivational forces or to increase the strength of forces that counter these or both.

- All interventions should have a clear specification concerning how far they are being used to achieve this, bearing in mind the likely current state of their motivational system.

- Moving individuals into new behavioural pathways (chreoids) will require changes to the motivational system that propagate throughout the system.

DUAL DIAGNOSIS

In recent years there has been increased focus on therapeutic programmes which integrate treatment of both substance misuse and severe mental illness. This is an important change to the earlier situation where the issues were considered in isolation; often individuals with complex needs would fall between the traditional mental health and substance misuse treatment services. This service gap contributed to the increasing number of clients with complex needs to be found in emergency accommodation and community programmes as described in Chapter 12. Integrated care pathways require more specialist resources than the single-issue services and may require radical redesign of service delivery systems.

Treatment programming for individuals diagnosed with a chronic mental illness and an alcohol use disorder could be enhanced by employing techniques that focus on aspects of the change process variables that are most strongly related to psychiatric distress. Prochaska and DiClemente's transtheoretical model (TTM, see above, p. 181) provides a useful framework within which to study these relations.

Velasquez *et al.* (1999) studied the associations between psychiatric severity and the TTM constructs of stages and processes of change. *Decisional balance, temptation* and *self-efficacy* were measured in 132 alcohol-dependent patients in an outpatient dual diagnosis programme. The researchers found that the participants' scores on the *temptation* subscale of the *Alcohol Absti-nence Self-Efficacy Questionnaire* were strongly related to psychiatric severity in that the greater the psychiatric distress experienced by an individual the more that person is tempted to drink, particularly in situations that trigger negative affect. *Decisional balance* scores were related to psychiatric severity; higher scores on the *Global Severity Index of the Brief Symptom Inventory* were associated with negative aspects of drinking.

A Cochrane review by Ley *et al.* (2000) has indicated that there is little evidence to support the current momentum for integrated programmes and that well-designed controlled clinical trials are needed to support the effective implementation of new specialist substance misuse services for those with serious mental illnesses. The reviews report that there is no clear evidence of one programme being superior to another and no significant advantage of any type of substance misuse programme for those with serious mental illness over the value of standard care was apparent.

In contrast to an integrated approach to severe mental illness a Cochrane review by Joy *et al.* (2000) focused on crisis intervention. In order to address the delivery of an acceptable level of care during the acute phases of severe mental illness *crisis intervention* models of care have been developed. This review failed to draw any robust conclusions on existing approaches and concluded that homecare crisis treatment, coupled with an ongoing home-care package, is a viable and acceptable way of treating people with serious mental illnesses.

CAPACITY FOR CHANGE

Behavioural change is an important process that allows humans and other animals to respond to the changing environment. This ecological perspec-tive suggests that both conscious and subconscious processes are active in bringing about appropriate adaptation to ensure survival. Maladap-tive behaviours, on the other hand, might result from either inappropriate choices being made or the inability to make choices due to cognitive dysfunction or the overriding influence of impulses and the lack of self-control.

Rational informed choice is thought to be based on a *cost-benefit analysis* by which behaviours are performed in the expectation that benefits will be gained by such actions. From this viewpoint we assume that a homeless person living and sleeping on the street, anaesthetised from the hostile envi-ronment by excessive alcohol consumption, would prefer not to live like this and only does so out of a lack of choice. This *Rational Informed Choice* (RISC) model of behaviour has been reviewed by Vuchinich and Heather (2003, see West 2006, p. 31). RISC theories include the theory of rational addiction (Becker and Murphy 1988), defined as 'a consistent plan to maximise utility over time'. This idea is based on stable rational preferences as explained by economists in describing addiction to substances at a community level to 'maximise utility'. The assumption here is that consumers expend resources according to their judgements about the benefits to them by acquiring or consuming the commodity, namely alcohol or illicit drugs.

In view of the high prevalence of comorbidity of mental health and substance misuse problems, it is conceivable that some people consume alcohol and other drugs as a way of coping or ameliorating adverse life experiences. The *Self-medication Model of Addiction* (Gelkopf *et al.* 2002) suggests that the use of drugs is an attempt to treat the psychological symptoms or needs experienced by the individual. Rational choice might not appear to be sensible, but it can be considered to be an adaptive behavioural response. A *cost-benefit* analysis, which includes expectations of the benefits of consumption of alcohol, may lead to excessive use.

In reviewing *expectancy theories* (Goldman and Darkes 2004) suggest that memory templates of the rewarding value of addictive behaviour may complement *beliefs*. There is an overlap between theories of expectancy and cognitive bias, which is used to explain maladaptive behaviours by biases in the cognitive system, including expectancies, beliefs, self-efficacy, attributions and attention (Ryan 2002). A particular aspect of cognitive bias is related to attention. Attentional biases can be conveniently measured using the Stroop test. This test has potential as a rapid measure of the signal-to-noise ratio, an important indicator of cognitive processing and attentional bias. This test is currently being developed for use in outcome monitoring in alcohol and related recovery programmes (Shaman and Luscombe, in preparation).

Adaptive behaviours become *habituated*, a form of learning which results in non-responsiveness in the absence of a stimulus. This is apparent when we first get dressed in the morning. Initially we are aware of the clothing on our skin, but within a short time our tactile receptors have *habituated* and we are no longer aware of the initial sensation. This aspect of learning is described in the *Opponent Process Theory* (Solomon and Corbit 1974), one of a number of explanations for the reduction in the effect of a drug and withdrawal symptoms during abstinence.

Rational and irrational choice theories rely upon an intact brain which has the capacity to assimilate external information and, after processing the information within a historical context, requiring a functional memory, brings about a response which might be construed as a change in behaviour. There is increasing evidence that homeless people, in particularly those with long-term alcohol problems or those with mental health problems, may be cognitively impaired. Impaired pathways in the brain may result in pathological changes in motives and conscious states that impel and restrain behaviour. Compulsion, craving and self-control underlie the *disease model of addiction* as described by Jellineck (1960). This rather dated model suggests that people do things against their will, a view not supported by Edwards *et al.* (1976) who, on commenting on lack of choice, propose that 'it is unclear . . . whether the experience is truly one of losing control rather than one of deciding not to exercise control'.

In developing a theoretical basis for the development of a philosophy of care, the forgoing reviews suggest that the concepts of rational and irrational choice, self-control and compulsion should be considered in relation to personality attributes, as proposed in Cloninger's *tri-dimensional personality theory* (Cloninger 1987), social identity (see Chapter 1) and a range of other psychosocial determinants. West (2006) has reviewed this wide range of theories relating to the development of a 'comprehensive theory' of addiction. This psychological analysis of many behavioural patterns, identified in socially excluded people, provides a useful insight into the motivational aspects of these maladaptive behaviours. Laudable as this *synthetic theory* is, it pays little regard to the biological status of homeless and socially excluded people whose plight has resulted from the chronic use of alcohol and other drugs, and consequential impact on cognitive functioning.

COGNITIVE FUNCTIONING IN THE HOMELESS AND SOCIALLY EXCLUDED

Spence *et al.* (2004) have carried out a systematic review of cognitive dysfunction in homeless adults. 'Cognitive function' depends on a number of neuropsychological processes that support mental activity. These include memory and attention, and executive functions which facilitate planning and control of behaviour. Spence's meta-analysis consisted of 3300 fully reported cases from around the world. Despite the methodological problems of comparing different studies, from a research design perspective, he found evidence of a link between homelessness and global neuropsychological impairment. Global neuropsychological impairment is likely to reduce the ability of a person to retain new information. Although executive (global) cognitive impairment has only been studied in a relatively small proportion of homeless people, this review does point to the need for more work in this area, as the behavioural consequences are highly relevant to the development of services.

In changing behaviour and circumstances, as discussed above, the learning of new skills and breaking down of destructive patterns of behaviour, executive functioning and cognitive flexibility are required. Cognitive dysfunctioning in clients receiving help from statutory and non-statutory services will lead to problems of compliance with the services offered. An important question arising from this critical review is whether cognitive dysfunction predisposes people to homelessness, or does it occur as a consequence of negative life styles of homeless and socially excluded people? Furthermore what implications are there for the process of rehabilitation and resettlement in those who are cognitively dysfunctional? Although these questions cannot easily be answered the high incidence of alcohol-related problems in homeless populations suggests that even moderate alcohol-related brain damage may be a significant factor in the loss of executive function. Additionally, smoking is associated with neurocognitive deficits in problematic alcohol users (Glass *et al.* 2005).

Structural and functional damage, due to long-term alcohol consumption, results in neuropsychological impairment, mood disorders and personality changes. Damage is normally located in temporal and prefrontal areas, regions that are specialised for memory, working memory, strategic planning, goal selection and response inhibition. Interference with these cognitive functions will undoubtedly mitigate against good outcomes in alcohol rehabilitation programmes (McCrady and Smith 1986; Roehrich and Goldman 1993). Current treatments aim to change behaviour and develop skills to prevent relapse and enhance psychosocial adaptation. Clearly attempts to arrest and hopefully reverse cognitive decline, improve mood (affect) and quality of life should be central to the strategy of rehabilitation, thereby increasing a sense of *meaning and belonging* in previously socially excluded individuals. Relapse occurs frequently in 'rehabilitated' clients and high-order measurements such as length of tenancy or social connectivity might not be the best indicators of the appropriate treatment regime, as attempted by project MATCH.

The implication of this work is that is seems imperative to assess the extent of cognitive impairment of those who use the various services aimed at increasing inclusion. A brief review of the development of neuropsychological assessment is given in Chapter 10.

NUTRITIONAL SUPPORT AND BEHAVIOURAL CHANGE

Behavioural therapies such as *cognitive behaviour therapy* (CBT) can lead to improved performance in the process of rehabilitation and resettlement of socially excluded people. However, these methods are likely to be limited in their effectiveness if the cellular mechanisms of brain function are compromised by nutritional imbalances. There are a number of possibilities for developing nutritional strategies, which might be used as adjuncts to cognitive and behavioural therapies; these have been reviewed by Bonner *et al.* (2003).

Chronic alcohol consumption, when an individual has adequate nutrition, results in subtle brain damage in cortical and subcortical regions (Cala 1982).

However, it has been well established that major neurological symptoms occur in cases of thiamine deficiency. Wernicke encephalopathy (WE) leading to Korsakoff's psychosis (KP) is perhaps the most widely known and best understood neuropsychiatric disorder associated with long-term alcohol misuse, the mechanisms of which might be considered to be *alcohol neurotoxicity* or *thiamine malnutrition* (Mulder and Joyce 2002). Supplementation of thiamine has been employed and shown to have a therapeutic benefit in alcohol-dependent subpopulations without severe KP as shown in the first reported randomised, double-blind, multidose study by Ambrose (2001). In a hospital setting patients suspected of having a poor diet should be treated as soon as possible with intravenous or intramuscular injections of B vitamins. This recommendation is based on evidence that 30–80 % of alcohol misusing patients have low circulating levels of thiamine (Cook *et al.* 1998). Thiamine uptake from oral doses is poor in these patients as intestinal absorption of thiamine is reduced by 70 %. This limited absorption can be further reduced by ethanol consumption by a further 50 %.

In addition to the role of vitamins and amino acids, other factors in the diet are known to have a significant effect on brain function, these include minerals such as zinc (Sandstead *et al.* 1978) and antioxidants (Bonner *et al.* 2003). There are some concerns about nutritional practice in hospitals, as reported in Chapter 9. In the homeless community the problems are probably far more acute.

In summary, this chapter has focused on various domains involving behavioural changes. Change comes from within, in terms of the motivation to seek change in behaviour or personal circumstances, and the transition to a new position in the client's perception of his or her world. The reader will note that behavioural change can be encouraged by low intensity counselling skills, involving active listening, or more sophisticated and complex counselling practice.

This review has drawn on work mainly developed in working with those who have addictive behaviour problems. This is justified on the grounds that a high proportion of homeless people are problematic alcohol and drugs users, and also the psychosocial interventions for these groups, which have been well developed over recent years, can be generalised to other groups of socially excluded people. In the case of the elderly, significant changes involve the loss of employment or a spouse. Changes in social networks due to death of peers or moving into retirement, care and nursing homes cause high levels of anxiety and personal adaptations. The description of attachment behaviour and the loss of secure base, as described above, provides a model for understanding the anxiety-prone changing situations which occur during the process of ageing. The capacity to respond to changing circumstances in both the elderly and younger people will be dependent on the level of cognitive function required to learn new things and to take executive decisions. Although, in the elderly there is an increased incidence of cerebral vascular problems (i.e. stroke) and Alzheimer's disease, other types of cognitive dysfunction might have some commonality between those ageing naturally and the premature ageing observed in many homeless people. Psychosocial therapies can be helpful to support the process of change, however, due consideration should be given to the cognitive capacity of the client to respond to change. The increasing evidence of links between neurocognitive dysfunction and nutrition suggests that appropriate assessments of both are required in order to maximise the effectiveness of interventions used in the rehabilitation and resettlement of homeless and socially excluded people.

REFERENCES

Ambrose, M. L., S. C. Bowden and G. Whelan (2001). Thiamine treatment and working memory function of alcohol-dependent people: preliminary findings. *Alcoholism: Clinical and Experimental Research*, **25**(1), 112–16.

Becker, G. S. and K. M. Murphy (1988). A theory of rational addiction. *Journal of Political Economy*, **96**, 675–700.

Bonner, A. B., A. D. Thomson and C. H. Cook (2003). Alcohol, nutrition and brain function. In: Watson R. R., V. R. Preedy and W. R. Watson (eds), *Nutrition and Alcohol*. Boca Raton, Florida: CRC Press.

Bowlby, J. (1977). The making and breaking of affectional bonds. I. Aetiology and psychopathology in the light of attachment theory. An expanded version of the Fiftieth Maudsley Lecture, delivered before the Royal College of Psychiatrists, 19 November 1976. *British Journal of Psychiatry*, **130**, 201–10.

Cala, L. A., F. L. Mastagali, B. Jones and B. Wiley (1982). The effects of alcohol in social drinkers. *Journal of Studies on Alcohol*, **43**(5), 614–15.

Cloninger, C. R. (1987). Recent advances in family studies of alcoholism. *Progress in Clinical Biology Research*, **241**, 47–60.

Cook, C. C., P. M. Hallwood and A. D. Thomson (1998). B vitamin deficiency and neuropsychiatric syndromes in alcohol misuse. *Alcohol and Alcoholism*, **33**(4), 317–36.

Davis, P. E. (1996). Cognitive and behavioural approaches to changing addictive behaviours. In: Bonner, A. B. and J. Waterhouse (eds), *Addictive Behaviour: Molecules to Mankind*. Basingstoke: Macmillan.

Donovan, T. and G. A. Marlatt (2005). *Assessment of Addictive Behaviours*. New York: Guilford Press.

Edwards, G., M. M. Gross, M. Keller and J. Moser (1976). Alcohol-related problems in the disability perspective. A summary of the consensus of the WHO group of investigators on criteria for identifying and classifying disabilities related to alcohol consumption. *Journal of Studies on Alcohol*, **37**(9), 1360–82.

Gelkopf, M., S. Levitt and A. Bleich (2002). An integration of three approaches to addiction and methadone maintenance treatment: the self-medication hypothesis, the disease model and social criticism. *Israel Journal of Psychiatry and Related Sciences*, **39**(2), 140–51.

Glass, J. M., K. M. Adams, J. T. Nigg, M. M. Wong, L. I. Puttler, J. M. Jester, *et al.* (2005). Smoking is associated with neurocognitive deficits in alcoholism. *Drug and Alcohol Dependence*, **82**(2), 119–26.

Goldman, M. S. and J. Darkes (2004). Alcohol expectancy multiaxial assessment: a memory network-based approach. *Psychological Assessment*, **16**(1), 4–15.

Goodchild, S. and J. Laurance (2006). Dependency Britain: we're in a major drugs crisis. Why it may be better to talk. *The Independent on Britain*, 16 April, 12–13.

Haynie, D. (2001). *Biological Thermodynamics*. Cambridge: Cambridge University Press.

Jellinek, E. M. (1960). Alcoholism, a genus and some of its species. *Canadian Medical Association Journal*, **83**, 1341–5.

Joy, C. B., C. E. Adams and K. Rice (2000). Crisis intervention for people with severe mental illnesses. *Cochrane Database System Review*, (2), CD001087.

Kent, R. (2004). Trust me, I'm a client – embracing motivational interviewing. *Drugs and Alcohol Today*, **4**, 37–42.

Ley, A., D. P. Jeffery, S. McLaren and N. Siegfried (2000). Treatment programmes for people with both severe mental illness and substance misuse. *Cochrane Database System Review*, (4), CD001088.

McCrady, B. S. and D. E. Smith (1986). Implications of cognitive impairment for the treatment of alcoholism. *Alcoholism: Clinical and Experimental Research*, **10**(2), 145–9.

Miller, W. and S. Rollnick (1991). *Motivational Interviewing*. New York: Guilford Press.

Mulder, R. T. and P. R. Joyce (2002). Relationship of temperament and behaviour measures to the prolactin reponse to fenfluaramine in depressed men. *Psychiatry Research*, **109**(3), 221–8.

Nemeroff, C. B. (1994). Evolutionary trends in the pharmacotherapeutic management of depression. *Journal of Clinical Psychiatry*, **55**(Supplement 3), 15; discussion 16–17.

Nunes, E. V. and F. R. Levin (2004). Treatment of depression in patients with alcohol or other drug dependence: a meta-analysis. *Journal of the American Medical Association*, **291**(15), 1887–96.

Prochaska, J. O. and C. C. DiClementi (1986). Towards a comprehensive model of change. In: Miller, W. R. and N. Heather (eds), *Treating Addictive Behaviours: Process of Change*. New York: Plenum Press, pp. 3–27.

Reading, B. (2002). The application of Bowlby's attachment theory to the psychotherapy of the addictions. In: Weegmann, M. and R. Cohen (eds), *The Psychodynamics of Addiction*. London: Whurr Publishers.

Roehrich, L. and M. S. Goldman (1993). Experience-dependent neuropsychological recovery and the treatment of alcoholism. *Journal of Consulting and Clinical Psychology*, **61**(5), 812–21.

Rollnick, S., N. Heather, R. Gold and W. Hall (1992). Development of a short 'readiness to change' questionnaire, opportunistic interventions among excessive drinkers. *British Journal of Addiction*, **87**, 743–54.

Rollnick, S., P. Mason and C. Butler (2002). *Health Behaviour Change, A Guide for Practitioners*. Edinburgh: Churchill Livingstone.

Ryan, F. (2002). Attentional bias and alcohol dependence: a controlled study using the modified Stroop paradigm. *Addictive Behaviors*, **27**(4), 471–82.

Sandstead, H. H., D. A. Strobel, G. M. Logan, Jr., E. O. Marks and R. A. Jacob (1978). Zinc deficiency in pregnant rhesus monkeys: effects on behavior of infants. *American Journal of Clinical Nutrition*, **31**(5), 844–9.

Solomon, R. L. and J. D. Corbit (1974). An opponent process theory of motivation. I. Temporal dynamics of affect. *Psychological Review*, **81**(2), 119–45.

Spence, S., R. Stevens and R. Parks (2004). Cognitive dysfunction in homeless adults: a systematic review. *Journal of the Royal Society of Medicine*, **97**(8), 375–9.

Stott, N. C., S. Rollnick, M. R. Rees and R. M. Pill (1995). Innovation in clinical method: diabetes care and negotiating skills. *Family Practice*, **12**(4), 413–18.

Team, T. U. R. (2001). United Kingdom Alcohol Treatment Trial (UKATT): hypotheses, design and methods. *Alcohol and Alcoholism*, **36**(1), 11–21.

Velasquez, M. M., J. P. Carbonari and C. C. DiClemente (1999). Psychiatric severity and behavior change in alcoholism: the relation of the transtheoretical model variables to psychiatric distress in dually diagnosed patients. *Addictive Behaviors*, **24**(4), 481–96.
West, R. (2006). *Theory of Addiction*. Oxford: Blackwell Publishing.
Winnicott, D. W. (1964). *The Child, the Family and the Outside World*. London: Penguin.

CHAPTER 12

INTERVENTIONS: SUPPORTING VULNERABLE PEOPLE

ACCOMMODATION

Seeking shelter is a basic motivational drive found in all animals, and humans have used various forms of shelter ranging from caves, used by troglodytes in France, to increasingly complex constructions. Shelters provide protection from adverse climatic conditions and predators and a base for the growth and nurturing of families. Domestic conditions do have a significant impact on a person's self-identity and the *territorial imperative* is a fundamental biosocial determinant. The Universal Declaration of Human Rights (1948) describes access to adequate housing as essential. UNICEF (Alson 1998) estimates that in the US 750 000 people are homeless, and before expansion of the EU, in 2004, approximately 3 million people were without a permanent home. In 2001, Shelter estimated that 440 000 were homeless in the UK. A Salvation Army/University of Surrey study (Moore *et al.* 1995) indicated the considerable methodological problems in measuring the various 'faces of homelessness in London'. This study indicated that 16 281 people were using the 286 hostels in London, 753 were visible sleeping in the streets, 30 000 were estimated to be living in squats, 5710 homeless people were in temporary hotel accommodation, about 75 % living as families. The total homeless population in London was estimated to be 75 000 at this time. Globally, about 1 billion people are poorly housed, of whom 100 million live on the streets (Begin *et al.* 1999).

Housing for people who are in transit or are homeless has evolved from the twelfth century when inns and churches provided shelter for most travellers. At this time there was a floating population of people visiting towns, attracted by local fairs in Britain. After the suppression of the abbeys, inns became popular. The rich crowded out the poor, and the hostel became the hotel. People who entertained strangers for a small charge became 'keeper of a common lodging house'. The stables of inns were the first common lodging houses, but accommodation here was only available for payment, and those without money begged in order to buy shelter. The destitute without money survived by begging. Vagabonds, homeless, nomadic unsettled people were considered in the sixteenth century to be worthless and not subject to control or restraint (OED 1973). These itinerant beggars, loafers or tramps were viewed as disreputable and good for nothing, and various Acts of Parliament were enacted in England and Scotland to control these people who were excluded from fixed communities. During the eighteenth century, cities such as London and Glasgow became more prosperous and the early industrial developments attracted groups of transient and nomadic people who became unskilled labourers wandering in search of food and shelter. This was a time when common lodging houses were opened in response to this influx of people from the countryside and other towns and cities, as various industrial ventures flourished and waned. In the nineteenth century the itinerant populations of towns and cities were increased by mass migration of the Irish after the failure of the Irish potato crop, resulting in the growth of poorly run temporary accommodation. Ferrier (1810) described the unhealthy state of Manchester lodging houses commenting that:

> ... great numbers of labouring poor ... tempted by the prospect of large wages.... flock into the principal towns, become diseased by getting into dirty infected houses on their arrival.... Others waste money without procuring employment, and sink under the pressure of want and despair. The horror of these houses cannot easily be described; a lodger fresh from the country often lies down in a bed filled with infection by its last tenant, or from the corpse of a victim's fever only removed a few hours before.

At this time epidemics of typhus, relapsing fever and cholera were quite frequent. Creighton (1894) reported that typhus did not cause high mortality in patients in the slums who were:

> ... hardened and inured to their circumstances.... and frequently developed a milder form of the disease. It was in those accustomed to better circumstances ... that the most fatal infections took place.

Reports in *The Glasgow Herald* (1907, 1908) from the Reverend David Watson commented on 'these places ... enabled men to shirk their duties ... and attracted wastrels and vagabonds from all parts'. He preached against drink and the immorality of lodging houses, and blamed 'parental inefficiency and a weakened sense of responsibility'. This initiated missions from the Church of Scotland and other churches to hold services in the lodging houses. In 1937 The Salvation Army opened a new lodging house for women in Clyde Street, replacing the old one in the high street. (The Salvation Army had previously established homeless centres in Edinburgh, Glasgow and London 50 years before this report). Between 1930 and 1940 there was a decreased demand for lodging houses, however, the quality of the reducing number of lodging houses gradually improved. A further reduction in lodging houses continued in 1940–54 due to a significant proportion of the lodging house population joining the armed forces.

Laidlaw (1954) undertook a survey of lodging-houses in Glasgow in the early 1950s. He made 700 visits and reported on interviews with 800 people using lodging houses during this period. This work provides important insights into the conditions and attitudes of the community at that time. He commented on the varying standards of the lodging houses:

> ... some achieving a high standard by refusing accommodation to dirty, drunken and disorderly characters. Others keep up their profits by admitting all. Summary justice is administered to those who start fights by the superintendent and the police are sometimes called. In Salvation Army Homes drinking and spitting are rigorously prohibited and a strict set of rules enforced.

Laidlaw reported that most of the lodging-houses had a shop and provided supplies for one meal only, to obviate the need for storage.

> The hostels run by the Salvation Army differ in having a canteen from which cooked food is served, and there are no cooking facilities for lodgers'. By this time there were few dormitories, and 'most of the sleeping accommodation is ... arranged in cubicles separated by wooden partitions and topped with wire netting which allows ventilation yet makes them secure against pilfering. Each lodger ... has a 7 feet high wooden partition ... to divide his cubicle from his neighbour's. . . . The minimum air space in dormitories was initially 330 cubic feet. . . . this was later increased to 435 cubic feet. The standard of cleanliness ... varies from one lodging house to another ... and

The First Labour Exchange was established in 1890, opportunities for employment were linked with accommodation. Within one year 20 similar schemes had been developed around the UK.

Source: Reprinted with permission from the Salvation Army International Heritage Centre, London.

many require visits from the disinfestation squad. Arrangements are made by which verminous lodgers can be cleansed at Belvidere Disinfection Station.

The Salvation Army hostels for men contained large dormitories providing accommodation for up to 250 men, usually managed by one or two officers. This type of provision was available until the 1960s.

MODERN HOUSING POLICY

With the advent of state intervention in the housing market lodging houses, later known as hostels, became restricted in number and a range of schemes including subsidised council housing provided an accommodation solution for those who could not afford to buy their own homes. By 1900 subsidised local authority housing was being criticised by New Liberals who regarded subsidies as mitigating against the 'independent working man'. In *Garden Cities of Tomorrow*, Ebenezer Howard (1902) argued that cheap land in rural areas could be used to build garden cities. Subsidised council housing and rent control were the main housing policies until 1979. This approach to building new towns with council-owned housing had little impact on the housing shortage after the First World War. Between 1915 and 1979 tenancies provided some stability to the accommodation problems in the UK. During this period successive UK governments assisted local authorities to build homes for 'general needs' in extreme housing shortages, a policy which encouraged subsidised housing within conurbations for those displaced from slum clearance.

During the 1960s and 1970s council high-rise estates were rapidly developed in an attempt to solve the UK's housing crisis. The social problems, which became apparent in these new housing developments, were ascribed to design by remote architects, speedy and poor quality construction methods and unsatisfactory living conditions. Stewart and Rhoden (2003) reported that these estates became seen as an inhumane environment for many residents, living in accommodation that soon became stigmatised and difficult to let due to their influx of residual households, creating majority welfare-dependent estates. The problems of social and economic exclusion became greater in these estates in comparison with traditional housing. Prior to the 1980s, there were no specific government policies to tackle housing regeneration on high-rise estates.

The Housing Act 1980 gave local authority tenants a statutory right to buy their homes at a discount rate. The 1988 Housing Act and Local Government Housing Act 1989 gave tenants the choices to transfer their homes to another landlord and promoted housing action trusts. This was not particularly popular. The main way in which council housing stock was reduced was by some local authorities transferring their stock into *housing associations*. By 1997 council stock had been reduced to 17 % of total housing, and the sector had become 'residualised' with a higher proportion of tenants without work and living on low incomes (Bingley and Walker 2001). The Housing Act 1988 changed the character of housing associations to *registered social landlords*, their properties were let under the same legal framework as private land-lords. *Registered social landlords* were allowed to borrow finance and a large proportion of their revenue was produced from the market, supported by Housing Benefit, and by 1997, 5 % of the housing stock was owned by social landlords. Housing Benefit was reformed in 1986, and was payable to a tenant if his income was below a set threshold, determined by rent officers. After this time Housing Benefit became more selective due to taper relief, a reduction related to each pound of income. Hills (1992) comments on this factor making a significant contribution to the 'poverty trap'.

In reviewing current government policy Monk *et al.* (2006) highlight the problems of gaining planning permissions and the quality of the housing (not specific to affordable housing).

INCOME SUPPORT AND HOMELESSNESS

In 2001, £11 billion was being spent on Housing Benefit in the UK. A reorganisation of the welfare benefits scheme was addressed in the Green Paper *Quality and Choices: A Decent Home for All* (DETR/DSS 2000). One of the proposals introduced in this paper suggested a flat standard local housing allowance to be introduced in the deregulated private rented sector. The problem with this idea was that new tenants, who could not find a low-priced property, would lose out and be moved towards the 'poverty trap'. This was one of the issues tackled by the Social Exclusion Unit (SEU), which was established in 1998. The SEU's report *Bringing Britain Together: A National Strategy for Neighbourhood Renewal* (SEU 1998a) high-lighted the design limitations with 'problem estates', and poor housing management. In reviewing housing problems, SEU concluded that previous strategies had failed due to a lack of coordination across government depart-ments, too many initiatives, a 'concentration on bricks and mortar' at the expense of 'social capital' and a lack of participation by residents. Increased coordination and resident participation formed significant aspects of the *New Commitment to Neighbourhood Renewal: National Strategy Action Plan* (SEU 2001).

In addition to housing-related benefits SEU turned its attention to those who were homeless, including rough sleepers. The response of the Conser-vative government in 1995, to the growing number of, mainly young, rough sleepers in city centres was to cut Housing Benefit to discourage sleeping on the streets. This policy was reversed by New Labour's SEU, which set out to reduce the number of rough sleepers by two-thirds by 2002. The *Rough Sleeper Initiative* (SEU 1998b) was allocated £143 million. By 2001 government data collection indicated that the number of rough sleepers had been reduced to 532, a figure disputed by many of the non-statutory organisations, working in the communities (Please and Quikars 1996). If this data is correct, it is a good achievement, however, the consequences of moving so many rough sleepers off the streets was bed-blocking in many of the hostels, and also the longer term issue, combating the continual flow of new people moving into cities such as London, had not been resolved (CRISIS 2003).

The Rough Sleeper Initiative funding was rolled up into a new system of income support called *Supporting People* (SP), in 2003. Unlike Housing Benefit, which was the main funding to support people in hostels and temporary accommodation, SP involved contracted services. In 1998–2002 transitional relief was available as Housing Benefit declined and SP contracts were negotiated with the registered private landlords, which was how community homeless services became classified. SP funding helps 1.2 million vulnerable people, and it is administered by 150 Administering Authorities, managing 37 000 contracts with in excess of 6000 providers of housing-related support.

The target groups initially identified for SP funding include rough sleepers, ex-offenders, people with physical or sensory disability, those at risk of domestic violence, problematic alcohol and drug users, teenage parents, elderly people, young people at risk, people with learning disabilities, people with HIV and AIDS, travellers and homeless families. The key objective of SP funding is to develop and sustain independence in these vulnerable groups. The SP commissioning bodies monitor the performance of service providers by means of the *Quality Assessment Framework* (ODPM 2004). This framework provides a means by which core service objectives can be measured on a scale A–D with respect to: needs and risk assessment; support planning; security; health and safety; protection from abuse; fair access; diversity and inclusion; and complaints.

BUILDING AND MAINTAINING COMMUNITY

The Homelessness Act 2002 directed local authorities to develop and implement a homeless strategy, and abolished the two-year limit on the provision of temporary accommodation. The Act also extended the priority groups. Following the rise in house prices between 1992 and 1996, the number of the statutory homeless population began to increase. Although a solution using bed and breakfast accommodation for roofless families and other vulnerable people was adopted, this policy ended in 2002.

The issues of homelessness were addressed within the 'social capital' strategy being developed by the New Labour government, via the Office of the Deputy Prime Minister. *Sustainable Communities: Settled Homes: Changing Lives* (ODPM 2005c) proposed a strategy to halve the number of households living in temporary accommodation by 2010, by significant investment in more social housing, an increase of 50 % in new homes by 2008, which involves building 75 000 new social homes. In addition to changes in planning regulations this target is being supported by an allocation of £80 million to local authorities for investment in homeless prevention initiatives.

In *Creating Sustainable Communities: Supporting Independence* (ODPM 2005a), the ODPM aims to refine the *Supporting People* funding initiative by focusing more on vulnerable groups and individuals ('there is no such thing as a typical service user'). The three groups requiring special attention are: 'people receiving care and support for whom housing related support underpins health and social care. . . . People living independently for whom a small amount of support (such as a warden or community alarm) makes a critical difference in remaining independent. . . . People experiencing risk of social exclusion, for whom housing plays an essential part in preventing or dealing with a crisis situation restoring independence in a sustainable way'. *Creating Sustainable Communities* (ODPM 2005a) recognises the success of SP but also identifies ways of building on this progress by ensuring greater integration with other local services needed by vulnerable people. This new approach to SP will provide more independence for local authorities to decide how best to effectively invest in services needed to support independent living by establishing a framework for commissioning services which are most appropriate and can be integrated to address the identified needs. Recognition of the role of the voluntary and community sector as key deliverers of services, will be supported within the new SP strategy.

The SP programme funds housing-related support and is aimed at helping people to maintain or improve their ability to live independently. It is part of a series of major government initiatives to combat social exclusion. These include:

- creating sustainable communities;

- tackling disadvantage and social exclusion;

- increasing choice for older people, people with disabilities (including learning difficulties) and people with mental health issues;

- reducing avoidable hospital admissions and assessing timely hospital discharge;

- reducing reoffending and the need for custodial sentence, thereby supporting community safety;

- reducing and preventing homelessness;

- reducing substance misuse;

- preventing and addressing antisocial behaviour.

In returning to the provision in the community of lodging houses (now called hostels), introduced at the beginning of this section, although there is a general trend to close down the large anonymous hostels, which were developed in the 1950s, this level of low threshold housing is still considered to be essential for certain groups of vulnerable people. However, the main change in approach between the support available from the 1950s to the end of the millennium, and the contemporary strategies is that a support plan is now required for each client. Traditionally, the average length of stay of hostel dwellers was seven years, with some people staying for 20–30 years. In contrast to this 'warehousing' policy, the present approach is to use the hostel as a temporary accommodation by which support and training can be made available to enable the service users to develop independence and move on into sustainable long-term housing. With reference to the current review of SP funding to focus more on specific vulnerable groups, special consideration should be given to problematic alcohol and drug users and those with mental health problems who form a large proportion of the contemporary hostel population. Sullivan and Burham (2000) have provided evidence which suggests that interventions most likely to improve the quality of life of homeless persons with mental illness 'include those that facilitate the maintenance of stable housing and provision of food and clothing, and that address physical health problems and train individuals to minimize their risk of victimization. Interventions that decrease depressive symptoms might also improve subjective quality of life'.

Currently the Office of the Deputy Prime Minister is engaged in a wide range of initiatives including the *Hostel Capital Improvement Programme* (ODPM 2005b). This source of money is intended to provide buildings that are innovative and which, by their high-quality design, are intended to give a positive message to the residents. In contrast to previous buildings, which had high levels of security and were designed as 'controlled environments', the new architectural designs are intended to increase a sense of self-worth and, rather than appearing to be a place of last resort, the buildings are to give a sense that this is the first step on the ladder.

The skill level and motivation of staffing of the residential services is paramount to their success. The problems of staff burnout, due to onerous shift rotas, night working and inadequate training opportunities are significant human resource problems. Frequently there is a conflict between the needs of the employer to provide the most cost-effective (and often minimum) training in contrast to the needs of the employee looking for career progression via a continuous professional development (CPD). This presents a problem for the organisation whose funding might be depending on short (1–2 year) funding cycles.

The *Hostel Capital Improvement Programme* aims to promote the design of buildings to give a positive environment for engagement and rehabilitation, and to provide services appropriate for those who are 'hard to engage'. These services include the imaginative delivery of basic skills. This might involve, for instance engaging clients in the simulation of managing a football team, which is reliant on the development of literacy and numeracy skills. Other examples include establishing a DJ (disc jockey) service, which requires the development of reading skills, in order to arrange the music tracks and organising the timing of the activity.

EMPLOYMENT

Employment has, since the nineteenth century, been considered to be an essential factor in alleviating poverty, adding to aspects of personal identity and providing a role for individuals. In addressing the issues of social exclusion related to disability, mental health problems and recovery from drug misuse, UK governments have tackled this issue from a socio-economic perspective. Despite the development of the welfare state, by the last two decades of the twentieth century, a significant proportion of the population were unemployed, impacting on their quality of life and leaving their families dependent on benefits with poverty extending into retirement. Unemployment on this scale was considered to be the basis of despair in communities containing people with low aspirations. After 1997 the New Labour government reorganised the Department of Work and Pensions with a number of strategies to help 'people build assets so that the welfare state becomes a ladder out of poverty, not just a safety net . . . by a commitment to self-reliance. . . . placing the drive to alleviate poverty at the heart of breaking intergenerational disadvantage and ensuring that social inclusion contributes to both individual well-being and the broader economic needs of society' (DWP 2005).

In addition to promoting work through a large investment of over £2 billion in combining the Benefits Agency and the Employment service into *JobCentre Plus*, other key objectives of the department also include 'promoting security and independence for pensioners, . . . improving the rights and opportunities for the disabled . . . and [ensuring] the best start for children by ending child poverty by 2020'. The *New Deal* (1998) approach to improving the prospects of the unemployed was a major component of the reform of the welfare state, a process that began in 1997 and still continues. During this time substantial numbers of people have moved from being on benefits back into work. The Green Paper *A New Deal for Welfare: Empowering People to Work* (DWP 2006) provides a strategy for achieving an employment rate of 80 % of the working age population, by reducing incapacity benefits by 1 million, helping lone parents into work and increasing the number of older workers by 1 million. This strategy is underpinned by the concern for the demographic change in the UK population age profile which is projected to result in 50 % of the population being over 50 years by 2024.

Various tax incentives have been developed to encourage people back to work, the tax credit scheme was reformed in 1999. This gives families with children and one partner working at least 16 hours per week up to £100 a week in tax incentives. An interesting corollary of this incentive is that single women with children are now more likely to get into a relationship where they would get a cash bonus. This has resulted in 50 000 more couples since 1999 (Anderberg 2006). This first study to estimate how tax credits affect family relationships indicated that nearly a quarter of children had been lifted out of poverty.

There are specific challenges for some groups trying to move into employment. These include post-treatment problematic alcohol and drug users, ex-offenders and ex-service personnel. *JobCentre Progress2work*, launched in 2001, has been developed to support the first two groups into employment. Ex-service personnel sometimes have multiple problems due to addictive behaviours which had been managed with their services institutional structure. Outside the supportive framework of the armed forces social exclusion frequently occurs, due to complex needs involving substance misuse and mental health problems. In particular post-traumatic stress disorder (PTSD), comorbid with alcohol dependence, mitigates against future employment as reported by Savoca and Rosenheck (2000).

EDUCATION AND TRAINING

Residential support is the first step leading through halfway housing to a tenancy in the community. There is a need for residential programmes to be sufficiently flexible to allow participants to move off into work at an appropriate time. Accommodation should not be seen as an end in itself. A 'purpose in life' provides a reason to get out of bed each morning. The importance of self-improvement through training and education is being rediscovered. A major obstacle in achieving the high employment rates suggested in *A New Deal for Welfare: Empowering People to Work* are the skills and competencies required in the workplace. Approximately 10 million working age adults are not qualified to full level 2 (further education credit framework), and about 5 million have literacy skills below level 1 (DWP 2006). Level 2 skills involve understanding, competence and knowledge to work effectively in retail and construction sectors.

A review of skills in the UK has recently been undertaken (Leitch 2005). This report comments on the need for improvements in skills in order to maintain the UK's long-term prosperity, and reduce 'social disparities'. The report notes that '. . . over one-third of adults do not have a basic school leaving certificate, double that in Canada and Germany. Five million people have no qualification at all; one in six do not have the literacy skills expected of an 11 year old and half do not have these levels of functional numeracy'. The review indicates that if the government targets are met by 2020, 'the proportion of working age people without any qualifications will fall to 4 %, and [those] holding a degree will increase from 27 % to 38 %; and this will have significant benefits for the economy'.

Addressing these training and educational deficits is a key objective set out in *Skills in the UK: The Long-term Challenge: the National Strategy for Improving Adult Literacy and Numeracy Skills* (Henderson 2006). The *Basic Skills Agency* (see www.basic-skills.co.uk) works 'at arm's length' for the Department of Education and the Welsh Assembly, which was established to improve the speaking and listening skills of children, young people and adults. This agency has been active during recent years in developing effective links between homeless services and mainstream training establishments such as the further education colleges.

REFERENCES

Alson, P. (1998). *Progress of Nations 1998: Industrialised Countries.* New York: UNICEF.
Anderberg, D. (2006). *Tax Credits, Income Support and Partnership Decisions.* London: Royal Economic Society.
Begin, P., L. Casavant, N. M. Chenier and J. Dupusi (1999). *Homelessness.* Library of Parliament (Canada), Parliamentary Research Branch.
Bingley, P. and I. Walker (2001). Housing subsidies and work incentives in Great Britain. *The Economic Journal*, **111**, 86–103.
Creighton, C. (1894). *History of Epidemics in Britain.* Vol. II. Cambridge: Cambridge University Press.
CRISIS (2003). *Mental Health and Social Exclusion: A Response to a Consultation Request from the Social Exclusion Unit.* London: CRISIS.
DETR/DSS (2000). *Quality and Choices: A Decent Home for All, The Housing Green Paper.* London: Department of the Environment, Transport and the Regions/ Department of Social Security.
DWP (2005). *Departmental Framework.* London: Department of Work and Pensions.
DWP (2006). *A Deal for Welfare: Empowering People to Work.* London: Department of Work and Pensions.
Ferrier, J. (1810). Medical history and reflections. In: *A History of Epidemics in Britain.* Cambridge: Cambridge University Press, p. 217.
Henderson, S. (2006). The National Strategy for improving adult literacy and numeracy skills: update. *Skills for Life*, 1–36.
Hills, J. (1992). *Unravelling House Finance: Subsidies, Benefits, Taxation.* Oxford: Clarendon Press.
Howard, E. ed. (1902). *Garden Cities of Tomorrow.* Reprinted in 1946, edited with a preface by F. J. Osborn and an introductory essay by Lewis Mumford. London: Faber and Faber.
Laidlaw, S. I. A. (1954). *Glasgow Common Lodging Houses and the People Living in Them.* Glasgow: Health and Welfare Committee of the Corporation of Glasgow.
Leitch, S. (2005). *Skills in the UK: the Long-term Challenge.* London: Leitch Review of Skills, HM Treasury.
Monk, S., T. Crook, D. Lister, R. Lovatt, A. N. Lauaigh, S. Rowley, *et al.* (2006). *Delivering Affordable Housing through Section 106: Outputs and Outcomes.* York: Joseph Rowntree Foundation.
Moore, J., D. Canter, D. Stockley and M. A. Drake (1995). *The Faces of Homelessness in London.* Aldershot: Dartmouth.
ODPM (2004). *Monitoring and Review of Supporting People Services: Quality Assessment Framework – Core Service Objectives.* London: Office of the Deputy Prime Minister.

ODPM (2005a). *Creating Sustainable Communities: Supporting Independence.* London: Office of the Deputy Prime Minister.

ODPM (2005b). *Hostels Capital Improvement Programme (HCIP).* London: Homeless and Housing Support Directorate, Office of the Deputy Prime Minister.

ODPM (2005c). *Sustainable Communities: Settled Homes: Changing Lives.* London: Office of the Deputy Prime Minister.

OED (1973). *The Shorter Oxford English Dictionary.* Oxford: Clarendon Press.

Please, N. and D. Quikars (1996). *Health and Homelessness in London: A Review.* York: Centre for Housing Policy, University of York.

Savoca, E. and R. Rosenheck (2000). The civilian labor market experiences of Vietnam-era veterans: the influence of psychiatric disorders. *Journal of Mental Health Policy and Economics,* **3**(4), 199–207.

SEU (1998a). *Bringing Britain Together: A National Strategy for Neighbourhood Renewal.* London: The Stationery Office.

SEU (1998b). *Rough Sleeping.* London: The Stationery Office.

SEU (2001). *A New Commitment to Neighbourhood Renewal: National Strategy Action Plan.* London: The Stationery Office.

Stewart, J. and M. Rhoden (2003). A review of social housing regeneration in the London Borough of Brent. *Journal of the Royal Society for the Promotion of Health,* **123**(1), 23–32.

Sullivan, G. and A. Burnam (2000). Quality of life of homeless persons with mental illness: results from the course-of-homelessness study. *Psychiatric Services,* **51**(9), 1135–41.

CHAPTER 13

HEALTH AND SOCIAL CARE IN THE COMMUNITY

THE DEVELOPMENT OF HEALTHCARE IN THE UK

A brief review of the development of the welfare state was presented in Chapter 1. This socio-political approach to addressing the social and health inequalities in the community was, in part, a response to the negative consequences of the growth of industry, stimulated by philanthropic activities of some of the beneficiaries of the wealth created by industrial development. Paradoxically, the industrial cities, the wealth-generating centres of the UK, provided employment and prosperity for many but also led to squalid living conditions, occupational health problems and problems associated with the greater availability of alcohol and other 'social evils' (Booth 1890, reprinted 1984).

The move from rural to urban-based employment provided more wealth but it also brought about a change in social structure and dissociation between individuals and the countryside. Communities developed near to the industrial activities and some of these were supported by benefactors, as in the case of Port Sunlight (near Liverpool) and Bourneville (near Birmingham) model urban villages. These community schemes were established at about the same time as the development of state-organised health care, which began with the Public Health Acts of the mid-nineteenth century. Improvements in sanitation and planning resulted in reduced mortality from infectious diseases such as cholera and typhoid. Public hospitals developed from the workhouses, provided under the poor law at a time when voluntary hospitals were being developed by religious organisations and charitable donations from the rich. During this period medicine was developing as a science and influenced health care in the voluntary hospitals towards the treatment of acute physical needs, at the expense of those with chronic illnesses or infections. The workhouses tended to support those who would not be accepted by the voluntary hospitals. The Metropolitan Poor Act (1867) encouraged the establishment of infirmaries, separated from the workhouses. The Local Government Act (1929) transferred workhouses and infirmaries to the control of local authorities, leading to the development of a local authority service. From 1845 local authorities were required to establish hospitals (asylums) for people with mental health and learning difficulties.

The National Insurance Act (1911) provided income during sickness and unemployment and free care from general practitioners, for some groups of workers earning less than £160 per year. The National Health Service Act was passed in 1946, a development from the Emergency Medical Services during the First and Second World Wars. This resulted in the control of local authority and voluntary hospitals being moved to a single, national system of administration. The National Health Service was designed to provide a comprehensive health service, free at the point of use and financed by general taxation. Various changes have occurred during the period 1948 to 1979, one of the most significant of which occurred in the 1960s with the advent of *community care*, in response to the Mental Health Act (1959). This brought about the replacing of some activities, which had been carried out in the large institutions, with more community-based approaches. Since that time an increasingly bureaucratic administration has grown and withered in reaction to various Conservative and Labour government initiatives. This has resulted in changes in the number and size of health authorities, which became increasingly separated from local authorities.

A major driver in the continued reorganisation of the National Health Service is towards greater financial efficiency, in view of the escalating costs of providing a modern health service. The White Paper, *Working for Patients* (DH 1989), led to the separation of purchaser and provider responsibilities, via the development of NHS trusts and GP fund-holders. At the same time a White Paper, *Caring for People* (HMSO 1989), gave local authorities the lead role in community care in collaboration with the NHS, voluntary and private sector bodies via the *NHS and Community Care Act* (HMSO 1990) and the creation of an internal market. These changes brought about by the Conservative government had mixed responses, one of which was the *Black Report on Inequalities in Health* (DHSS 1980). This report suggested a number of recommendations to reduce social class inequalities, including improving housing conditions and increasing child benefits. No action was taken to implement the Black Report. However, with the spread of HIV/AIDS there was an increasing community focus, which sought to encourage people to change their behaviour and life style. The White Paper, *The Health of the Nation* (DH 1992), set targets for health improvement in coronary heart disease and stroke, cancer, mental health, HIV/AIDS and sexual health and accidents.

While a strategic approach to health in the community was welcomed, there are major criticisms regarding over-ambitious targets and the reluctance to tackle social inequalities and deprivation. Significant omissions in the strategy were health problems related to smoking and alcohol consumption (Baggot 2000). In contrast to the lack of action on social inequalities and deprivation, there was growing encouragement for private health provision.

From 1970 to 2002 there was a tripling of the number of people benefiting from private health insurance (ONS 2002).

Since 1997, the New Labour government has begun to address the problems of funding the NHS and organisational issues such as the effective use of primary health services, and the growing social class inequalities in mortality and morbidity (see Chapter 4). Modernisation of the health service was initiated following the White Paper, *The New NHS, Modern, Dependable* (DH 1997). This new direction in health policy included the controversial *private finance initiative* (PFI), the reforming of primary care and increased expenditure on the health service. A significant development was the creation of Primary Care Trusts (PCTs), which were made independent of health authorities and were directed to provide a full range of community services. PCTs were given the power to commission hospital and other community services. This transition of 15 % of the NHS budget, held by GPs in the 1990s, to PCTs having 75 % of the NHS budget by 2004, has had a major impact on the delivery of health care in the community.

Other structural changes include the provisions for the reduction in waiting times and highly controversial plans for *foundation hospitals.* Health Action Zones (HAZs) have been identified as initiatives reflecting the 'third-way' policies developed by the UK New Labour government. Like other area-based or zone initiatives, HAZ programmes are designed to tackle inequalities and exclusion in some of the most deprived areas of the UK. These locally based strategies encouraged partnerships between the public, private and voluntary sectors, and most significantly, communities themselves. HAZs embrace communities and attempt to foster involvement in health improvement, often using established community development models. Crawshaw and Bunton (2003) have reviewed the development of one zone in the north-east of England with respect to community involvement in practice.

The creation of the National Institute for Clinical Excellence (NICE) in 1999, was initially intended to improve best practice across health technologies, including medicine, medical devices, diagnostic techniques and procedures. However, the remit of NICE has now been extended beyond these traditional medical areas to include educational and social domains. This is demonstrated by the current exercise designed and aimed at producing guidelines for working with young people with substance misuse problems. It is interesting to note again that alcohol is not included in this scoping activity.

In parallel with changes in the commissioning and inspections for social services (see Chapter 12) the Commission for Health Improvement (CHI) was set up in 1999. The CHI is an independent inspection body for England and Wales, responsible for monitoring and reviewing the implementation of standards presented in the National Services Frameworks.

HEALTH SERVICES FOR THE HOMELESS AND SOCIALLY EXCLUDED

During recent years there have been a number of significant policy developments that are having and will have an impact on homeless and socially excluded people. *The Health of the Nation* (DH 1992) promoted a rather narrow biomedical approach that did not particularly address the needs of the homeless, who were already seen as undeserving and were held responsible for their own health problems. In *Our Healthier Nation* (DH 1998a) the key aim was to 'improve health of the population as a whole by increasing the length of people's lives and the number of years people spend free of disease'. In 2005 the life expectancy of rough sleepers was still only 42 years, in comparison with the general population who live to an average age of 80 years.

Earlier chapters in this book demonstrate that homelessness and social exclusion are often preceded by an extensive series of life events and disadvantages, which are associated with poverty and family breakdown leading to homelessness. Health and social inequalities span generations such that children who have been homeless have considerable problems in breaking the cycle of a disadvantaged life (see *Breaking the Cycle: 3*, SEU 2004a). At the beginning of the new millennium, health inequalities and poverty became central features of government policy. In the *Priorities and Planning Framework 2003–6* (DH 2002), health inequalities were made a key priority for the NHS. Those groups, particularly families and those facing social exclusion, who were disadvantaged in accessing and receiving healthcare provision, were given priority. Homeless people were identified as a particularly vulnerable group requiring targeted interventions as defined in *Cross-Cutting Review on Tackling Health Inequalities.* This initiative was developed further in the Wanless report, which identified local objectives based on national objectives and local needs.

The Wanless report, *Securing Good Health for the Whole Population*, recommended changes in the function of Primary Care Trusts (PCTs), which presently commission and provide the delivery of primary and community health care, as part of their prime responsibility for improving the health of people living in their locality. The PCTs' Public Health Directorate is responsible for taking a lead role in providing public health leadership for health improvement by working in partnership with Local Strategic Partnerships (LSPs) and the local community. This was to be achieved by delivering a range of public health services and programmes in their communities, and providing expert public health advice and support. PCTs are required to develop a *local delivery plan*, which should include a homelessness strategy. Aspects of the local delivery plan should include:

• reductions in health inequalities;

• better services for drug users;

- reduction in teenage conceptions;

- mental health services;

- shorter waiting times in Accident and Emergency departments;

- improved access to primary care.

Presently there are a number of health-focused homelessness strategies in various parts of England. The most effective of these are complementary to other statutory and non-statutory strategies. The key outcomes that health and homeless partnerships are working towards are:

- Improving healthcare for homeless families in temporary accommodation.

- Improving access to primary health care for homeless people.

- Improving substance misuse treatment for homeless people.

- Improving mental health treatment for homeless people.

- Preventing homelessness through appropriate, targeted health support.

The roles of PCTs are currently evolving into solely commissioning functions and the delivery of services will be open for tender by statutory and non-statutory services. For example Help the Aged might tender to deliver services for older people in a particular area. These recommendations are given as advice notes to local authorities, PCTs and other partners in *Achieving Positive Shared Outcomes in Health and Homelessness* (ODPM 2004). These changes in government policy, with a focus on improving the health of the homeless and socially excluded, are to be welcomed but there are a number of obstacles to negotiate, some of which have been identified in *Health and Homelessness in London: A Review* (Please and Quikars 1996). This review highlighted the considerable problems that homeless people have in accessing mainstream health services. These include: stereotypes and prejudice; the geographical decentralisation of the NHS (mitigating against continuity of care for a relatively mobile population); procedures in the NHS (including the need for a permanent address, and lack of staff training for work with homeless people); social marginalisation of the homeless (communication problems and difficulties in coping with authority); and relative scarcity of healthcare provision (including access to GP services, acute beds, mental health and related services).

The lack of response to the Black Report on *Inequalities in Health* (1980) was emphasised in the Acheson Report (1998), which noted that health inequalities had increased since the Black Report. In addition to responding to this in *Our Healthier Nation* (see above) the government focused action on tobacco in a White Paper on Tobacco (*Smoking Kills: A White Paper on Tobacco* 1998) and a strategic planning process to address problematic drug use in the community.

ANTI-SUBSTANCE MISUSE STRATEGIES

Substance misuse is a major factor contributing to homelessness and social exclusion, as discussed in Chapter 8. Although consumption of alcohol and other drugs presents significant threats to health, there has been an increasing tendency to deal with these issues within a criminal justice agenda. The current UK government's concern with antisocial behaviour is being linked with the evolving strategies to address problematic alcohol and drug use in the community.

The first joined-up approach was initiated in 1995 by the appointment of a US-styled national anti-drugs coordinator (or drugs czar). Keith Hellawell's task was to coordinate anti-drug-related activities across government departments. This was to be achieved by means of a number of targets as set out in the 10-year strategy *Tackling Drugs Together* (1995). This strategy was relaunched in 1998, with the publication of *Tackling Drugs Together.* (1998) and then updated in 2002 (*Tackling Drugs: Updated Strategy* 2002). The initial strategies in the 1980s focused on: *young people*, helping them to resist drug misuse; *communities*, by protection from drug-related anti-social and criminal behaviour; *treatment*, enabling people with drug problems to overcome them and live healthy, crime-free lives; and *availability*, by stifling the availability of illegal drugs on our streets. The updated strategy in 2002 indicated a more robust approach to Class A drugs, and more emphasis on education, prevention, enforcement and treatment. A measure of the government's concern over drug misuse in the community is demonstrated by the increasing budget targeted at these initiatives.

Currently the government is spending £1.5 billion annually on tackling drugs. The strategy was initiated by the joint action between the Home Office and the Department of Health, and is presently jointly managed by the operation of the Criminal Justice Intervention Programme (CJIP) and the National Treatment Agency (NTA). The NTA is a Special Health Authority and is empowered to manage the delivery of the treatment services in England. By means of regional management teams it works with the Drugs Prevention Advisory Service (DPAS), which is integrated into the government offices in the regions. The NTA and DPAS are responsible for the development and quality control of services and the development of a workforce to deliver treatment services.

Quality assurance standards have been developed over recent years, these are documented as Quality in Alcohol and Drug Services (QuADs) (2002). Workforce development is being modelled on Drug and Alcohol National Occupational Standards (DANOS, 2006). Currently there is some confusion as how QuADs and DANOS should be implemented. In the case of quality of standards for service delivery, there is growing concern that agencies and projects are being overinspected. Implementation of DANOS is problematic due to the need for assessors to validate the competencies of staff in the workplace. Although a National Vocational Qualification (NVQ) scheme is being recommended, this approach is not well accepted by the treatment agencies, due to the expense of engaging in workplace assessment, and there is a dearth of trained assessors available to carry out this work. A further complication relates to the lack of coordination between the further education (FE) sector, which is equipped to undertake NVQs but is generally not experienced in delivering alcohol and drug training programmes, and the higher education (HE) institutions, some of which are well equipped to provide training but are not ready to deliver work-based NVQs.

Alcohol, the neglected strategy

Despite advice from the medical and health-related professions, alcohol misuse was not included in the UK anti-drug strategies. In view of the extensive ill health, social problems, criminality and costs to society, it has seemed irrational that effective strategies to reduce alcohol-related harm have been poorly developed by successive UK governments. There are approximately 7 million people in England drinking excessively and over 1 million who experience alcohol dependence. The cost of alcohol-related harm is £20 billion per annum. Drummond (2005) has reported that indices of alcohol-related harm have increased in the past 10 years in the UK related to greater affordability and consumption of alcohol. The greatest increase has been seen in young people, and young women in particular.

Proposals for a *National Alcohol Strategy* have been developed by a number of professional groups and non-governmental agencies such as Alcohol Concern (1999). These proposals include increased taxation on alcohol, restricting availability, restricting the density of outlets, minimum drinking age, blood alcohol limit for driving and the provision of brief interventions and treatment for those affected. However, there are many competing interests for governments in deciding on alcohol policy, not least being the revenue and employment generated by the production and sale of alcohol.

The *Alcohol Harm Reduction Strategy for England* (2005) emphasises the responsibility of the individual drinker and the alcohol industry. The new Licensing Act (2003) is unlikely to make a positive impact on alcohol-related harm. Drummond (2005) concluded that 'consideration needs to be given to whole population measures to reduce alcohol consumption and positive lessons from tobacco policy need to be translated to the alcohol field . . . Alcohol strategies therefore need to balance the rights of the majority of the population not to be affected by the misuse of alcohol by a minority, against the freedom of the individual to use alcohol in any way he or she chooses'.

MENTAL HEALTH SUPPORT IN THE COMMUNITY

In addition to problematic alcohol and drug misuse, mental health issues are frequently found in homeless and socially excluded people (see Chapter 6). Untreated mental health problems can be a cause of social exclusion, conversely such problems might be the consequence of social isolation or might be a component of the complex needs occurring in vulnerable people. Adults with mental health problems are one of the most excluded groups in society, and have the lowest rates of employment compared to the main groups of disabled people (SEU 2004b), with only 24 % of these adults being employed. Lack of work is linked with social isolation, a significant risk factor for deteriorating mental health and suicide. This is exemplified by the fact that two-thirds of males under 35 with mental health problems who die by suicide are unemployed.

Affective disorders, which include depression, anxiety and phobias have been found in up to one-sixth of the population, with the highest rates in deprived areas. Although more severe mental health problems such as schizophrenia are comparatively less frequent in the population, there is increasing evidence that the levels of psychosis in the homeless population are higher than previously known (van den Bree *et al.*, in preparation). The main causes of social exclusion of individuals with mental health problems, identified by the SEU, are: stigma and discrimination; low expectations of what people with mental health problems can achieve; lack of clear responsibility for promoting vocational and social outcomes; lack of ongoing support in employment; and barriers to engaging in the community. There is particular concern for adults with complex needs, such as substance misuse (see Chapter 8), and lone parents. Mainstream mental health services are not easily accessible to black ethnic minorities, due to alienation and other reasons including language problems and perceived discrimination due to controversial diagnosis. Another vulnerable group is young men with a high risk of dropping out of education and work due in part to mental health problems. These young men are at high risk for criminal behaviour and suicide.

A review and reorganisation of mental health services has been a key task emanating from the White Paper, *Modernising Mental Health Services* (DH 1998b). An additional budget of £700 million was made available to enable the implementation of the *National Service Framework for Mental Health* (DH 1999). This service framework is directed at the mental health needs of working age adults up to 65 years. The needs of children and young people and older people are being addressed by means of other frameworks. There are five areas in which standards have been developed. These are: mental health promotion; primary care and access to services; effective services for those with severe mental health problems; individuals who care for people with mental health problems; and action to reduce suicides.

By focusing on these targets, health and social services are accountable to the government for delivering these new national standards. The main objectives of the *National Service Framework for Mental Health* (DH 1999) are contained in the service framework listed below.

Standard 1: Mental health promotion

- Promote mental health for all, working with individuals and communities.

- Combat discrimination against individuals and groups with mental health problems, and promote their social inclusion.

Standard 2: Primary care and access to services
Any service user who contacts their primary healthcare team with a common mental health problem should:

- Have their mental health needs identified and assessed.

- Be offered treatments, including referral to specialist services for further assessment, treatment and care if they require it.

Standard 3: Any individual with a common mental health problem should:

- Be able to make contact round the clock with the local services necessary to meet their needs and receive adequate care.

- Be able to use NHS Direct for first-level advice and referral to specialist helplines or to local services.

Standard 4: All mental health service users on Care Programme Approach (CPA) should:

- Receive care which optimises engagement, prevents or anticipates crisis, and reduces risk.

- Have a copy of a written plan.

- Be able to access services 24 hours a day, 365 days a year.

Standard 5: Each service user who is assessed as requiring a period of care away from their home should have:

- Timely access to an appropriate hospital bed or alternative bed.

- A copy of a written aftercare plan agreed on discharge, which sets out the care and rehabilitation to be provided, identifies the care coordinator and specifies the action to be taken in a crisis.

Standard 6: All individuals who provide regular substantial care for a person on CPA should:

• Have an assessment of their caring, physical and mental health needs.

• Have their own written care plan, which is given to them and implemented in discussion with them.

Standard 7: Local and health and social care communities should prevent suicide by:
Addressing Standards 1–6, above, plus:

• Supporting local prison staff in preventing suicides among prisoners.

• Ensuring that staff are competent to assess risk of suicide among individuals at greatest risk.

• Developing local systems for suicide audits to learn lessons and take any necessary action.

To support the development of the new national strategies to tackle mental health issues in the community, the *National Institute for Mental Health in England* (NIMHE) has been set up. The main aim of NIMHE is to improve the quality of life of people of all ages who experience mental distress, by providing a gateway to learning and development and offering new opportunities to share experiences. The key strategic priorities of NIMHE are: to ensure that the mental health care system is appropriate for the provision of effective care and treatment, to facilitate workforce development and to develop practice for rapid access to best possible care.

JOINED-UP STRATEGIES

In order to promote social inclusion, links between NHS and other government departments have been facilitated via the Office of the Deputy Prime Minister (ODPM) through the development of the Social Exclusion Unit (SEU), established in 1997. The SEU was set up with the objectives of tackling poverty and deprivation by addressing the cycles of disadvantage which underpin social exclusion, as noted in Chapter 12. One of the first strategies involved people sleeping on the streets (SEU 1998). The *Rough Sleepers Initiative* was aimed at getting people off the streets. This resulted in bed blocking and lacked a follow-on strategy to support the rehabilitation of those who were encouraged to move off the streets, see Chapter 12. Other initiatives included reducing teenage pregnancies and increasing the tax benefits for the poorest families.

Currently, the SEU is reviewing ways by which the lives of adults with mental health problems can be improved. This work involves a partnership with NIMHE as described in *Action on Mental Health: A Guide to Promoting Social Inclusion* (SEU 2005).

In an attempt to break the cycle of deprivation, there has been an increasing focus on children and families living in disadvantaged areas. The *Connexions Service* has been set up to provide all young people 13–19 with access to a personal advisor, working with them to develop a strategy to address their needs. The *Sure Start* local programmes have been established to make available 'high-quality services from the start of a child's life, right through school and beyond'. These local programmes have been reported to have benefited over 400 000 children and to have contributed to a reduction in the number of schools where less than 65 % of the pupils achieved level 4 or higher at key stage 2. Local Sure Start programmes are proposed to be the foundations of Children's Centres – 'by 2008 and 2010, the targets for establishing one Children's Centre in each community, are 2500 and 3500, respectively'. These centres are 'intended to bring together a range of integrated early-learning, health and parent services and to promote the physical and intellectual and social development of young children' (TSO 2004).

A greater focus on the early years is encapsulated in *The Children Act* (2004). This joined-up approach to providing integrated services will be overseen by a Children's Commissioner, and the establishing of Local Safe-guarding Children Boards (LSCBs) in England and Wales. LSCBs should include representatives from the local authority, the police, the proba-tion service, the youth offending team, the Strategic Health Authority and Primary Care Trust, the NHS, the Learning and Skills Service, the Children and Family Court Advisory and Support Service, the governor of a local secure training centre and the governor of any local prison. *The Children's Act* also calls for the appointment of a director of children's services, to be responsible for all children's services, including the educational service, in each local authority and to be accountable to the Secretary of State.

A new initiative launched in 2006 is *Sure Start to Later Life* (SEU 2006), 'preventing a cycle of decline and promoting the cycle of well being'. This new agenda, initiated by the Social Exclusion Unit, builds on the similar strategy used in Sure Start for children's services. It originated from the analysis of the *English Longitudinal Study of Ageing* which found that 7 % (1.2 million) of older people were found to be excluded on three or more indicators of exclusion, 13 % were excluded on two indicators and 29 % were excluded in one dimension such as social relationship.

This integrated approach aimed at reducing exclusion in the elderly will bring together a full range of services being delivered in one place, using a single accessible gateway to services. The scheme will be initiated by means of a pilot programme called *Link-Age Plus*, which will include local part-nerships supported by a new *White Paper on Primary and Community Care.*

Working with the Department of Work and Pensions, pursuing the take up of benefits such as the Pension Credit, Housing Benefit and Attendance Allowances, the ODPM will be developing an integrated system of health and social care for older people. The main thrust of this policy will be to help more old people remain independent and active for as long as possible, and the prevention of homelessness.

REFERENCES

Alcohol Concern (1999). *Proposals for a National Alcohol Strategy for England.* London: Alcohol Concern.
Alcohol Harm Reduction Strategy for England. (2005). London: The Prime Minister's Strategy Unit.
Baggot, R. (2000). *Public Health: Policy and Politics.* Basingstoke: Palgrave.
Booth, W. (1890, Reprinted 1984). *In Darkest England and the Way Out.* London: The Salvation Army.
Crawshaw, P. and R. Bunton (2003). Health Action Zones and the problem of community. *Health and Social Care in the Community,* **11**, 1136–44.
DANOS (2006). Drugs and Alcohol National Occupational Standards (DANOS). Available: http://www.skillsforhealth.org.uk/danos/ [accessed 28 August 2006].
DH (1989). *Working for Patients.* London: Department of Health.
DH (1992). *The Health of the Nation.* London: Department of Health.
DH (1997). *The New NHS, Modern, Dependable.* London: Department of Health.
DH (1998a). *Our Healthier Nation.* London: Department of Health.
DH (1998b). *Modernising Mental Health Services.* London: Department of Health.
DH (1999). *National Service Framework for Mental Health: Modern Standards and Service Models.* London: Department of Health.
DH (2002). *Improvement, Expansion and Reform – the Next 3 Years: Priorities and Planning Framework 2003–6.* London: Department of Health.
DHSS (1980). *The Black Report. Inequalities in Health: Report of Research Working Group.* London: Department of Health and Social Security.
Drummond, C. (2005). Alcohol and government policy. In: Bonner, A. B. (ed.), *European Society for Biomedical Research into Alcoholism.* Canterbury: University of Kent.
HMSO (1989). *Caring for People: Community Care in the Next Decade and Beyond.* London: HMSO.
HMSO (1990). *NHS and Community Care Act.* London: HMSO.
ODPM (2004). *Achieving Positive Shared Outcomes in Health and Homelessness.* London: Homelessness and Housing Support Directorate, Office of the Deputy Prime Minister.
ONS (2002). *Social Trends 32.* London: The Stationery Office.
Please, N. and D. Quikars (1996). *Health and Homelessness in London: A Review.* York: Centre for Housing Policy, University of York.
SEU (1998). *Rough Sleeping.* London: The Stationery Office.
SEU (2004a). *Breaking the Cycle: Taking Stock of Priorities for the Future.* London: Social Exclusion Unit, Office of the Deputy Prime Minister.
SEU (2004b). *Mental Health and Social Exclusion.* London: Social Exclusion Unit, Office of the Deputy Prime Minister.
SEU (2005). *Action on Mental Health: A Guide to Promoting Social Inclusion.* London: Social Exclusion Unit, Office of the Deputy Prime Minister.

SEU (2006). *Sure Start to Later Life: Ending Inequalities for Older People.* London: Social Exclusion Unit, Office of the Deputy Prime Minister.
Smoking Kills: A White Paper on Tobacco. (1998). London: The Stationery Office.
Tackling Drugs Together. (1995). London: HMSO.
Tackling Drugs: Updated Strategy. (2002). London: Home Office/ODPM/DES/DH/ DWP/FCMO/HM Customs and Excise.
TSO (2004). *Children Act 2004.* London: The Stationery Office.
TSO (1998). *Tackling Drugs to Build a Better Britain.* London: The Stationery Office.
van den Bree, M., A. B. Bonner, C. Luscombe and D. R. A critical analysis of clients with a psychotic diagnosis in homeless hostels in Cardiff, London and Glasgow. *In preparation.*

CHAPTER 14

SOCIAL EXCLUSION: IS THERE A WAY OUT?

UNDERSTANDING SOCIAL EXCLUSION

Social exclusion is a wide-ranging concept used to describe a situation that might occur at any period during, or in some unfortunate people, throughout the whole life cycle. Exclusion is experienced when a person has problems with one of a number of factors relating to health, wealth, accommodation and relationship with family and friends. Perhaps the most important needs contributing to a sense of *inclusion* are feeling useful, having a role and being treated with respect. To understand the all-pervading nature of exclusion a whole life-cycle approach should be used. Chapter 3 has provided an insight into the roots of later life health and social problems, which are laid down even before our birth.

Childhood deprivation and abuse are frequently cited by excluded and homeless people as major components of their problematic life styles. Moving from childhood into adolescence provides many challenges and psychosocial changes, which can be more difficult for some individuals than others. The incidence of childhood depression is increasing, a problem that has biological and psychological components, as demonstrated by the not uncommon problem of self-image, for example in young people seeking treatment for acne. The observation that treatment with a retinoid-based medication, such as Accutane, can cause severe depression and suicide in some young people (Margin *et al.* 2005), exemplifies the powerful biological forces underpinning mental health. Young people from all socio-economic backgrounds are subject to a wide range of challenges and opportunities; their response to these will depend on their peer group, family and cultural background (Cook *et al.* 1997). The opportunity for children to obtain illicit drugs and access 'inappropriate' internet or digital television programmes causes a great concern to many parents. These are not irrational fears in view of the occasional report in the media of children as young as nine years of age being treated in alcohol detoxification clinics.

Leaving home to find work, study or joining the armed forces can be a very lonely experience, and the development of a positive social network is a critical stage in the process of 'being included'. A significant proportion of homeless people using hostels have been adversely affected at this stage of socialisation. Some of these problems result from experience in the armed forces. In the initial training phases and in operational situations stress levels are high, and the availability of large quantities of alcohol leading to intensive binge drinking between operational duties, linked with family issues, is managed, to some extent, within the institutional setting. When the soldier leaves the services after contracts of 3, 6 or 12 years the lack of institutional support, a possible underlying alcohol problem and the experiences of warfare considerably increase the possibility of exclusion from society. Approximately 10–20 % of UK Salvation Army hostel residents are ex-service personnel (Luscombe and Brook 2005). Some ex-service men have particular problems of post-traumatic stress disorder (PTSD) and other mental health problems.

In mid-life, exclusion can result from a wide range of situations relating to family, work and health, all of which are interconnected, and require well-developed coping skills to maintain a good quality of life. The traditional family structure has changed during recent decades. Between 1996 and 2004, cohabiting and lone-mother households increased to 2.2 and 2.3 million, respectively. At this time, of the 17 million families in the UK, the number headed by a married couple decreased by 500 000. Changes in family structure have resulted in 7 million people living alone, four times as many as in 1961. In 2001 136 000 children were living in households with adults or other relatives who were not their parents. At this time 52 000 children under 16 years of age lived in children's homes or similar communal agencies (ONS 2005).

Growing old can lead to exclusion and can be particularly acute in those who have been excluded in mid-life. A change in life style in retirement, bereavement, loss of mobility, moving into care and nursing homes can all cause increasing levels of anxiety. Coping in old age will very much depend on physical and mental health and the levels of support available to help maintain independence.

Throughout the life cycle there will be a wide range of individual differences in an individual's ability to become included and maintain their inclusion in society. These individual differences will depend on the complex interactions between genetic background, learned experiences and the social environment.

COMMUNITY RESPONSES

The issues considered in Part II of this book suggest that a wide range of physiological and psychological factors contribute to effective individual functioning, a prerequisite to *belonging* to a community. Clearly these biopsychological factors interact with a plethora of social and community factors that facilitate inclusion into society. For many vulnerable people their living conditions, educational opportunities, employment prospects and involvement in the community mitigate against inclusion. In a civil society, an appropriate community response would involve an awareness of the needs of its members and a response that would provide an appropriate support for those who are in need. Chapter 12 provides an overview of the evolving response of the UK government in terms of housing policy and income benefits that are related to employment, moving to a situation where only those people who are not able to engage in work will receive financial support from the state. In anticipating the escalating costs of health and social support as the UK demographics change towards a relatively more elderly population profile, current government social policies are being directed at facilitating a greater community response via family support and increased community participation. Such alternative strategies for providing support in the community, now being promoted, are based around the concept of *social capital*. To provide a simple explanation of *social capital*, Field (2003) suggests that this concept can be summarised in two words: 'relationships matter'. The development of social capital involves people, often sharing common interests, connecting via networks, which become a resource. In addition to the immediate utility of a social network, this stock of capital can be beneficial in other settings. 'The more people you know, and the more you share a common outlook with them, the richer you are in social capital' (Field 2003). Although formal and informal organisations are managed through rules and procedures, often people bypass the set procedures in order to make things happen. It is easier to call on trusted friends or acquaintances than 'officials' to solve a problem. Sharing values and helping others provides a sense of *meaning and belonging*.

The concept of social capital has developed from the writings of the following: de Tocqueville (1832), who commented on the 'vibrant associational life that underpinned American democracy and economic strength'; Emile Durkheim (1933), who described the transition from 'mechanical solidarity' to 'organic solidarity'; Bourdieu (1960), whose Marxist perspective led him to make the link between social relationships, hierarchies and economic capital; Coleman (1994), influenced by rational choice theory (see Chapter 11), considered educational attainment as a major driver in the development of social capital via human capital; and Putnam (2000), who focused on civic engagement, in particular the importance of this dynamic in the 'decline in social capital' in the US since the 1940s.

Of all these writers Putnam has had the greatest impact on social policy in the US and the UK. Putnam's book, *Bowling Alone*, influenced the then president of the US, Bill Clinton, to consider the social disaffection and apparent fracturing of the US society, epitomised by the epidemic of drug dependency and soaring crime rates, as indicators of

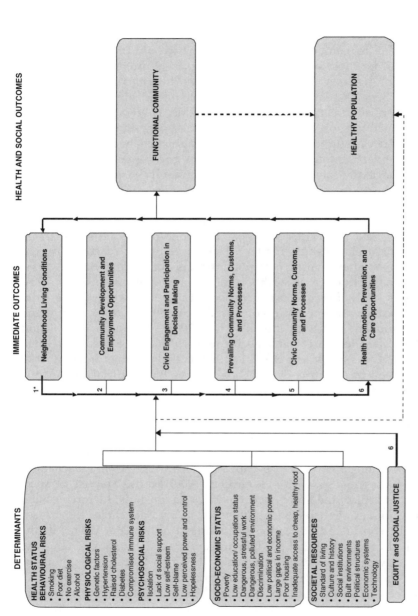

Figure 14.1 Logical framework analysis of community development, from a biopsychological perspective, focusing on the facilitation of social capital.

Source: Reprinted with permission from *Speaking of Health: Assessing Health Communication Strategies for Diverse Populations,* © 2002 by the National Academy of Sciences, courtesy of the National Academies Press, Washington, DC.

the lack of social cohesion. The reasons for this loss of social capital were ascribed to the lack of political and civic participation, which was mirrored in a decreasing participation in membership of associations, participation in religious groups, volunteering, charity, work-based socialising and informal socialising, all of which appeared, from Putnam's data, to be declining synchronously. Explanations for these societal changes included the pressures associated with two-career families, sheer busyness and the reduced time that women, in particular, can devote to community involvement. Putnam suggested that civic disengagement was also related to home-based computer entertainment, television and 'generational change'. Putnam's storyline sounds convincing but there have been a number of criticisms, not the least that his ideas are based on evidence collected in the US.

Halpern (2005) provides a useful review of social capital. His review provides an insight into how social capital can be measured, the links between health, well being, crime, education and social capital. He concludes that 'in roughly descending order of importance, people who are married, have close friends, go to church or are members of clubs have significantly better health than those who do not... [These] bio-psycho-social pathways explain how personal relationships generally act to protect [physical and mental] health'.

The concept of social capital has been embraced by policy makers including the Organisation of Economic Cooperation and Development (OECD), which provides a forum for policy discussion by the economically advanced countries in the world, and also the World Bank. In the UK, the concept has influenced New Labour policy, in answering such questions as 'how to build solidarity in a secular society exposed to the full rigours of a global market and committed to the principle of individual choice' (Leadbetter 1997). The political attractiveness of activating a community response is conceivably a sound ethical way to reduce, or at least contain, welfare spending. Additionally, it provides a set of models for understanding the complex dynamics of society and a possible critical analysis of those aspects that can be changed, by either a community response or state intervention.

Figure 14.1 shows a logical framework analysis (see Chapter 10, p. 171) of the health-related and socially determined factors that impact on the social inclusion and the health of community, from a *social capital* perspective. This analysis provides a simplistic view of the possible areas for change to facilitate an increase in social capital.

FAITH AS SOCIAL CAPITAL

Increasing educational attainment, improved physical and mental health, lower levels of crime, better functioning labour markets and economic growth, together with more active citizenship, are all thought to significantly contribute to social capital. During the last 15 years both Conservative and Labour governments have considered faith communities as key partners in the development of social policies and regeneration programmes. Recent world events have focused the long-standing debate on the beneficial and negative aspects of the social impact of religion. Religious understanding promotes strong boundaries that facilitate coherence in social groups. This can be divisive, on the other hand the major faiths have core principles which could be used to facilitate bridge-building and the development of community relationships. The doctrines of all faiths have commitments to peace, justice, honesty, service, community, personal responsibility and forgiveness. The assets of faith communities include: buildings; 'spaces' for religious reflection, motivation, understanding and participation in worship; formal governance and partnerships; and participation in the public domain. Each of these assets is not without its problems, as discussed by Furbey *et al.* (2006).

The concept of *human capacity development* (HCD) has been used in developing countries for some years. HCD involves community facilitation approaches, used in conjunction with or independently of development projects, which are normally externally sponsored and controlled by donor agencies. A combination of these approaches is used by organisations such as the Salvation Army, in promoting the development of *social capital* in developing countries. An example of this is reported by Campbell and Campbell (2005), in relation to 20 years of responses to HIV/AIDS. Development projects involve interventions from outside local communities which often are insufficient, in themselves, to bring about sustained change. An alternative approach is HCD. 'HCD refers to the elicitation of the will, skills, abilities, and systems in response to risk. It asserts that people in the home and local neighbourhood environment are capable of responding to risks and opportunities; so that they make progress with expansion of care and of prevention. Also, people in organisations can learn from local experience and adapt approaches so that local community strengths are the foundation for the organisational response'. The complex set of cofactors in increasing HIV-related risk in all countries is compounded by alcohol and drug misuse. Building local community capacity to respond to HIV/AIDS by addressing multiple risks inclusive of substance misuse, is proposed as a way of addressing the economic devastation of HIV/AIDS and building social capacity through integrated home care, community counselling and institutional support (Campbell and Campbell 2005). This approach used by the international Salvation Army and other non-governmental organisations, provides an example of how a faith-based organisation can have a positive influence on community health.

BELIEVING IS BELONGING

The concept of social capital, as introduced above, is based on the development of networks of relationships. Relationships between therapist and client were highlighted as a critical factor in developing a *therapeutic alliance*, as discussed in Chapter 11. Relationships are also important in self-help groups, which form the basis of one of the most successful forms of long-term support for those with substance misuse problems, known as the twelve-step movement. Alcoholics Anonymous (AA) developed from the work of Bill Wilson and Dr Bob in 1935. This 'non-religious . . . but spiritual approach' peer support group's approach to alcohol dependency involves twelve steps of personal development which include:

1. 'we admitted that we are powerless over alcohol'

2. '[we] came to believe that a Power greater than ourselves could restore sanity'

3. '[we] made a decision to turn our will and lives over to the care of God, as we understand him'

The basic principles of AA are set out in *The Big Book* (AA 2001). In 1940 there were 2000 AA members, by 1990 the membership had risen to 2 000 000 in 70 000 fellowship groups in 115 countries. Currently the growth rate in the UK is 15 % per year. Of the global membership 30 % is in Latin America. These statistics reflect the potential of this approach to 'offer a new way of life' for many millions of people. The underlying philosophy of AA has led to an increasing number of self-help groups, which include Al-Anon (for spouses and friends), Al-Ateen (for teenage children), ACOA (Adult Children of Alcoholics) and a number of co-dependency movements and mutual aid groups such as Women for Sobriety, Secular Organisations for Sobriety (SOS) and Rational Recovery (RR). The twelve-step approach is not based on a scientific method, and some commentators have suggested that harm to people and society results from this 'dependency culture', however, many referrals are made to AA by medical professionals. Although AA is a 'non-religious . . . but spiritual approach' its origins were in the Christian society of the nineteenth century, as were the *temperance movements* (Berridge 2005). In 1835 1.5 million inhabitants in the US had 'signed the pledge' and in the UK, the Band of Hope, a temperance organisation for young people had 16 000 societies and 2 million members in 1889. This movement, which originated as a response to the problems of excessive alcohol use, became politically very influential in US and led to prohibition of alcohol in the 1920s.

Nick Heather (1987) has reviewed the development of the changing concepts of alcohol and the 'alcohol epidemic'. He suggests that problematic and excessive use of alcohol are reflections of the change in social control of deviant behaviour. 'The role of the Church and civic authorities were replaced by science and medicine'. In relation to the discussion in the preceding paragraphs it might also be suggested that the decline of these important community influences resulted in a significant loss of *social capital*.

Not withstanding the criticisms of the AA twelve-step approach to helping people through their journey of recovery, the continuing success of this approach for many should be considered. The development of *relationships* through AA is clearly an important aspect of this group activity. However, the development of a belief in a 'higher power' is central to development of a *purpose of life* in those who previously had little hope and were helpless. Seligman (1978) described *helplessness* as a learned response to overwhelming external challenges, a situation which is not uncommon in many socially excluded people. In highly stressful situations, especially, ongoing relentless struggles, as described in Chapter 5, *helplessness* is accompanied by a low self-worth and loss of self-respect. This is the antithesis of Maslow's *self-actualisation* (see Chapter 2), a concept explored by Engel (1975). This author proposed that the search for meaning, as described by Maslow, was an important aspect of spiritual change and transformation, and was a 'being need' rather than a 'deficiency need'.

The linkage between believing and belonging is therefore a central axis, which appears to be a unique human attribute. Lewis Wolpert (2006) has commented that religion is a natural consequence of how we are genetically wired as human beings in that we have 'belief engines', and what differentiates us from other animals is that we have 'causal beliefs'. *Causal beliefs* referring to the insight that if, for instance, a community worker provides a cup of soup for a homeless person on the street, then the recipient will become warmed up both physically and psychologically by that altruistic action. Although animals have been reported to display altruistic behaviours (Dawkins 1976) they do not have the capacity to *believe* in the consequences of an intended behaviour. Through the process of evolution, humans became significantly more sophisticated than their animal cousins, through the use of tools and with increasing brain processing capacity they wanted to know e.g., why the sun shone or disappeared, why people became ill, what happens when we die? Wolpert suggests that these human behavioural changes led to the origin of belief, but he differentiates *causal beliefs* from *moral beliefs*, which are the foundation stones of ideologies and religions. He states that, 'I believe that religious beliefs are at least partly genetically determined. How else can you explain the fact that there's no society ever discovered that didn't have some sort of religious belief?'. There is evidence that people with religious beliefs are healthier, have fewer psychological problems and are less depressed (Koenig 2005).

Depression is characterised by false *causal beliefs*. Clearly a relationship exists between belief systems and increased feelings of well being, but the paradox is that church attendance in the UK is decreasing on the one hand and yet there appears to be an increase in people seeking a spiritual dimension to their lives (Gill 2002). Grace Davie (1994) comments that, 'The discrepancy between believing and belonging . . . is at its sharpest in urban working-class areas, and above all in the inner city. Here belief persists (albeit in a depressed form), but the expected reluctance to practise religion is compounded by a further factor, mistrust of institutional life of whatever kind, the churches included'. It is interesting to note that in global faith-based organisations such as the Salvation Army there is an increasing membership in the developing countries but a decline of church membership in the developed countries, despite significant increases in the Salvation Army social services, globally. In consideration of the contemporary relevance of this historically old organisation, Mingay (2005) has reviewed the problems of organisational change in the local community. He attributes resistance to change to fear of transition, power and control factors. From an affiliative behaviour perspective (see Figure 11.1) parent– child factors, object loss factors, child loss factors and personal fear of death (of the organisation) are also considered to be significant factors in the resistance to change.

In contrast to the reported decline in church attendance in the UK, black churches are booming (accounting for two-thirds of churchgoers in London; 12 % of the population in London is black compared to 2 % in the UK); and the Alpha course, which originated and is still based in the Holy Trinity Church, Brompton, London, is continuing to attract an increasing number of wealthy middle class and young to middle aged people. These significant expressions of spiritual awareness in the UK in 2006 have been attributed to 'an increasingly desperate pursuit of any kind of transcendence. . . .The Alpha course presents Christianity as therapeutic and self actualising in an attempt to appeal to precisely those values that most preoccupy the modern imagination' (Appleyard 2006).

The previous paragraphs point to Maslow's 'being need' which appears to be a fundamental human motivational drive, and is possibly an important constituent of the cement which helps to bind people into social groups. It therefore follows that a spiritual dimension should be considered in developing a holistic and integrated biopsychosocial perspective in addressing the needs of socially excluded people.

IN *DARKEST ENGLAND*

Substantial amounts of money and the development of highly complex social and health policies in the UK are presently directed at reducing social exclusion (see Chapters 12 and 13). In addition to this state intervention there are a large number of voluntary organisations working independently of, or in partnership with, statutory services to support the needs of the socially excluded. Despite this large-scale government and non-statutory investment in social capital, there is still a great number of unmet needs and community disaffection in the UK in 2006. In the concluding section of this book a comparison between the social problems in the late 1800s, when the Salvation Army began its 'social mission', and the current time seems apposite. When William Booth, a Christian evangelist, laid the foundations for a global movement involving social action and social reform in 1865, there were 500 charitable societies providing £3.5 million for the relief of social problems in the East End of London. However, Booth's mission was different. Volunteers were vital and his growing community church developed in the context of Booth's outspoken social reformist views:

> [D]ay by day the mass of pauperism is becoming intensified. Hunger and misery reign supreme in the homes of the poor . . . sickness and fever tread closely on the heels of want, and in the thin, pinched features of many a little one, in their wasted arms and shrunken head, we read the saddening story of parental privation and suffering. Another danger is sprung up. Large numbers of young women, usually employed in the manufacture of articles of clothing, find themselves deprived of work, and having no friends or resources, are being helplessly driven into a life of shame and misery.

A careful distinction was made between the funds used to maintain the Christian Mission and money given for the 'general relief' of the poor. Even at this early time before the Christian Mission became The Salvation Army, in 1878, an important guideline was that 'no benefit will be conferred upon any individual except under extraordinary circumstances without some return being made in labour'.

In England the socio-political climate was influenced by Thomas Huxley, the Earl of Shaftsbury, and those who were trying to understand human social behaviour in terms of the new Darwinism. Social Darwinism, developed from the revolutionary ideas in *The Origin of the Species* (Darwin 1872), suggested that giving relief to the poor was to be resisted as they were unlikely to survive because of their poverty, poor health and lack of skills. Relief given to the poor would lead to dependency of increasing numbers of potentially riotous masses. In contradiction to social Darwinism, religious and secular charitable organisations, including the Salvation Army began to address the needs of the socially excluded.

A consequence of the religious zeal of the early Salvationists was the small-scale innovations that led to a series of global social actions. An example of this was Eliza Shirley, who, with her family, began work in Philadelphia in 1879; this was followed by the opening of the US National Headquarters in 1880, by Commissioner George Scott Railton and seven women officers. By 1890, 410 Salvation Army centres had been established in 35 states. These developments involved revival services and a social mission comprising casework, advocacy, emotional and spiritual support, comforting the sick, homeless and lonely. The importance of this work was acknowledged by invitations for The Salvation Army leaders to the White House in 1886. At this time 'Pioneer officers did not accept that social and religious activities were not perfectly harmonious; both served the great cause of saving souls' (Bollwahn 2000).

The formal social work of the Salvation Army developed in various locations around the world. In Glasgow, a rescue home for women was opened in 1883; a halfway house for released prisoners was started in Melbourne, Australia in 1883; a rescue home for prostitutes was established in Whitechapel, East London in 1884; a treatment centre for women alcoholics opened in Canada, 1886; and a child day centre was set up in a 'slum port' in London. The first social enterprise in America was a rescue home for 'fallen women' and a shelter for homeless men was opened in New York in 1886. At this time, well before the emancipation of women, W.T. Stead reported in the *Pall Mall Gazette* on the international trade in underage girls to please specific buyers. 'Girls were drugged and sent in nailed coffins to specific-order clients. Sometimes a victim would awake during the voyage, only to die in terror clawing at the wooden coffin'. In the first of its advocacy roles the Salvation Army influenced the British

Salvation Army 'Farthing Breakfasts', Hanbury Street, London, 1880.
Source: Reprinted with permission from the Salvation Army International Heritage Centre, London.

Parliament, with 393 000 signatures, to pass a bill in 1885, which raised the age of consent to 16, virtually stopping the intercontinental traffic in girls. In 1888, the first food and shelter depot was opened in Limehouse, East London, and prison gate brigades were started at this time. By 1889, 10 000 low-priced meals were served to starving dockers in East London. During the previous six years the women of Booth's Cellar, Gutter, and Garret Brigade lived in filthy tenements of Whitechapel, serving the poor and caring for the elderly. This group later became known as the 'Slum Sisters', a name still used in Scandinavia today.

At this time shelters, or common lodging houses (hostels), were being re-established (see Chapter 12), and the Salvation Army opened the first labour exchange in the UK in 1890, see photograph on p. 197. Within 12 months 20 such exchanges had been established around the UK. Labour yards were set up next to the hostels; here men were guaranteed eight hours of work, making benches, patching boots or providing other domestic service (Collier 1965).

The National Commander in the US, Commissioner Frank Smith, had been influenced by the socialist philosophy of Henry George, and on returning to Britain in 1890, encouraged Booth to undertake an 'intense' study of the homeless population. Booth now recognised that 'a man's first step toward salvation was to regain his self-respect so that even men who have touched zero could earn the price of a night's bed and board'. Salvation of the soul through salvation of the body was now his belief, based on reality and experience (Green 1989). With help from Frank Smith, Booth gathered data and formulated the scheme for social action and salvation, documented in *In Darkest England and the Way Out*, in 1890. In this book he laid down the principles that would address the complex needs which he considered to be caused by:

> [D]ifficulties which heredity, habit, and surroundings place in the way of its solution, but unless we are prepared to fold our arms in selfish ease and say that nothing can be done, and thereby doom those lost millions to remediless perdition in this world, to say nothing of the next the problem must be solved in some way. . . . I lay down what must be the essential elements of any scheme likely to command success:

1. Every scheme must change the man when it is his character and conduct which constitute the reason for his failure in the battle of life.

2. The remedy must change the circumstances of the individual when they are the cause of his wretched condition and lie beyond his control.

3. Any remedy worthy of consideration must be on a scale commensurate with the evil with which it proposes to deal.

4. Not only must the scheme be large enough, but it must be permanent.

5. But, while it must be permanent, it must also be immediately practicable.

6. The indirect features of the scheme must not be such as to produce injury to the persons whom we seek to benefit.

7. While assisting one class of community, it must not seriously interfere with the interests of another (Booth 1890, pp. 84–7. Reprinted 1984).

The *Darkest England* scheme aimed to create communities in which people could receive help to increase their physical, moral, spiritual and employment capacity, to learn to govern themselves, and to build a sustainable society to provide for others as they became independent. The communities would be developed as a City Colony, the Farm Colony and an Overseas Colony. These proposals were vehemently opposed by Thomas Huxley and those who were influenced by social Darwinism. Nevertheless the *Darkest England* scheme began with £100 000 from public donations and government support. With these non-evangelical funds, homes for unwed mothers, hospitals, children's homes, summer camps and rehabilitation centres were built. The scheme was supported in America and Australia and slowly gained acceptance by the establishment, even to the extent of recognition by Oxford University, which considered the scheme of social and spiritual redemption as a unique contribution to society and awarded Booth a Doctorate of Civil Law in 1907. The public and the press had mixed views about these developments, but kindly used the slogan 'Soup, Soap, and Salvation', to encapsulate the style of the rapidly developing international organisation, which today is one of the largest voluntary charitable organisations in the world, see Appendix A.

The author has been impressed by examples of the *Darkest England* scheme in various continents, for example, in Costa Rica, where a number of Salvation Army social activities supporting the homeless and vulnerable people in the capital city San Jose are operated daily. Just outside the city is a 200-acre residential centre for young people with substance misuse problems. This Salvation Army centre has a programme run by clinical psychiatrists and Salvation Army officers who integrate the rehabilitation programme with work therapy using the productive pig farm and the well-equipped woodwork factory, which produces in excess of 20 solid wood house doors each week. Like many work-based projects in South America, South Africa, India and other countries these projects have been operating since 1912 or thereabouts. Similar industrial-scale work-based schemes are involved in the manufacture of furniture and textiles (e.g. sleeping bags) in Scandinavia. In Sweden one of the many social action projects is a Salvation Army owned island, Kuron (the island of hope), just off the coast of Stockholm. This community provides a comprehensive work-based rehabilitation scheme for problematic alcohol and drug users, a *Darkest England* project that was established in 1920.

Hattersley (1999) has critically reviewed the internal and external struggles which have been part of these fascinating historical developments of

The Salvation Army. However, despite many hindrances to the *Darkest England* scheme, the global legacy of William Booth still provides a successful model of work-based rehabilitation, and a child/family-centred approach, delivered within a faith-based context. It is interesting to reflect that current UK government strategies, in 2006, are focusing on employment-related schemes and programmes to support lone parents and children. A principle, which underpins Booth's social action, is that, in addition to having an ambulance at the bottom of the cliff, a strong fence should be constructed at the top of the cliff to prevent the descent into misery and sorrow.

FROM *DARKEST ENGLAND* TO *COOL BRITANNIA*

The UK in 2006 is a very different place from the England in which Booth and other social reformers began their work in the late nineteenth century. The UK now has a strong economy with low rates of unemployment compared to other European countries. There has been a significant transition from the politics of individualism and competition generated in the contract culture of Margaret Thatcher in the 1990s, symbolised by her comment that 'there is no such thing as society', to the *Modernising Britain* of Tony Blair in the years since 1997. In Blair's *Cool Britannia* the principles of a market economy have been maintained, and increased spending on public services has been underpinned by performance-based strategies. New financial and work-related provisions are being made for single parents and families, and the Children's Act has very significant implications for the integration of children's services. In tackling the problems of housing shortage, the ODPM is leading an extensive house-building scheme throughout the country. The reader might begin to perceive that a light is beginning to shine in *Darkest England.*

The government targets for abolishing child poverty by 2020 appear to be more or less on track with child poverty presently estimated to be 3.5 million, compared with a government target for 2004/5 of 3.1 million. However, the proportion of children living in workless households in the UK is the highest in Europe. Furthermore, significant health inequalities remain: infant deaths in manual households are 1.5 times greater than in non-manual households; deaths under 65 years from heart disease and lung cancer are twice as likely in manual workers compared to non-manual workers (Palmer *et al.* 2005). One in six children suffer from depression, and one in 15 children cause self-inflicted harm. Self-harm in young people is a growing problem, which appears to be culturally related. Recent research undertaken at the University of Glasgow indicates that self-harm is four times more likely in teenage 'Goths' in that 53 % of Goths (identified with black clothes and dark music) had self-harmed, compared to 24 % of Punks and 14 % of all young people (Young 2006).

In the latest British Crime Survey (BCS) (Nicholas *et al.* 2005), a sample of 22 463 people showed that 26 % of women and 17 % of men have experienced at least one incident of domestic violence since they were 16. The BCS shows more than a million victims each year in England and Wales. The definition of domestic violence includes threats of force of a non-sexual nature. The researchers estimate that the underlying rate is at least five times higher than disclosed in the BCS study. Violent domestic incidents can lead to death; half of all female murder victims are killed by their partners or ex-partners. These statistics do not represent single events, as the BCS survey showed that victims have on average 20 incidents a year, 16 involving force. In a third of the women, violence started in pregnancy; if a man has been abusive, before the pregnancy, it becomes escalated during and after the pregnancy. Home Office research shows that, on average, a woman endures 35 incidents of domestic violence before making a complaint to the police. There are growing concerns regarding the increased consumption of alcohol by girls and also the influence of alcohol on fights, work and homelife/marriage (Anderson and Baumberg 2006) (see Figures 14.2 and 14.3).

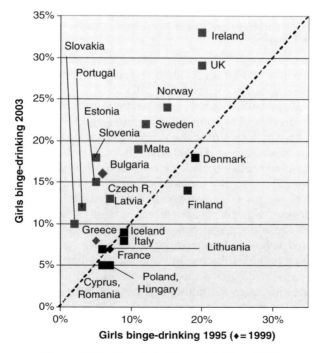

Figure 14.2   Trends in binge drinking, 1995.
Source: Reproduced from Anderson, P. and B. Baumberg (2006). *Alcohol in Europe*. London: Institute of Alcohol Studies.

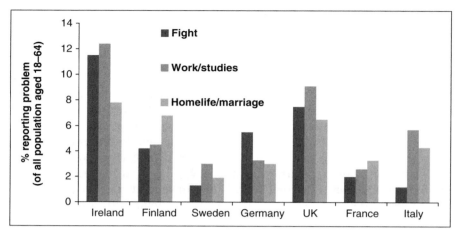

Figure 14.3   Significant effects of alcohol on personal and domestic functioning.
Source: The ECAS survey plus an added survey conducted in Ireland (as reported in Hope and Ramstedt 2004).
Note: 'Fight': the percentage of people reporting that they had been in fights while drinking. 'Work/studies': the percentage of people reporting that drinking had harmed their work or studies. 'Homelife/marriage': the percentage of people reporting that drinking had damaged their marriage or homelife.
Source: Reproduced from Anderson, P. and B. Baumberg (2006). *Alcohol in Europe*. London: Institute of Alcohol Studies.

There has been a reduction in suicide rates, which have now fallen to the lowest levels since records began (DH 2006). In 1995 the number of suicides was 9.2 per 100 000, this was reduced to 8.56 deaths per 100 000 in 2004. Highest rates of suicide occur in men aged 30–39, 800 men killed themselves last year, four times the number of women. The rate in young men has fallen from 20 per 100 000 in 1995 to 17 per 100 000 in 2004. The government aims to reduce suicide rates by one-fifth of 1995 levels by 2010. Changes in suicide reflect the mental health of the community.

The new UK is indeed a very different multi-ethnic, libertarian and permissive society from that described in *Darkest England*. However, many 'social ills' still cause great concern. The levels of anti-social behaviour and linked increased levels of binge drinking have been responded to by new legislation which includes the use of Anti-Social Behaviour Orders (ASBOs) and zero tolerance strategies adopted by the police. In Europe the UK has the highest rates in young people of alcohol use, binge drinking, drunkenness, marijuana and problem drug use (ESPAD 2003; FSS 2000). Furthermore the rates of illicit drug use among young adolescents have nearly doubled in the last few years. The UK is among the European countries with the highest rates of problem drug use. There are an estimated 266 000 drug-addicted individuals in Great Britain, a ratio of about 1 in 200. The highest risk is in young males, with over 50 % of persons presenting for treatment in England, Scotland and Wales being under age 30, with a 3:1 male:female ratio. Lifetime illicit drug use has been estimated at 22% among 13–14 year olds and 42% among 16–19 year olds in the UK. Currently there is increasing concern about the increasing rates of binge drinking in girls in the UK, see Figure 14.2.

Although we might commend the investment of £1.6 million in the anti-drugs programme, £600 million for *Supporting People*, £3 billion for mental health services and £600 million on the criminal justice services, this is surely an indictment on modern society that such spending is required to tackle very significant problems. Globalisation and the development of computer technology and advances in mass media have brought about large numbers of benefits in education (for example in supporting those with learning disorders), bridging the gap across communities and widening opportunities for the disabled. The benefits of increased global markets and the raised awareness of poverty in third-world countries are offset by the global problems of drug trafficking, internet pornography and the trafficking of sex workers (Munro 2066).

Several tendencies seem to be emerging. One relates to changing family structure and the increase in lone-parent families. This demographic change has created a major shortage of houses, hence the need for an extensive government building programme. A related issue is the apparent increase in disaffected young people (Newburn and Shiner 2005). There are many contributing factors leading to these early developmental problems, one which is not normally acknowledged publicly is the absence of a father figure to provide a role model in the family home. The all pervasive problems, apparent in Darkest England, still exert a significant negative influence on personal and domestic functioning, see Figure 14.3. Problems related to modern society are reflected in the mental health of the community. From this perspective it is interesting to note that 3.5 million people in the UK are receiving prescriptions for Prozac (the so-called 'happy pills', which work via serotonin brain systems, see Chapter 7). Prescriptions for Prozac and Zoloft have more than doubled during the last decade. Currently, the Department of Health is set to expand 'talking therapies' services (psychosocial interventions) as an alternative to the pharmacological treatments, which presently cost £400 million per year. The locations chosen for pilot projects are in areas where there is a high proportion of people claiming incapacity benefit, a third of whom are thought to be suffering from depression. The new 'talking therapies' will include marriage counselling and jobs advice. According to the so-called 'happiness czar', Professor Lord Richard Layard, 10 000 new therapists are required (Goodchild and Laurance 2006). Is this an indicator of deficits in *social capital*?

CONCLUSION

Reducing social exclusion is a key government target. The considerable budgetary and strategic resources being used to increase the inclusion of young people, adults and the elderly in the community, is a reflection of the socio-political and economic importance of increasing community safety and reducing the financial deficits of health and social services for all. From an individual perspective consideration should be given to the enormous amount of human sadness and sorrow, which is probably not so different since the time of Booth's *In Darkest England Scheme*, in 1890. Many of the social problems (described as 'evils' by Booth) have their origins in hedonistic pursuits or are consequences of extremely difficult and oppressive living and working conditions, and possibly dysfunctional family situations.

Behaviours that are 'reward mediated' as described in Chapter 2, can lead to excessive use of alcohol and other drugs (self-medication hypothesis), addictive behaviours and a variety of psychopathologies. This book has attempted to explore the cascade of internal and external development factors that underlie such personal features, which increase or decrease an individual's likelihood of being a member of an inclusive community. Successful inclusion in the community therefore is highly complex and dependent on the life history of the individual. A life story is central to the determination of our *social identity* and provides a sense of 'meaning'. The development of *meaning and belonging*, in those being helped, should underpin the philosophy of social care services, a role which faith-based organisations have been adopting over many years. Individual functioning within the group or community will be more or less effective according to an individual's contribution to the group. Clearly one of the most effective ways of *belonging* to the group is to contribute by adopting a role and 'doing work'.

Since the beginning of the millennium it has been gratifying to note the change in UK government strategy in addressing the health needs of the homeless, child poverty, the provision for an ageing society, and to generally move from welfare handouts to the promotion of independence. The Children's Act (2004) provides a strong focus on the integration of children's services and other related measures and will hopefully increase resilience and reduce disaffection in young people. In this evolving strategy based on the concept of *social capital*, it is interesting to see the attention of the Social Exclusion Unit being attracted to the role of *faith communities* (JRF 2006). This, together with the *Respect* agenda, indicates a rediscovery by the government of the importance of *belief* and *value* systems in communities, apparently neglected in previous state interventions. These were and are central elements of the *Darkest England Scheme*. Booth, writing in Victorian times when colonial attitudes prevailed, was very much aware of the rigid class structure and the limited aspirations of many UK citizens. The UK, in 2006, is by no means a classless society, but the chances of social mobility are now much greater. The concepts of 'meaning' and 'belonging' therefore need to be considered within this changing social structure.

A person waking-up in his/her owner-occupied or social housing accommodation needs to be motivated by a 'purpose'. A 'purpose in life' might be related to working to support the family, being paid to work or volunteering. 'Purpose in life' might have a spiritual meaning in the case of someone recovering from substance misuse, assisted by a twelve-step support group, or engaging with a faith community. In Chapter 1, the historical discourse into the mind, body and soul may provide an insight into 'meaning, belonging and purpose'. The concept of the human soul has been debated by philosophers and theologians since the time of the Ancient Greeks. A view of someone who has been 'de-souled' as a result of the alcohol-related brain disease WKS, provides a sad image of someone without a life story and without a purpose. Thankfully, many people can regain their purpose in life, an essential aspect of rehabilitation into the community.

REFERENCES

AA (2001). *Alcoholics Anonymous Big Book*, 4th edition. New York: Alcoholic Anonymous World Services.

Anderson, P. and B. Baumberg (2006). *Alcohol in Europe*. London: Institute of Alcohol Studies.

Appleyard, B. (2006). Religion: who needs it? *New Statesman*, 10 April, 20–2.

Berridge, V. (2005). *Temperance: Its History and Impact on Current and Future Alcohol Policy*. York: Joseph Rowntree Foundation.

Bollwahn, P. (2000). *William Booth: The Development of His Social Concern*. Washington: National Headquarters, The Salvation Army.

Booth, W. (1890, Reprinted 1984). *In Darkest England and the Way Out*. London: The Salvation Army.

Campbell, I. and A. R. Campbell (2005). Responding to HIV/Aids, alcohol and drug misuse – developing local community capacity for care, prevention and transfer. *Alcohol and Alcoholism*, **40**(Supplement 1), 3.

Coleman, J. S. (1994). *Foundations of Social Theory*. Cambridge, MA: Belknap Press.

Collier, R. (1965). *The General Next to God*. London: Collins.

Cook, C. C., D. Goddard and R. Westall (1997). Knowledge and experience of drug use amongst church affiliated young people. *Drug and Alcohol Dependence*, **46**(1–2), 9–17.

Davie, G. (1994). *Religion in Britain since 1945*. Oxford: Blackwell.

Dawkins, R. (1976). *The Selfish Gene*. Oxford: Oxford University Press.

DH (2006). *Lowest Suicide Rates since Records Began*. London: Department of Health.

Engel, J. F. (1975). *What's Gone Wrong with the Harvest?* Michigan: Grand Rapids.

ESPAD (2003). *The European School Survey Project on Alcohol and Other Drugs (ESPAD)*.

Field, J. (2003). *Social Capital*. London: Routledge.

FSS. (2000). *Drug Abuse Trends*. London: Forensic Science Service.

Furbey, R., A. Dinham, R. Farnell, D. Finneron and G. Wilkinson (eds) (2006). *Faith as Social Capital*. London: The Policy Press.

Gill, R. (2002). *Changing Worlds: Can the Church Respond?* Edinburgh: T and T Clark.

Goodchild, S. and J. Laurance (2006). Dependency Britain: we're in a major drugs crisis. Why it may be better to talk. *The Independent on Britain*, 16 April, 12–13.

Green, R. J. (1989). *War on Two Fronts*. Atlanta: The Salvation Army.

Halpern, D. (2005). *Social Capital*. Cambridge: Polity Press.

Hattersley, R. (1999). *Blood and Fire: William and Catherine Booth and Their Salvation Army.* London: Abacus.

Heather, N. (1987). Problem drinkers. In: Harrison, L. (ed.), *Alcohol Problems in the Community.* London: Routledge.

JRF (2006). Faith as social capital. Available: http://www.jrf.org.uk/knowledge/findings/socialpolicy/0136 [Accessed 20 April 2006].

Koenig, H. (2005). *Faith and Mental Health.* West Conhohokem, PA: Templeton.

Leadbetter, C. (1997). *The Rise of the Social Entrepreneur.* London: DEMOS.

Luscombe, C. and A. Brook (2005). Prevalence of alcohol abuse in homeless populations: the use of holistic assessments in the non-statutory sector. *Alcohol and Alcoholism,* **40**(Supplement 1), S02–4.

Margin, P., D. Pond and W. Smith (2005). Isotretinoin, depression and suicide: a review of the evidence. *British Journal of General Practice,* (February), 132–8.

Mingay, R. (2005). *The Challenge of Change: What Factors Constitute a Fear of Transition in The Salvation Army?* University of Nottingham.

Munro, G. (2006). *An Exploratory Research Study into the Substance Misuse and Health Related Needs of Migrant and Trafficked Women Engaged in Prostitution in Tower Hamlets and the City.* London: The Research Department, The Salvation Army.

Newburn, T. and M. Shiner (2005). *Dealing with Disaffection: Young People Mentoring and Social Inclusion.* Portland: Willan Publishing.

Nicholas, S., D. Povey, A. Walker and C. Kershaw (2005). *Crime in England and Wales 2004/2005.* London: Home Office.

ONS (2005). *Focus on Families: Dependent Children.* London: Office for National Statistics.

Palmer, G., J. Carr and P. Kenaway (2005). *Monitoring Poverty and Social Exclusion.* York: Joseph Rowntree Foundation.

Putnam, R. (2000). *Bowling Alone. The Collapse and Revival of American Community.* New York: Simon & Schuster.

Seligman, M. E. (1978). Learned helplessness as a model of depression. Comment and integration. *Journal of Abnormal Psychology,* **87**(1), 165–79.

Wolpert, L. (2006). *Six Impossible Things Before Breakfast.* London: Faber and Faber.

Young, R. (2006). Goth culture may protect vulnerable children. *British Medical Journal,* **332**, 909.

APPENDIX A

INTERNATIONAL STATISTICS OF THE SALVATION ARMY (SA)
(WITH PERMISSION FROM THE SALVATION ARMY YEAR BOOK, 2006)

Countries and other territories where SA serves	111
Languages used in SA work	175
Churches, outposts, societies	14,918
Goodwill centres	442
Officers	26,055
Active	17,295
Retired	8,760
Auxiliary officers	1,801
Theological students	992
Employees	107,726
Church members	1,041,461
Associate members	188,180
Young members	386,185
Trainee officers/cadets	42,414
Senior band musicians	23,956
Senior songsters	98,335
Other senior musical group members	66,856
Senior and young people's leaders	136,180
Women's ministries – members	1,199,498
League of Mercy/community volunteers	102,187
SA Medical Fellowship – members	7,381
Over-60 clubs – members	104,990
Men's fellowships – members	53,287
Young people's musicians – members	245,374
Sunday schools – members	351,601
Junior youth groups (scouts, guides, etc. and clubs)	145,120
Senior youth groups – members	74,746
Corps-based community development programmes	762
Beneficiaries/clients	865,376

(continued)

Thrift stores/charity shops (corps/territorial)	1,496
Recycling centres	27

Social programmes
Residential

Hostels for homeless and transient	618
Capacity	32,429
Emergency lodges	207
Capacity	9,565
Children's homes	215
Capacity	9,568
Homes for the elderly	191
Capacity	13,060
Homes for the disabled	47
Capacity	1,615
Homes for the blind	8
Capacity	339
Remand and probation homes	60
Capacity	1,106
Homes for street children	29
Capacity	643
Mother and baby homes	40
Capacity	1,348
Training centres for families	19
Capacity	252
Care homes for vulnerable people	55
Capacity	953
Women's and men's refuge centres	98
Capacity	2,004
Other residential care homes/hostels	399
Capacity	5,402

Day Care

Community centres	638
Early childhood education centres	195
Capacity	23,092
Day centres for the elderly	211
Capacity	23,471
Play groups	161
Capacity	4,707
Day centres for the hearing impaired	14
Capacity	246
Day centres for street children	20
Capacity	5,120
Day nurseries	145
Capacity	6,817
Drop-in centres for youth	291

Other day care centres	279
Capacity	42,951

Addiction dependency

Non-residential programmes	63
Capacity	2,129
Residential programmes	205
Capacity	12,734
Harbour Light programmes	40
Capacity	2,934
Other services for addictions	46
Capacity	2,903

Services for the Armed Forces

Clubs and canteens	22
Mobile units for service personnel	38
Chaplains	21

Emergency disaster response

Disaster rehabilitation scheme	38
Participants	7,199
Refugee programmes – host country	43
Participants	26,110
Refugee rehabilitation programmes	8
Participants	22,892
Other response programmes	2,020
Participants	295,650

Services to the community

Prisoners visited	298,124
Prisoners helped on discharge	143,107
Police courts – people helped	249,801
Missing persons – applications	12,405
Number traced	8,165
Night patrol/anti-suicide – number helped	269,286
Community youth programmes	548
Beneficiaries	72,539
Employment bureaux	
Application	477,893
Initial referrals	141,169
Counselling – people helped	481,418
General relief – people helped	15,644,817
Emergency relief (fire, flood, etc.) – people helped	3,954,668
Emergency mobile units	1,447
Feeding centres	39,635
Restaurants and cafes	41
Thrift stores/charity shops (social)	1,263
Apartments for elderly	2,170
Capacity	7,514

(continued)

Hostels for students, workers, etc.	64
Capacity	3,992
Land settlements (SA villages, farms etc.)	47
Capacity	1,939
Social services summer camps	130
Participants	19,049
Other services to the community/unspecified	126
Beneficiaries	30,179,664

Health programmes

General hospitals	20
Capacity	2,439
Maternity hospitals	11
Capacity	302
Other specialist hospitals	16
Capacity	1,582
Specialist clinics	46
Capacity	369
General clinics/health centres	181
Capacity	838
Mobile clinics/community health posts	50
Inpatients	158,971
Outpatients	989,574
Doctors/medics	946
Invalid/convalescent homes	30
Capacity	572
Health education programmes (HIV/AIDS, etc.)	5,134
Beneficiaries	331,578
Day care programmes	10

Education programmes

Kindergarten/sub primary	680
Primary schools	1,011
Upper primary and middle schools	192
Secondary and high schools	193
Colleges and universities	14
Vocational training schools/centres	104
Pupils	478,793
Teachers	15,649
Schools for the blind (included in above totals)	23
Schools for the disabled (included in above totals)	9
Boarding schools (included in above totals)	29
Evening schools	10
Colleges, universities, staff training and development study and distance learning centres	18

Source: Reproduced with permission from *The Salvation Army 2006 Year Book*.

SUMMARY OF ASSESSMENTS FOR SOCIALLY EXCLUDED POPULATION

Purpose	Domain/construct	Instrument (s)	Author (s)
Screening	Screening for alcohol problems	CAGE	Ewing (1984)
		AUDIT	Saunders *et al.* (1993)
		AUDIT-C	Gorden *et al.* (2001)
		TWEAK	Russell (1994)
		RAPS-RAPS4	Cherpitel (1995, 2000)
Problem assessment	Diagnosis of alcohol and other drug problems	DIS-IV	Robins *et al.* (2000)
		SCID-I/P	First *et al.* (1996)
		PRISM	Hasin *et al.* (1996, 1998)
		CIDI-SAM	Robins *et al.* (1995)
		SSAGA	Bucholz *et al.* (1994)
		SCAN	Wing *et al.* (1990)
	Severity of alcohol and other drug dependence	ADS	Skinner and Allen (1982)
		EDSS	Babor (1996)
		SADQ	Stockwell *et al.* (1983)
		SDSS	Miele *et al.* (2000)
	Severity of substance dependence	ASI	McLellan (1992)
	Alcohol consumption	QF measures	
		GF	Midanik (1994)
		LDH	Skinner and Sheu (1982)
		CLDH	Russell *et al.* (1997)
		TLFB	Sobell and Sobell (1992,
		Form 90	2000)
		Daily Diary	Miller (1996)
		IVR/EMA	
	Alcohol biomarkers	Ethanol tests	
		GGT	
		CDT	
	Severity of alcohol withdrawal	CIWA-Ar	Sullivan *et al.* (1989)
		AWS	Wetterling *et al.* (1997)

(continued)

Purpose	Domain/construct	Instrument (s)	Author (s)
	Cocaine craving questionnaire		Tiffany(1993)
	Subjective Opiate Withdrawal Scale	SOWS	Handelsman (1987)
	Severity of Selective Cocaine Assessment	SDSS	Miele (2000)
	Desires for Drug Questionnaire	DDQ	Franken (2002)
	Alcohol-related consequences	DrInC	Miller *et al.* (1995)
		RAPI	White and Labouvie (1989)
Personal assessment	Readiness to change	URICA	DiClemente and Hughes (1990)
		SOCRATES	Miller and Tonigan (1996)
		RTCQ-TV	Heather *et al.* (1999)
	Antecedents to drinking	IDS	Annis *et al.* (1987)
		RFDQ	Zywiak *et al.* (1996)
		RPI	Litman *et al.* (1983)
		AWARE	Miller and Harris (2000)
	Self-efficacy	SCQ-39	Annis and Graham (1988)
		DRSEQ	DiClemente *et al.* (1994)
		SARA	Young and Knight (1991)
		ISS	Schonfield *et al.* (1993)
			Miller *et al.* (1994)
	Coping skills	CBI	Litman *et al.* (1983)
		CRI	Moos (1992)
		ASRPT	Monti *et al.* (1993)
	Cocaine risk Response Test		Carroll (1999)
	Drinking outcome expectations	AEQ	Brown *et al.* (1980)
		DEQ	Young and Knight (1989)
		CEOA	Fromme *et al.* (1993)
		NAEQ	Jones and McMahon (1994)
		AEQ-A	Christiansen *et al.* (1982)
	Spirituality and religiosity	RBB	Connors *et al.* (1996)
		PIL/SONG	Crumbaugh (1969, 1977)
	Twelve-step affiliation	AAI	Tonigan *et al.* (1996)
		Steps	Gilbert (1991)
		B-PRPI	Brown and Peterson (1994)
		AAAS	Humphrey's *et al.* (1998)

Craving	YBOCS-hd	Modell *et al.* (1992)
	OCDS	Anton *et al.* (1995)
	AUQ	Bohn *et al.* (1995)
	ACQ-Now	Singleton (1996)
	PACS	Flannery *et al.* (1999)
Comorbid	BDI-II	Beck *et al.* (1996)
psychopathology	CES-D	Radloff (1977)
	STAI	Spielberger *et al.* (1983)
	BAI	Beck *et al.* (1988)
	BSI	Derogatis and Melisaratos (1983)
Neuropsychological deficits	WCST	Heaton (1981)
	Shipley	Zachary (1986)
	WMS	Wechsler (1987)
	CVLT	Delis *et al.* (1987)
	Trail Making	Halstead (1947)
	Digit Symbol	Wechsler (1981)
Multidimensional measures	ASI	McLellan *et al.* (1992)
	CASI-A	Meyers *et al.* (1995)
	CDP	Miller and Marlatt (1984)
	AUI	Horn *et al.* (1987)
	PEI-A	Winters (1996, 1999)
Patient placement	ASAM criteria	Mee-Lee *et al.* (2001)
Situational Confidence Questionnaire (Heroin Users)		Barber (1991)

Source: Reproduced from Donovan, T. and G. A. Marlatt (2005). *Assessment of Addictive Behaviours*. New York: Guilford Press.

REFERENCES

Annis, H. M. and J. M. Graham (1988). *Situational Confidence Questionnnaire (SCQ-39) User's Guide*. Toronto: Addiction Research Foundation.

Annis, H. M., J. M. Graham and C. S. Davis (1987). *Inventory of Drinking Situations (IDS) user's guide*. Toronto: Addiction Research Foundation.

Anton, R. F., D. H. Moak and P. K. Latham (1995). The Obsessive Compulsive Drinking Scale: A self-rated instrument of the quantification of thoughts about alcohol and drinking behaviour. *Alcoholism: Clinical and Experimental Research*, **19**, 92–99.

Babor, T. F. (1996). Reliability of the ethanol dependence syndrome scale. *Psychology of Addictive Behaviors*, **10**, 97–103.

Barber, J.G., B. K. Cooper and N. Heather (1991). The Situational Confidence Questionnaire (heroin). *International Journal of the Addictions*, **26**, 565–75.

Beck, A. T., N. Epstein, G. Brown and R. Steer (1988). An inventory for measuring clinical anxiety: Psychometric properties. *J of Consulting and Clincial Psychology*, **56**, 893–7.

Beck, A. T., R. A. Steer and G. K. Brown (1996). *Beck Depression Inventory-II*. San Antonio TX: Psychological Corporation.

Bohn, M. J., D. D. Krahn and R. A. Staehler (1995). Development and initial validation of a measure of drinking urges in abstinent alcoholics. *Alcoholism: Clinical and Experimental Research*, **19**, 600–6.

Brown, H. P. and J. H. Peterson (1991). Assessing spirituality in addiction treatment and follow-up: Development of the Brown-Peterson Recovery Process Inventory (B-PRPI). *Alcoholism Treatment Quarterly*, **8**, 21–50.

Brown, S. A., M. S. Goldman, M. S. A. Inn and L. Anderson (1980). Expectations of reinforcement from alcohol: Their domain and relation to drinking pattern. *J of Consulting and Clincial Psychology*, **48**, 419–26.

Bucholz, K. K., *et al.* (1994). A new, semistructured psychiatric interview for use in genetic linkage studies; A Report of the reliability of the SSAGA. *J. of Studies on Alcohol*, **55**, 149–58.

Carroll, K. M., C. Nich, T. L. Frankforter and R. M. Bisighini (1999). Do patients change in the way we intend?: Treatment specific skill acquisition in cocaine-dependent patients using the Cocaine Risk Response Test. *Psychological Assessment*, **11**, 77–85.

Cherpitel, C. J. (2000). *A brief screening instrument for problem drinking in the emergency room: The RAPS4*. Vol. 61.

Christiansen, B. A., M. S. Goldman and A. Inn (1982). Development of alcohol-related expectances in adolescents: Separating pharmacological from social-learning influences. *J of Consulting and Clincial Psychology*, **50**, 336–44.

Connors. G. J., J. S. Tonigan and W. R. Miller (1996). Measure of religious background and behavior for use in behavior change research. *Psychology of Addictive Behaviors*, **10**, 90–6.

Crumbaugh, J. C. (1969). *Purpose in Life Test*. Murfreesboro TN: Psychometric Affiliates.

Delis, D. C., J. H. Kramer, E. Kaplan and B. A. Ober (1987). *The California Verbal Learning Test*. New York: Psychological Corporation.

Deorgratis, L. R. and N. Melisaratos (1983). The Brief Symptom Inventory: An Introductory report. *Psychological Medicine*, **13**, 595–605.

DiClemente, C. C., J. P. Carbonari, R. P. G. Montgomery and S. O. Hughes (1994). The Alcohol Abstinence Self-Efficacy Scale. *J. of Studies on Alcohol*, **55**, 141–8.

DiClemente, C. C. and S. O. Hughes (1990). Stages of change profiles in outpatient alcoholism treatment. *J of Substance Abuse*, **2**, 217–35.

Donovan, T. and G. A. Marlatt (2005). *Assessment of Addictive Behaviours*. New York: The Guilford Press.

Ewing, J. (1984). Detecting alcoholism; The CAGE questions. *J. American Medical Association*, **252**, 1905–7.

First, M. B., R. L. Spitzer, M. Gibbon and J. B. Willaims (1996). *Structured Clinical Interview fro DSM-IV Axis I Disorders-Patient Edition (SCID-I/P, version 2.0)*. New York City: Biometrics Research Department, New York State Psychiatric Institute.

Flannery, B. A., J. R. Volpicelli and H. M. Pettinati (1999). Psychometric properties of the Penn Alcohol Craving Scale. *Alcoholism: Clinical and Experimental Research*, **25**, 1289–95.

Franken I. H. A., V. M. Hendriks and van den Brink W. (2002). Initial validation of two opiate craving questionnaires: The Obsessive Compulsive Drug Use Scale and the Desires for Drug Questionnaire. *Addictive Behaviors*, **27**, 675–85.

Fromme, K., E. Stroot and D. Kaplan (1993). Comprehensive effects of alcohol: Development and psychometric assessment of a new expectancy questionnaire. *Psychological Assessment*, **5**, 19–26.

Gilbert, F. S. (1991). The development of a "Steps Questionnaire". *J of Studies on Alcohol*, **52**, 353–60.

Gordon, A. J., S. A. Maisto, M. McNeil, K. L. Kraemer, R. Ol. Conigliaro, M. E Kelley and J. Conigliaro (2001). Three questions can detect hazardous drinkers. *J. of Family Practice*, **504**, 313–20.

Halstead, W. C. (1947). *Brain and Intelligence: A quantitative study of the frontal lobes.* Chicago: University of Chicago Press.

Handelsman L., K. J. Cochrane, M. J. Aronson, R. Ness, K. J. Rubinstein and P. D. Kanof (1987). Two new rating scales for opiate withdrawal. *American Journal of Drug and Alcohol Abuse*, **13**, 293–308.

Hasin, D. S., K. D. Trautman and J. Endicott (1998). Psychiatric Research Interview Substance and Mental Disorders: Phenomenologically based diagnosis in patients who abuse alcohol or drugs. *Psychopharmacology Bulletin*, **34**, 3–8.

Hasin, D. S., K. D. Trautman,G. M. Meile, S. Samet, M. Smith and J. Endicott (1996). Psychiatric Research Interview for Substance and Mental Disorder (PRISM): Reliability for substance abusers. *American Journal of Psychiatry*, **153**, 1195–201.

Heather, N., A. Luce, D. Peck, B. Dunbar and I. James (1999). The development of a treatment version of the Readiness to Change Questionnaire. *Addicion Research*, **7**, 63–8.

Heaton, R. K. (1981). *Wisconsin Card Sorting Test Manual.* Odessa FL: Psychological Assessment Resources.

Horn, J. L., K. W. Wanberg and F. M. Foster (1987). *Guide to the Alcohol Use Inventory.* Minnieapolis: National Computer Systems.

Humphreys, K., L. A. Kaskutas and C. Weisner (1998). The Alcoholics Anonymous Affiliation Scale: Development, reliability, and norms for diverse treated and untreated populations *Alcoholism: Clinical and Experimental Research*, **22**, 974–8.

Jones, B. T. and J. McMahon (1994). Negative and positive alcohol expectancies and predictors of abstinence after discharge from a residential treatment program: A one-month and three-month follow up study in men. *J of Studies on Alcohol*, **55**, 543–8.

Litman, G. K., J. Stapleton, A. N. Oppenhein and M. Peleg (1983a). An instrument for measuring coping behaviours in hospitailised alcoholics: Implications for relapse prevention treatment. *British Journal of Addiction*, **78**, 269–76.

Litman, G. K., J. Stapleton, A. N. Oppenhein, M. Peleg and P. Jackson (1983b). Situations related to alcoholism relapse. *British Journal of Addiction*, **78**, 381–9.

McLennan, A. T., H. Kushner, D. Metzger, R. Peters, I. Smith and G. Grissom (1992). The fifth edition of the Addiction Severity Index. *J of Substance Abuse Treatment*, **9**, 199–213.

Mee-Lee D., G. D. Shulman, M. Fishman, D. R. Gastfriend and J. H. Griffith (2001). *ASAM Patient Placememt Criteria for the treatment of substance-related disorders, second edition-Revised (ASAM PPC-2R).* Chevy Chase MD: American Society of Addiction Medicine.

Miele G. M., K. M. Carpenter, M. S. Cockerham, J. D. Trautman, J. D. Blane and D. S. Hasin (2000). Substance Dependence Severity Scale (SDSS): Reliability and validity of a clincian-administered interview for DSM-IV substance use disorders. *Drug Alcohol Depend*, **59**, 63–75.

Meyers, K., *et al.* (1995). The development of the comprehensive addiction severity index for adolescents (CASI-A): An interview for assessing multiple problems of adolescents. *J of Substance Abuse Treatment*, **12**, 181–93.

Midanik, L. T. (1994). Comparing usual quantity/frequency and graduated frequency scales to assess yearly alcohol consumption: Results from the 1990 US National Alcohol Survey. *Addiction*, **89**, 407–12.

Miele G. M., K. M. Carpenter, M. S. Cockerham, J. D. Trautman, J. D. Blane and D. S. Hasin (2000). Concurrent and predictive validity of the Substance Dependence Severity Scale (SDSS). *Drug Alcohol Depend*, **59**, 77–88.

Miller W.R. and G.A Marlatt. (1984). *Manual for the Comprehensive Drinker Profile*. Odessa FL: Psychological Assessment Resources.

Miller W.R. and J. S. Tonigan (1996). Assessing drinkers' motivations for change: The Stages of Change Readiness and Treatment Eagerness Scale (SOCRATES). *Psychology of Addictive Behaviors*, **10**, 81–9.

Miller, W. R. (1996). *Form 90: A structured assessment interview for drinking and related behaviors*. Rockville, MD., National Institute on Alcohol Abuse and Alcoholism.

Miller, W. R. and R. J. Harris (2000). A simple scale of Gorski's warning signs for relapse. *J of Studies on Alcohol*, **61**, 759–65.

Miller, W. R., J. S. Tonigan and R. Longabaugh (1995). *The Drinker Inventory of Consequences (DrInC): An instrument for assessing adverse consequences of alcohol abuse*. Rockville, MD., National Insitiute on Alcohol Abuse and Alcoholism.

Modell, J. G., F. B. Glaser, Z. M. Mountz, S. Schmaltz and L. Cyr (1992). Obsessive and compulsive characteristics of alcohol abuse and dependence: Quantification by a newly developed questionnaire. *Alcoholism: Clinical and Experimental Research*, **16**, 266–71.

Monti, P. M., D. J. Rohsenow, D. B. Abrams, W. R. Zwick, J. A. Binkoff and S. M. Munroe (1993). Development of a behavior analytically derived alcohol specific role play assessment instrument. *J of Studies on Alcohol*, **54**, 710–21.

Moos, R. H. (1992). *Coping Response Inventory: Adult form manual*. Palo Alto, CA.: Centre for Health Care Evaluation, Stanford University and Department of Veterans Affairs Medical Centres.

Radloff, L. S. (1977). The CES-D scale: A self-report depression scale for research in the general population. *Applied Psychological Measurement*, **1**, 385–401.

Robins, L. N., L. B. Cottler and T. Babor (1995). *CIDI substance abuse module*. St Louis MO: Washington University School of Medicine.

Robins, L. N., L. B. Cottler, K. K. Bucholz, W. M. Compton, C. S. North and K. M. Rourke (2000). *Diagnostic Interview Schedule for the DSM-IV (DIS-IV)*. St Louis, MO.: Washington University School of Medicine.

Russel, M. (1994). New assessment tools for drinking in pregnancy: T-ACE, TWEAK, and others. *Alcohol Health and Research World*, **18**, 55–61.

Russel, M., J. R. Marshall, M. Trevisan, J. L. Freudenheim, A.W. Chan, N. Markovic, J. E. Vana and R. L. Priore (1997). Test-retest reliability of the Cognitive Lifetime Drinking History. *Am. J. of Epidemiology*, **146**, 975–81.

Saunders, J. B., O. G. Asland, T. F. Babor, J. R. de la Fuente and M. Grant (1993). Development of the alcohol use disorders identification test (AUDIT): WHO collaborative project on early detection of persons with harmful alcohol consumption-II. *Addiction*, **88**, 791–804.

Schonfield, L., R. Peters and A. Dolente (1993). *SARA: Substance Abuse Relapse Assessment: Professional manual*. Odessa FL: Psychological Assessment Resources.

Singleton, E. G. (1996). Alcohol Craving Questionnnaire (ACQ-NOW) [Abstract]. *Alcohol and Alcoholism*, **32**, 344.

Skinner, H. A. and B. A. Allen (1982). Alcohol dependence syndrome: Measurement and validation. *J. Abnormal Psychology*, **91**, 199–208.

Skinner, H. A. and W. J. Sheu (1982). Reliability of alcohol use indices: The Lifetime Drinking History and the MAST. *J. of Studies on Alcohol*, **43**, 1157–70.

Sobell, L. C. and M. B. Sobell (1992). Timeline Follow-back: A technique for assessing self-reported alcohol consumption. In R.Z. Litten and J. Allen (Eds), *Measuring Alcohol Consumption: Psychosocial and Biological Methods*. Towota NJ: Humana Press.

Sobell, L. C. and M. B. Sobell (2000). Alcohol Timeline Followback (TLFB). In A. P. Association (Ed.), *Handbook of psychiatric measures*. Washington DC: The American Psychiatric Association.

Speilberger, C., R. Gorsuch, R. Lushene, P. Vagg and G. Jacobs. (1983). *Manual for the State-Trait Anxiety Inventory*. Palo Alto CA: Consulting Psychologists Press.

Stockwell, T., D. Murphy and R. Hodgson (1983). The Severity Alcohol Dependence Questionnaire. *British Journal of Addiction*, **78**, 145–56.

Sullivan, J. T., K. Sykora, J. Schneiderman, C. A. Naranjo and E. M. Sellers (1989). Assessment of alcohol withdrawal: The revised Clinical Institute Withdrawal Assessment for Alcohol scale (CIWA-Ar). *British Journal of Addiction*, **84**, 1353–7.

Tiffany S. T., E. G. Singleton, C. A. Haertzen and J. E. Henningfield (1993). The development of a cocaine craving questionnaire. *Drug Alcohol Depend*, **34**, 19–28.

Tonigan, J. S., W. R. Miller and G. J. Connors (1996). Alcoholics Anonymous Involvement (AAI) scale: Reliability and norms. *Psychology of Addictive Behaviors*, **10**, 75–80.

Wechsler, D. (1981). *WAIS-R manual*. New York: Harcourt Brace Jovanovich.

Wechsler, D. (1987). *Wechsler Memory Scale-Revised*. New York: Psychological Corporation.

Wetterling, T., R. D. Kanitz, B. Bestiers, D, Fischer, B. Zerfass, U. John, H. Spranger and M. Driesssen (1997). A new rating scale for the assessment of the alcohol-withdrawal syndrome (AWS scale). *Alcohol and Alcoholism*, **32**, 753–60.

White, H. R. and E. W. Labouvie (1989). Toward the assessment of adolescent problem drinking. *J of Studies on Alcohol*, **50**, 30–7.

Wing, J. K., T. Babor, T. Brugha, J. Burke, J. E. Cooper, R. Giel, A. Jablenski, D. Regier, and N. Sartorius, N (1990). SCAN. Schedules for Clinical Assessment in Neuropsychiatry. *Arch Gen Psychiatry*, **47**(6), 589–93.

Winters, K. C. (1999). A new multiscale measure of adult substance abuse. *J. of Substance Abuse Treatment*, **16**, 237–46.

Young, R. M. and R. G. Knight (1989). The Drinking Expectancy Questionnaire: A revised measure of alochol-related beliefs. *J. of Psychopathology and Behavioural Assessment*, **11**, 99–112.

Zachery R. A. (1986). *Shipley Insitiuet of Living Scale: Revised manual*. Los Angeles: Western Psychological Services.

Zywiak, W. H., G. J. Connors, S. A. Maisto and V. S. Westerberg (1996). Relapse research and the Reasons for Drinking Questionnaire: A factor analysis of Marlatt's relapse taxonomy. *Addiction*, **91** (Suppl), 121–30.

INDEX